The Power of PRAISE *and* WORSHIP

D0094395

The Power of
PRAISE and
WORSHIP

TERRY LAW With JIM GILBERT

DESTINY IMAGE® PUBLISHERS, INC.

P.O. Box 310, Shippensburg, PA 17257-0310

"Speaking to the Purposes of God for this Generation and for the Generations to Come."

This book and all other Destiny Image, Revival Press, Mercy Place, Fresh Bread, Destiny Image Fiction, and Treasure House books are available at Christian bookstores and distributors worldwide.

For a U.S. bookstore nearest you, call **1-800-722-6774.**

For more information on foreign distributors, call **717-532-3040.**

Reach us on the Internet at **www.destinyimage.com.**

ISBN 10: 0-7684-2676-6
ISBN 13: 978-0-7684-2676-2

For Worldwide Distribution, Printed in the U.S.A.

1 2 3 4 5 6 7 8 9 10 11 / 12 11 10 09 08

Endorsements

Traveling the world with Terry Law for 15 years—serving first as a musician, and eventually as a worship leader for his ministry—I have personally experienced the life-changing message found in *The Power of Praise and Worship*. Birthed out of personal triumph and deep personal tragedy, Terry shares profound, yet simple truths in *The Power of Praise and Worship* that transcend denominations, cultures, and generations. I believe this book will change your life as it has mine.

Don Moen
Integrity Music Worship Leader

Terry carries God's anointing and is a living example, and leader, in *The Power of Praise and Worship*. His book is dynamic. Its truths move me to God, and you will be moved, too.

Oral Roberts

Contents

PART II

PART I

Introduction

by Terry Law

In the spring of 1969 my friend, Larry Dalton, and I concocted an idea that was radical for its time: we would use contemporary music in evangelism. Seniors at Oral Roberts University in Tulsa, Oklahoma, we assembled a few fellow students and formed a band called Living Sound, that would minister on weekends for the duration of the semester. Our *modus operandi* was a one-hour concert of Larry's musical arrangements, followed by my preaching, and concluding with an invitation to follow Christ.

1969 may have been the year of Woodstock and hippies, but electric guitars were a rarity on church platforms, and drums were even rarer. (One pastor said we could use them, but only if we put them in the baptistry behind the choir risers where no one could see them.) Nevertheless, we determined to sing for anyone who would have us, as long as we could be back on campus for classes by Monday morning.

Our call to full-time ministry and the nations came quickly, and at the end of the semester we began itinerating across the USA and Canada, raising funds through church concerts until we had enough money to ship our equipment to the nation of South Africa. Now we were going to be "musicianaries!"[1]

Living Sound spent most of 1970 singing and preaching to black, white, and mixed-race audiences in every town and city across South Africa's troubled landscape, to spectacular results. We sang and proclaimed the Gospel in high schools, churches, and rented auditoriums, from Johannesburg's Coliseum Theatre to the Capetown City Hall, in many cases setting attendance records that stood for years. Much more importantly, nearly 7,000 people committed their lives to follow Jesus, and the South African church itself was rejuvenated, if not revolution-ized, in its paradigm of worship and outreach.

The Hippie Movement came and went, but we kept going. Over the next seventeen years there were as many as four Living Sound teams traversing the world simultaneously. In November 1972, we made our first foray behind the Iron Curtain, into communist Yugoslavia and Poland. In 1973, we launched a second team with a four-month, nine-nation tour of Southeast Asia, including the war zone in Vietnam.

In 1978 we ventured into the Soviet Union for the first of many missions. Two years later, while the United States and sixty-four other nations boycotted the Olympics in Moscow, Russia, to protest the Soviet invasion of Afghanistan, we wrote and recorded the official anthem for the games. The Soviets were desperate to save face, and any American input was a plus for them, even if it meant giving a Christian group some leeway. The gambit paid off, and our exposure on Soviet television propelled our ministry all over the Eastern Bloc.

In 1980 Pope John Paul II, who had loved us when he was a Cardinal in Poland, invited us to sing to his Tuesday audience of 60,000 people at the Vatican, heartily endorsing us and opening the door for us to minister throughout the Roman Catholic world.

The darkest period of my life commenced in 1982 with the sudden, accidental death of my wife, Jan. I entered a period of indescribable loneliness, a time tunnel of grief, not knowing that the eventual light at the end would bring me into an incredible revelation about praise and worship. The result was a total paradigm shift in my approach to ministry, resulting in a drastic modification in strategy for our teams. My music director, Don Moen, threw out 90 percent of our repertoire and began writing the praise songs for which he has since become so renowned. Living Sound was transformed into one of the world's pioneer "worship bands," fulfilling King David's charge to "declare His glory among the nations, His wonders among all peoples" (Ps. 96:3). Again, the results were dramatic and fruitful. Yet I sensed a change was coming.

By 1987, after our teams had ministered in at least 60 nations on every continent but Antarctica, I realized that our concert approach had run its course. I disbanded the teams, and Living Sound became Terry Law Ministries. For a while I continued conducting the praise and healing meetings that had become our signature, with Don Moen leading worship from the piano. Within a short time, however, it became clear that I needed to release Don to fulfill his own expanding calling, and he joined Integrity Communications' Hosanna! Music as an artist and producer. Don rose to new heights both spiritually and professionally, eventually becoming president of the company before launching his own venture in 2008.

In 1992 Terry Law Ministries took the added name "World Compassion," as I replaced our musical strategy with one of humanitarian aid. I saw that the wars and natural disasters that plague so many needy nations presented us with an opportunity not only to clothe bodies and feed hungry stomachs, but also to distribute the true bread of life, the Gospel of Jesus Christ, through thoughtfully designed literature. To that end I commissioned a 16-page illustrated booklet, *The Story of Jesus*, a kind of harmony of the Gospels with storybook illustrations. At the time of this writing our ministry, in cooperation with others, has distributed more than 270 million copies of that little book, in 72 languages in dozens of countries, including Russia, Vietnam, China, and Iraq. We have also distributed millions of Bibles in several languages, including Russian and Arabic, in various formerly closed nations. By coupling the gifts of these Bibles with the distribution of food, medicine, and clothing, we have found favor with various governments, as well as some of the highest Islamic authorities.

This book was first released in 1985, before most of these adventures had taken place, and before the transformation of Living Sound into World Compassion Terry Law Ministries. I intend to tell many of these stories in the following pages. But there is one story that, even with the passage of more than 25 years, I have not been able to put into words—the accidental death of my wife, Jan, in 1982, while I was overseas. Although in the first edition I alluded to it briefly, there were two reasons I did not delve into the details of that tragedy. First, I wrote the book primarily as a teaching tool, not an autobiography.

The second reason lay in the pain that I knew would be dredged up with a fuller treatment. In one sense I had overcome it, of course. Indeed that was the main reason I *could* write the book. But the residue of pain often is the blur it leaves behind, like a protective coating on the memory. To be honest, I could not precisely recall the external details of those days, because of the internal war I had fought.

In addition, I released the book during the period that coincided with meeting and marrying my second wife, Shirley. I could not have known that ten years later I would face a second devastation whose retelling would be equally impossible to convey.

There are, however, a few close friends who lived both stories with my children and me, among them Jim Gilbert, a comrade in arms for nearly 40 years. Jim was the youngest charter member of Living Sound, and we have shared many formative experiences, including those dark days more than two decades past.

Jim knows me well, and his remarkable powers of recall persuaded me that he should open both Parts I and II of this new edition by chronicling what I could not. We have done this because everything I have learned about praise and worship to God has been born out of these two episodes.

The following chapter is Jim Gilbert's account of my darkest hour.

ENDNOTE

1. The term is not mine. As far as I can determine it was coined by singer/missionary Bobby Michaels.

Chapter 1

Dark Night of the Soul

by Jim Gilbert

After yet another fitful night it was finally time for the memorial service. Married for only 13 years, 39-year-old Terry Law was about to bury the wife of his youth.

~

"Who's going to tell him? Do you want to, Jim?"

"No, David. You tell him. I don't think I can."

David Weir and I walked down the drafty, wood-floored hallway into the pitch black of Terry Law's upstairs room. Living Sound's headquarters in western England was a former convent, and its heavily treed countryside location made for dark and quiet nights. As was Terry's custom after his transatlantic "redeye" flight, he had stayed awake as long as possible before taking an over-the-counter sleep aid that would keep him dreaming until the sun rose on Greenwich mean time the next morning.

I flipped on the light and stared at his soundly sleeping figure for a moment. The bright glare did not stir him in the least. *We're about to destroy this man's entire world in a single moment,* I thought, *and there's not a thing I can do to stop it.*

David roused Terry, shaking him hard and telling him to sit up. Whether in an act of mercy or merely to keep from losing his nerve, he wasted no time. "Terry, we've just received some terrible news," he said in his deliberate Scottish brogue. "Jan has been killed in a car accident." His words sliced the chilly night air as swiftly as a guillotine, and they might as well have been one.

Terry struggled to waken and gather his wits. "Leave me alone you guys. This is a dream," he groused, and mumbled something about jet lag as he rolled back onto his pillow.

"No, Terry, this is real," one of us said, while wishing we were indeed just a figment of his long journey. "You have to wake up."

His eyes were open now, blinking back sleep and registering the shock. Reality was slamming him in the chest, slapping his face. Suddenly he grimaced, this man I loved so dearly, and with instant fury and a primeval wail, rammed a curled fist into the hard plaster wall. He was dying the first of a hundred deaths to come before dawn.

The horrible news had come minutes earlier with an overseas call from Living Sound's Executive Director, Don Moen, who was between tours at the main office in Tulsa, Oklahoma. He was still in shock from the sad tidings he now bore.

"My office phone rang, and a voice on the other end said, 'Mr. Moen, this is the emergency room at St. Francis Hospital. Do you know someone named Janice Law?'"

"Yes. What's wrong?"

"Are you a friend of Ms. Law?"

"Yes. Why? What's the matter?"

"Mr. Moen, are you a very close friend of the family?"

"Yes. Yes. Please, what's wrong? Has something bad happened?"

"Yes, Mr. Moen. Janice Law is dead. She was killed in an automobile accident a few minutes ago."

"I was so stunned I couldn't think," Don said later. "I stood there mute for a moment, and then just blurted out, 'That's not possible; you're wrong,' and slammed down the receiver. My adrenalin was pumping so hard, and then I realized I'd better call back. They asked me the same questions again, and then explained that they'd found my name and number on a card in Jan's purse. They told me where the helicopter personnel had found her; the accident had happened less than a mile away."

The shock of hearing Jan's name and the excruciating suddenness of the call sent Don reeling. In years to come the church world would know this young man as one of his generation's most gifted worship leaders and songwriters, but right now praising God was the last thing on his mind. *How can I do this?* he thought as panic swept over him. How could he? How do you tell a man his wife is dead? It wasn't fair. Anger mingled with fear, and might have overtaken him, but for the realization that there was much to be done, and done quickly, especially about the Laws' children.

Misty, Scot, and Rebecca were probably still standing by the curb in front of the school, awaiting their mom. They wouldn't be too worried yet; life in the Law household routinely followed the "hurry up and wait" rule. The accident had happened shortly before three o'clock, and someone in the office had observed that Jan must have been on her way to fetch them. Don decided to call Gordon and Stella Calmeyer, former team members and still close friends of the ministry. The kids trusted "Auntie" Stella, and she would take good care of them until Gordon could get their dad on the phone.

"At first I was thrilled to see Uncle Gordon," recalls Misty, who was a precocious 11-year-old at the time. "We hadn't been to their house for some time, and I knew we'd have fun. But after a while I knew something must be wrong. Why hadn't Mom picked us up? Then when I saw Pastor Daugherty walk in the front door, I suddenly knew why. I knew my mother was gone. After that, everything seemed to move in slow motion."

Meanwhile in England, Terry convulsed with sorrow. Again and again he cried out in disbelief, his hoarse complaint shattering the quiet of the old cloister. For a few minutes it seemed he might not make it, that he might utterly disintegrate, until the same urgent remembrance pressed him into duty. His children needed him. Oh God, they needed him, right there in Tulsa, not on the other side of the world!

Terry steeled himself, gathering strength and testing his voice, while we all waited for the Calmeyers' call from America. At last the hallway telephone rang.

The next few minutes were indescribably sad, yet more filled with the glory of God than almost any time I had ever witnessed. "God does all things well, children," Terry told Misty, his eldest, and Scot, his 8-year-old son. Little Rebecca was listening in too, but mainly for the reassurance of Daddy's voice because everyone else was crying. "We've got to remember, kids. God didn't do this to

Mommy. Satan is the destroyer. We can still trust God. He does all things well." His voice cracked repeatedly, and I could hear him reaching deep within himself for faith and strength, not only for their sakes, but also to see if there were any left in him. He needed to hear himself say it. "We can still trust Him. He does all things well." *Oh God, let it be true.*

It was after midnight when my wife, Dolly, went to work arranging Terry's flight back to Tulsa, while David Weir collected his still-packed luggage, hastily gathering his own as well. There was no way our friend, now awash in grief, could cross the Atlantic alone. David would drive Terry the 90 miles back to London's Gatwick Airport, and together they would take the first flight home the next morning.

As for me, I knew what I had to do, and simply sat in the downstairs parlor with my widowed friend, while the fog of death rolled in upon his soul. Words now failed the wordsmith, replaced by groans, mournful melodies of the Holy Spirit Himself, making intercession. It was an ugly song, but it was the only one in him, and it had to be sung, every torturous note of it. And all of it came.

Eventually exhausted from crying, Terry sank into silence, blankness. He stared into space, as if the walls and ceiling were an open sky. Time slowed, hung in suspension for a moment, then flung furiously backward, rewinding to David's voice and that awful announcement. "Wake up...terrible news...Jan's been killed." He flinched, reality assaulting him again—his kids needed their dad *now*, not tomorrow. Oh God, their mother was dead, and their father wasn't there either. He had to get home! What time was it? Could David get the car ready now? How would he ever raise them without their mother, especially 4-year-old Rebecca?

How could he go on traveling and preaching? How could he ever preach again?

"And the Lord was with Joseph." I remembered the punch line of one of Terry's most enduring sermons, taken from Genesis chapter 39. Jacob's favorite son, having survived kidnapping and slavery before rising to a place of privilege in Pharaoh's palace, now stood falsely accused of the attempted rape of his employer's wife. Surely Jehovah God would deliver Joseph once again. After all, he had visions yet unfulfilled, and a "word" to stand on. And even if he were convicted and sent to prison, his father was Israel, a "prince with God." Joseph's speedy deliverance was sure. The promise of God was certain.

Yet Joseph spent the next 12 years in prison. There were no miracles, no earthquakes, no bonds falling off his wrists, not even a visiting angel to comfort him. The Bible offers only one brief sentence, one consolation: "And the Lord was with Joseph."

But that was enough, Terry had often preached. What else ultimately do we need, or even have, besides God's presence? *What else indeed*, I thought, and gently comforted my mentor with his own words. After all, if they were real, they had to be real now. And they were. The Lord was with Terry that awful night. And though we could not tell it at the time, it was enough.

LONG JOURNEY HOME

Transoceanic flights can be tedious, especially when west-bound, because the sun stays high in the sky for several hours longer than normal. And if the previous night had seemed the longest of his life, Terry found his flight back to America the next day agonizingly endless. He ached to hold his children, to find solace in the smiles and arms of old friends, hundreds of whom were already making their way to Tulsa from all corners of the earth to honor Jan. The airplane, though it was streaking homeward, nonetheless felt like a prison in the sky, the clouds below a barrier between him and where he wanted to be. He didn't want to fly home; he wanted to *be* home.

Yet he also dreaded getting there, dreaded walking through the door and feeling the chill of Jan's absence. Terry and his dad had rebuilt that dilapidated old house on 91st Street with their own hands, bumped out the living room, and added a second floor with a large master suite. Jan's warm touch was everywhere, on every wall and table, in every color, in the very softness of every fabric. And the kitchen—it was *her* kitchen, newly renovated and barely broken in, yet already it seemed imprinted with her smile and sunny disposition. Terry wasn't sure he could ever step back into that kitchen. How could home ever again really be home without Jan?

The tedious flight was giving him too much time to think and no way to act. This was a man used to seizing the moment, to barging through obstacles and taking new ground for God's Kingdom. Now he was *being* seized, battered senseless with every tick of the clock by a single, awful fact: His wife, his faithful, patient, selfless Jan, was gone. And no airplane in any heaven could take him to her.

Terry claimed later that he had quit the ministry a hundred times on that flight. David Weir, the faithful friend who accompanied him that day, says that's no exaggeration.

"It was a ten-and-a-half hour flight, and every minute was a grind," he remembers. "Terry was suffering wave after wave of emotion: extreme anger, deep sorrow. He would softly repeat the names of his three children over and over; then he'd look at me and ask how God could do such a thing to him. He had served as faithfully as he could, he said, but now he was quitting the ministry. He was finished. He reiterated it so many times."

But Terry repeated something else too, a phrase that brought the gentle Scotsman reassurance that his devastated colleague would not quit after all. It was a verse from the Book of Job: "But He knows the way that I take; when He has tested me, I shall come forth as gold." Faith was already peeking through the ashes, like the flowers that had sprouted on the slopes of Mount Saint Helens after her eruption, surprising the pundits who had predicted a lunar-like landscape for years to come. David Weir marveled at his friend. He marveled at God even more.

Shortly after take-off he had spoken with the cabin crew, explaining the situation, and asking for their forbearance ahead of time. "They were exceptionally kind," he remembers, "bypassing us at mealtime when it was obvious that Terry couldn't eat. Later they brought us the finest food on the plane, from up in first class."

David's voice breaks to this day when he remembers those hours. "You run out of things to say to someone in such grief. Much of the time I just sat there and cried with him, but that was the only way I could show my sympathy. It must have been a strange sight, two grown men sitting together in the coach cabin, quietly sobbing."

Terry and David were crossing the Atlantic Ocean for the second time in two-and-a-half days, having spent the first night flying and the second preparing to return home. Both men were exhausted, and at length Terry grew sleepy. At last his adrenalin-ridden system was loosening its grip. "The flight wasn't very full," recalls David, "so the attendants moved him to an empty row in business class, and he slept hard for a while."

The grieving husband—widower—would need his rest. Awaiting him at home were the immediate needs of his children, a funeral to arrange, and hundreds of guests to receive. Don Moen met him at the airport, as did Living Sound team leader Joel Vesanen, who brought ORU professors Dr. Howard Ervin and Dr. Charles Farah, one of the ministry's spiritual fathers.

Both men hugged him tightly. "I can't tell you how sorry I am, Terry," said Chuck Farah. That was about the extent of it. Being together was the important thing right now, not talking. Psalm 133:1 says, "Behold, how good and how pleasant it is for brethren to dwell together in unity!" Maybe dwelling together was "good and pleasant" from Heaven's point of view, but today, down at ground level, it was critical.

FIELD OF BLOOD

Dolly and I arrived in Tulsa the next day, ready to serve Terry and his children in any way their fragile state might require. We prayed to be able to anticipate the unexpected hard steps before they came, those small moments that hit you when you're relaxing between battles.

One of those moments came when I took Terry to retrieve Jan's personal effects, which had been transferred from the hospital to the funeral home along with her body. The undertaker handed Terry Jan's handbag, and suddenly I realized its contents might hold more heartbreak, a dozen little things that could add up to one big one. After all, these were the everyday items of a life that hadn't planned on ending.

Anything that hit me hard would hit Terry harder, so I decided to rummage through Jan's purse first. There were her car keys, useless since the silver Peugeot wagon had been totaled in the accident. I left them in the bottom for later removal when Terry would not notice. Her wallet contained the usual kid pictures, charge cards, and some cash, not a big problem.

Then I saw her driver license. It was unexpired, still "valid." Yet she *had* expired. I choked back tears—this was my Jan too, my beloved honorary sis—and brought up the irony right then to diffuse the impact it might have made later. It worked, and I sighed with relief at having disarmed an emotional bomb.

Some moments would be crushing no matter how firmly Terry braced himself. And he knew the arrival of Jan's parents, Albert and Marian D'Arpa, would be such a time. "I looked out the front window and saw them slowly walking up the sidewalk to our door," Terry softly recalls. "They were devastated, and as much as I mourned for myself, I grieved for them at the loss of their daughter."

Like all parents, the D'Arpas could not have expected to outlive a child, especially Albert, who was already in his seventies. Jan had been the joy of his life, doubly delightful for having caught his passion for missions. His princess had become a heroine.

Marian's love for her daughter was no less fervent. "My Jan," she always called her. Ever the prayer warrior, this gentle lady carried Terry's ministry close to her heart, and Jan's reliance on that fact had only drawn them closer. Her prophetic insights often proved invaluable; not much took her by surprise. But she had been blindsided by Jan's death, and to her son-in-law, appeared utterly demolished.

Yet with all this, one of Terry's hardest moments still lay ahead. I knew that sooner or later he would want to go to the scene of the accident. He would insist on knowing the details of his wife's death, no matter how brutal it might have been.

I had already walked the sequence through on the phone with Don Moen, who had taken pains to learn the details. In similar anticipation of Terry's wishes, Gordon and he personally had cleaned up the accident site, leaving a few less violent markers untouched. Terry needed to find something out there, needed in some measure to encounter Jan's death exactly where it had taken place.

Terry's dad, his brother-in-law, Lorne Taylor, and Brian Stiller, his good friend from childhood, joined us for the drive to the two-lane bridge where Jan's car had left the road. Terry gathered his courage, and asked me to reconstruct the accident for him in as much detail as possible.

I explained what I had learned from Don, showing him the bridge railing and abrupt asphalt shoulder that together had grabbed the wagon's right front tire, causing Jan to lose control. The car had shot across the road and onto an earthen dam, where it flipped and threw her out. She had struck a large V-shaped tree before landing in the weeds some 40 feet away. There probably had been no suffering.

I searched the grass ahead of Terry while he stood looking at that awful tree, and soon found two broken ammonia packets. And blood. Here was Jan's blood, in the tall grass of an Oklahoma pasture. It had turned powdery, which gave it the appearance of not having completely dried.

I called Terry over, and showed him what I had found. The agony of the scene before me, although somewhat muted, almost rivaled that of his phone call to the children two nights earlier in England. He knelt, and crying quietly, stared at his precious wife's blood, which now stained the thumb and fingers of his right hand. It was all of Jan that he could touch, but at least something of her to hold.

I stood over my stricken friend and wept with him. I thought of my own sweet Dolly, and tried to imagine being the one kneeling in that field. But no matter how hard I tried, I could not fathom the thought.

A FAMILY GATHERS

Meanwhile Terry's mother had just arrived from Canada to take over from Stella in caring for the children. A few other Living Sound "aunties" were lending a hand as well, and on the eve of the funeral it fell to my wife, Dolly, to watch over Rebecca, Terry's youngest.

Hundreds of well-wishers from all over the world now gathered at the funeral home as dusk settled over eastern Oklahoma. A reception was being held in the main salon, where Terry and the children would receive the consolation of friends, although in reality every first look into a familiar face brought another burst of tears from eyes they thought had wept themselves dry.

The children seemed to be doing well under the circumstances. Misty was already unconsciously filling in for her mom. At 11 years old she had mastered Jan's comforting smile, and at the least could mimic her mother's poise and grace. But she needed to be a hurting little girl right now, not a strong woman.

Eight-year-old Scottie, on the other hand, was as quiet and affable as always, as though the heaviness of his mother's demise had not yet settled on him. In fact he looked to me as though he were in shock, insulated by a child's incapacity to comprehend it all. I was glad, and hoped he'd lose himself riding his bike or watching his beloved Dallas Cowboys win another big game. I learned years later that in fact it was a Cowboys *loss* that helped Scot to cope with his mother's death.

"I remember replaying in my mind the final two minutes of a Dallas Cowboys football game, and how I had wished the great 'Captain Comeback,' Roger Staubach, could suddenly come out of retirement and win the game," he said in a recent e-mail. "But of course he could not come back, and there had been no game-winning drive. Now, I realized, I had to face the fact that my mom could not come back to me."

Rebecca, Terry's 4-year-old, had spent less time away from her mother than her older siblings. Yet she was the easiest to console. She was happy to learn that Mommy was with the Lord.

"I want to meet Jesus," said the elfin blonde.

"What, honey?" Dolly replied, not sure she'd heard Becca correctly.

"I want to meet Jesus. He's right there in that room, where Mommy is sleeping."

Dolly quickly realized that her little charge had been given conflicting explanations. Someone had told her Mommy was with Jesus, while someone else had said Mommy was in the next room sleeping. She hadn't been to school yet, but she was already adding one plus one.

The older children were asking to see their mother's body. Terry knew such closure was normally wise, but he was torn about taking them into the viewing room. Jan's face had been disfigured, and although the embalmer had done his best, she really did not look like herself. The children might not understand. But they insisted, and their exhausted father at length decided to take the risk. More than 20 years later he still questions the wisdom of that decision.

THE TOUCH OF HEAVEN

After yet another fitful night, it was finally time for the memorial service. Married for only 13 years, 39-year-old Terry Law was about to bury the wife of his youth. He struggled to get dressed. How many "longest" days must a man face? He felt as though he had aged ten years in the past five days.

There was no such thing as "widescreen" television in 1982, but the panoramic picture window that fronted the Laws' 91st Street home might as well have been one. Only two days ago Terry had witnessed the sorrowful procession of Jan's aging parents come to mourn their daughter. Now a long, black hearse sat parked on the lawn, a macabre gateway to the grave that would enfold his wife's body after her final journey in a few hours. Were it not for the children, he could have wished to join her.

The Woodlake Assembly of God sanctuary filled to capacity that morning with an assemblage of relatives, various dignitaries, fellow ministers, and friends from far and near. Gordon Calmeyer began the sad proceeding, and after Kenneth Hagin Jr. offered a fitting prayer, David Weir and other close friends spoke words of tribute to Jan and comfort to the family.

The rest of that day is lost on a sea of salty tears, not only to me but also to everyone I have interviewed about it. Searching our minds years later yields few facts, though we have sought them with new tears in recent days. Don Moen remembers the poignant heaviness of the coffin that he and his fellow pallbearers bore down the center aisle. David can recollect some of the eulogy he delivered. Pianist Larry Dalton, who had known Jan even before she met Terry, recalls only that he was a "basket case."

Four brief minutes and not a minute more still live in my heart from that day, because I sang one of Jan's favorite songs, "My Tribute," by our legendary friend, Andrae Crouch. I remember it vividly because I so feared attempting to sing it. I had been strong for Terry's sake all week, but now my own grief was heavy upon me. I wasn't sure I could muster the self-control to sing that big melody and its powerful declaration:

"To God be the glory…for the things He has done. With His blood…."

Blood. The memory of Terry kneeling in that open field, weeping at the sight of Jan's blood on his fingers, kept coming back to me, and I wept every time. I did not want to falter while singing; emotions all around were raw, and a break in my voice could multiply the sorrow.

I was to precede Oral Roberts and Terry's pastor, Billy Joe Daugherty; it was time to sing. "Put your emotion *into* the song instead of fighting it," a Voice said as I walked to the podium. I obeyed, and the result was the kind of tribute my beloved Jan deserved. It remains, to this day, my finest rendition of that modern classic.

Pastor Daugherty delivered his message ahead of Oral, who was—and still is—at his best by simply being himself, a singular soul who breathes healing even when he isn't talking about it. And as Oral spoke, something began to arise within Terry, as if the voice of Jesus were commanding his spirit to come forth, out of the pit of despair that threatened to become his tomb.

And then he rose, from a second-row pew that on this day had become a mourner's bench, to the pulpit, and then past it, to another place, a heaven that most of us had never known, but all of us needed.

"For years I've said that my dream is someday to stand before the Lord, and to hear Him say to me, 'Well done, good and faithful servant.'" He sounded haggard, weary. "That dream has never changed. But now it appears that my wife has achieved my dream ahead of me. She has already heard the words I long to hear."

He spoke about Joseph, whose brothers mocked him as "this dreamer," and what sometimes happens on the road to fulfilling a dream. Hearkening back to our conversation in England on the night of Jan's death, he told about Joseph's unjust imprisonment, about the various ordeals that looked like multiple derailments from his destiny. And then he consoled his fellow mourners with the very same words we had remembered together: "And the Lord was with Joseph."

Then his tone toughened. I could tell there was a fire in his belly, at least for now. "Satan has tried to kill me, to stop me from preaching the Gospel. But it hasn't worked, so he's trying to harm my family." He still spoke quietly but with steel in his voice. "The devil is not going to win, and I'm not quitting. I'm going on." He spoke not just with determination, but with authority, prophesying that hell itself would regret its decision.

And then he descended the platform to the sanctuary floor, and back to earth.

Years later Oral Roberts would tell him, "I saw iron in you that I didn't know was there. I realized that there was something important that God had for you to do."

THE DESCENT

But the battle was not over. In some ways, in fact, it had just begun. The death and burial of a spouse are traumatic, of course, but their pain is easily rivaled later on when, after all the well-wishers have gone home and resumed their lives, a dull, aching absence invades—*pervades*—one's home. And in Terry's case, that ache came bundled with accusation.

"I often quoted Psalm 91 as a covering for my family before going on trips," he remembers, "especially verses ten through twelve: 'No evil shall befall you, nor shall any plague come near your dwelling; for he shall give His angels charge over you, to keep you in all your ways. In their hands they shall bear you up, lest you dash your foot against a stone.' I was building the proverbial hedge of protection around them.

"Living in Tulsa means constantly rubbing elbows with members of the 'Word of Faith' movement," he continues. "And I had learned to appreciate the value of a good confession, of claiming and appropriating God's promises."

Terry had in fact struck up a friendship with well-known Bible teacher, Kenneth Hagin. He was blessed by Hagin's kind, midwestern manner, and the genuine *largeness* of his faith. His enthusiasm for confessing Scripture—he called it "saying God's Words after Him"—was contagious. Terry delighted in his company, and considered him a true mentor in the area of faith.

But there are also those for whom the Bible is a cheap decoder ring that lets them find a "why" for everything, assigning credit for a good confession and, even worse, attaching blame to bad results. After all, God's Word cannot fail. "This stuff works," some have claimed with unmitigated triteness. So there must be another explanation when things go wrong.

Such a formulaic approach to faith is not faith at all—it is an emotional gun to the temple.

The gun went off one afternoon not long after Jan's funeral, with the ring of the doorbell at the Law family home. It was obvious, the uninvited visitor informed the family friend who had answered the door, that Terry Law was to blame for his wife's death. He must have been secretly living in sin.

Even before the funeral, on the long flight home from England, this accusation had accosted Terry's shattered psyche. "What have I done wrong?" he agonized. "Where did I make a mistake? No evil is supposed to befall my family; that's what God's Word says. *No evil, not even dashing your foot against a stone.*" The crisis of his wife's passing had become a full-blown crisis of faith. He was wracked with doubt, with the feeling that Jan's death was his fault, that there must be some sin for which he had not repented.

Now, even after a glorious memorial service, the torment had returned, no doubt exacerbated by the unwelcome "revelation" of a stranger. Maybe other people thought the same thing, he worried. Maybe they were right.

The elder Kenneth Hagin had visited with the grieving evangelist at some length a few days earlier. Don't torture yourself, the "father" of the faith movement had advised him. Sometimes bad things happen and there are no good answers. We'll never know this side of Heaven.

They were comforting words, a balm on Terry's scorched soul, and certainly worth a lot more than the snide observations of a total stranger. Still, it was like being both caressed and mugged. Within a few days the soothing truth of Dad Hagin's words had faded, while the soreness of the assault remained.

If he had ascended the heavens during Jan's memorial, Terry Law was falling like lightning from them now. He was, in fact, entering the abyss.

Chapter 2

The Crucible of Praise

by Terry Law

~

I could not have known that the far side of this particular desert stretch, and the route home to peace, would come with a phone call.

~

Jan's funeral had proven the adage that, no matter what the trial, divine grace is sufficient for us. Infused with God's glory and the Spirit's comfort, it had been not only consoling, but catalytic. I would carry on in ministry, yes, but more than that, I fully believed satan would rue the day he had tried to use Jan's death to harm my children and derail my calling. The Holy Spirit had moved on me so mightily that I had even prophesied in the midst of mourning her. Surely the children and I would know a great healing, and God's Kingdom would experience great growth.

Yet within minutes of the end of the service, the tormenting accusation had returned that my lack of faith had caused Jan's death. By the next morning a paralyzing numbness had settled over me. My sister Lois and her husband Lorne, more a brother than brother-in-law, were staying over for a few days to keep me company, as was Brian Stiller, my buddy from boyhood. In addition, my mom had already begun moving her things down from Canada, having decided to take over housekeeping chores on a more permanent basis.

But there was no evading Jan's absence. Being at home was as horrible as I had imagined. She was there in every room, but not there. Our kitchen, two weeks new, had been built to her specifications; the wallpaper, the cabinets, every item on the counters, reflected her tastes, her sunny disposition, reflected *her.*

The living room begged for her presence. It felt utterly empty, blank, except for the big front window that constantly re-played the memory of that ugly black hearse sitting just beyond it, like death at my door.

Friends had been gracious enough to remove Jan's possessions from our bedroom, and her clothing, which still held her fragrance, from our closet. But it felt more like an amputation than help. Our hearts had grown together over the years; God had *joined* us, and now we had been ripped apart. The nerves and vessels of my very soul were exposed and dangling, and the slightest emotional breeze felt like a sandstorm in the face. So I just went numb.

I couldn't think. I couldn't cry. And worst of all, I could not pray.

Many Christians find prayer a difficult discipline to develop, but to me it had always been like breathing. I took seriously Saint

Paul's admonition to "let this mind be in [me] which was also in Christ Jesus" (Phil. 2:5). Although I spent more time on the go than on my knees, I prayed constantly, sharing every thought with the Lord and then listening for His thoughts in return. But now…now God seemed as absent from my life as Jan. I felt doubly alone.

Nights were particularly awful. Our master suite had been a refuge in days past, especially after long trips. But now it was a prison, a torture chamber in cedar tones. For one thing, there was the irony of needing to talk to Jan about the pain of missing her, of starting to call her name out of sheer reflex, and then swallowing the words when the reality of her absence landed on me yet again. The impulse hit me so many times, but then how do you stop a reflex? Or kill one? Worst of all there was a hole in our bed, a spot where only *she* belonged, where nothing else fit, especially not an unrumpled pillow. I hated the undisturbed neatness of that half of the bed.

Since I couldn't sleep I decided to drive. I suppose spending so much time on the road had made driving as relaxing to me as stretching out on the couch is to others. In any case I found it therapeutic. Or at least I had in the past.

The roads skirting Tulsa's southern suburbs were often deserted late at night, and sometimes they just worsened my loneliness. But often they seemed to provide a place *for* it, like solitary without the confinement. Occasionally, on warm nights with the windows down, I could almost sense God's presence out there. Almost.

In the long run, I knew I could not simply drive forever. Every road comes to an end, and for better or worse, the one I was on must as well. But I could not have known that the far side of this particular desert stretch, and the route home to peace, would come with a phone call.

THE GRAVE CLOTHES COME OFF

Oral and Evelyn Roberts were no strangers to grief, their elder son, Ron, having passed away only a short time prior to Jan. This was five years after losing their daughter, Rebecca Nash, and her husband Marshall, in a plane crash. Yet Oral seemed more resilient than I, and he was recovering with a grace I did not possess, and in fact found bewildering. Now he called to invite me to his top-floor campus office, with its beautiful panoramic view of Oral Roberts University.

I got to know Oral shortly after arriving at ORU early in 1968, when I was asked to lead the song services for his West Palm Beach crusade. Working with this great man, a true giant in his faith, began to stretch my thinking and enlarge my vision.

A 24-year-old junior, I already had garnered some ministry experience, having assisted in my father's pastorate in Canada. I had also traveled throughout South Africa with fellow Canadian Dennis Bjorgan, preaching and singing to black and white audiences alike in a land rife with racial tension. The ministry there had been so fruitful that I planned on returning as soon as my university education was complete.

At first my sudden switch from preacher to student frustrated me; I was impatient to develop my own world outreach. Now, with a literal front-row seat on greatness, and the priceless education of our behind-the-scenes friendship, I realized how truly unprepared I was to take on the world. So I settled happily into campus life, serving President Roberts' ministry on weekends and traveling with him during semester breaks.

One trip came in the summer of 1968, when I was sent to Europe with a World Action Team, a musical cadre of ORU's best and brightest. I was there to play bass, and to my delight, to preach on several occasions. But God had a greater reason for my being there, since it was during a sightseeing trip to London, England, that I met Jan.

The ministry work had also afforded me a new friendship with Oral's crusade organist, a musical genius named Larry Dalton, whose great passion was to use his remarkable gift in evangelism, particularly overseas missions. The following February, a month after Jan and I married, Larry and I cofounded the weekend ministry team that soon became Living Sound.

We were a first at ORU. There had been other student groups, other musicians that Oral had raised up and sent out to fulfill God's mandate to him, the chief purpose for the university's very existence: "Raise up your students to hear My voice, to go where My light is dim, My voice is heard small, and My healing power is not known, even to the uttermost bounds of the earth. Their work will exceed yours, and in this I am well pleased."

But Living Sound was the first team of students that God had raised up without Oral's personal direction. He was, in a way, being bypassed, and for a time was uneasy about our initiative and youthful bravado, until a sense of being the ministry's proud "granddad" replaced his initial apprehension.

Oral had witnessed my appointments with destiny, indeed had been an instrument of God in bringing them to pass. I owed him so much, and was honored to have become his friend. Thus, when in my darkest hour, he called to invite me to his private campus sanctuary, I got in my car and drove straight there. After I arrived we just sat together for a couple of hours sharing our pain. If there were any comfort, it would be found in this man's company. I was glad to be a Timothy to his Paul.

President Roberts once remarked that when God called him to build ORU, he had no idea how to do it. He spoke of hiking around the more than 600 acres of rolling hills and woods on South Lewis Avenue, asking God to show him how to build a university. And then he built the sparkling, futuristic campus that became home to a world-class institution of learning.

Yet the secret of Oral's success, the way his instructions had finally come, was so simple as to seem foolish: He prayed in the Spirit, and then waited for God to make his mind "fruitful" to give him the interpretation of his spiritual groanings. Now, as I sat in his capacious office, he was standing over me, pointing his finger and exhorting me to do the same.

"Terry, if you do what I say, it could save your life. Go home, get down on your knees, and start to pray in the Spirit. You have got to begin to praise the Lord!"

I was flabbergasted. How in the world could I do that? I was numb on the inside, dead as dead could be, as though the grave had swallowed me too. "I can't," I protested.

But Oral was insistent. "You have to do it, Terry. You have to."

The next morning my alarm sounded before daybreak. I responded like a boot camp trainee, with unfeeling obedience, and knelt by my bed. How should I begin?

"Hallelujah," I said. The word was hollow, an empty echo both in the room and in my chest. "I praise You, Lord."

With that, the numbness began to give way to a hint of something else. Pain…a kind of cramp. And with it an accusation: "You're a hypocrite, Terry Law. How can you praise God after He killed your wife?" The thoughts felt like mine, but, of course, they were not. They came anyway. "You're lying. You don't mean a word you're saying."

"I praise You, Lord." I said it again, and the cramp worsened. Again. More pain. More accusation. I wanted to give up. The knot in my gut was becoming unbearable. Cursing would have been easier, or at least more honest. But I went on, mouthing goodness I didn't mean.

I watched the clock the way people do when they want to leave. Fifteen minutes passed, but it felt like a lifetime. "I bless You, Lord," I said, as Psalm 34:1 came to me: "I will bless the Lord at all times; His praise shall continually be in my mouth."

"You're ridiculous, Law," said the accuser, though I still thought it was me. "You might as well give up. There's no hope for you."

I pitied myself. And why not? Hadn't I risked my life for God time and again on mission fields all over the world? I had good reason to feel sorry for myself. This whole mess just wasn't fair. None of it.

"I will bless the Lord at all times; His praise shall continually be in my mouth." The verse came again, and I began to realize there was a war of words going on in my soul. I had to take sides.

I spoke aloud this time. "Lord, I will bless You at all times." Something happened deep inside my spirit, a slight sense of satisfaction, as if I had hit a target.

But the battle wasn't over. More thoughts taunted me. "You're not really praising God. You don't mean a word of this. You're lying."

Now I realized that even though the inner voice had sounded like my own, it was really satan attacking me. So I spoke louder. "Lord, I bless You at all times." The battle was on. Victory still seemed impossible, but at least I was fighting back.

I waited for some sort of emotional release, a breakthrough like you read about in books. It didn't come. I was still acting on sheer determination. But having identified the enemy, I was fighting now, and did not intend to stop.

I praised the Lord in obedience to His Word, with not a shred of feeling, for 30 minutes more…then an hour…an hour and a half…two hours. Still, I felt nothing.

Then, after nearly two-and-a-half hours, a pressure started to build inside me. It felt like water building up behind a dam. I kept praising God, and the pressure kept rising. It felt like the dam might explode.

Finally it did, and there came a great gush of hot, stinging tears. My shoulders started to heave. The awful cramp in my stomach had at last released, and I was sobbing, crying harder than I had ever cried in my life. I raised my hands…

I don't know how long I prayed, because I never looked at the clock again. The spirit of prophecy came upon me, and I began to proclaim my own healing. The oil of gladness poured over my fractured, torn emotions, and I began to rejoice. God was fitting my soul with a garment of praise that would once and for all replace the spirit of heaviness that for weeks had clung to me like cold, wet clothes.

I was free!

A NEW SONG

The weeks that followed my spiritual breakthrough are hard to describe. My relationship with God felt as new as my first day in Christ. More than refreshed, I felt recreated, in some ways as innocent and untroubled as a newborn. Even though I still suffered occasional bouts of grief, I loved being at home again, loved sitting in Jan's living room while the sun shone in. And when haunting thoughts tugged at me, I would simply start to praise the Lord.

Ephesians 1:14 refers to the Holy Spirit as the "guarantee [or earnest] of our inheritance," a down payment on eternal life—in other words, our "Heaven on earth." And He certainly brought Heaven to my heart. I entered a dimension in prayer, a place of flowing in the Holy Spirit that can best be described as divine teamwork. Some days I spent many hours just praying in the Spirit, harmonizing with the Lord, learning what it meant to "let that mind which was in Christ Jesus be also in" me (Phil. 2:5) .

One day I was worshiping God in my bedroom, the sanctuary that so recently had been a cell, when the spirit of prophecy came upon me. I had learned by now to pray in the Spirit until I was "finished," until I felt fully expressed, and then to speak out what the Holy Spirit was giving me, to describe the pictures He painted on my soul.

Today, though, it was unusual, different by degrees. I spoke boldly, but this time I was as hungry to hear the words as to speak them. And what followed was a divine mandate—*the* mandate—for my ministry, and for that matter for the writing of this book.

"I am going to use you to bring salvation, healing, and deliverance to people everywhere through the message of praise and worship."[1]

Ideas, philosophers are wont to say, have consequences. And I knew that what I was prophesying was a big idea, with bigger consequences than I could imagine. But I could not—*dared* not—stop. God had overhauled my spirit, and now it was clear—He was about to overhaul my ministry, my theology, my entire life.

Almost immediately I began to realize that God had been preparing me for this massive spiritual realignment even before Jan died. For several weeks I had been bombarded with the words "praise and worship" on two fronts.

On one side there was Don Moen, Living Sound's executive director, who was devouring a set of cassette tapes one of his pastors had brought home from an early August worship conference in Detroit, Michigan. The International Worship Symposium had been a five-day event that, during the day, featured gifted teachers such as Dr. Sam Sasser and Fuschia Pickett, while the evening meetings were devoted to extravagant experiments in spontaneous praise and worship.

On the other side was an exuberant Jim Gilbert, who had attended that same conference, just prior to joining me in Nova Scotia to fill in for Don in meetings there. He claimed the symposium had changed his life and ministry, something I did not take lightly coming from an experienced colleague.

Don and Jim were not aware of their simultaneous paradigm shift, nor that it had come from the same Source. But together they were God's voice to me in stereo.

At first I had trouble connecting the message of praise and worship with the ministry of healing and deliverance. After all, worship is for God, not us, while healing is for people; God doesn't need it. The two were, in my opinion, mutually exclusive.

I struggled to connect the dots. If praise and healing were related, why hadn't the great healing evangelists discovered it? I had watched one of them, Oral Roberts, up close, but had never seen him minister healing through the avenue of praise.

Nevertheless, even in my ignorance, I was pledged to obedience and took immediate action. On the same day God spoke to me at home, I called the office and told Don what had happened, that we were going to set a new course. I instructed him to take every lead sheet, every arrangement of every song we had sung for 13 years, out of the filing cabinets and examine their content.

I knew we would have to be single-minded in presenting our new message to the public. We would drop anything that wasn't exclusively and explicitly an expression of praise and worship. This didn't mean that our previous music had been wrong or uninspired, but simply that its season was finished.

Don, who was tracking right along with me in his own renewal, followed my orders to a tee. He deleted approximately 90 percent of our previous repertoire, and gave himself to writing and arranging songs of praise. Most important, Don gave himself to a *life* of praise and worship to God. I believe that is why so many of his compositions have become standards in the Church worldwide.

My next step was to print posters and flyers promoting praise and healing meetings. This was a leap of faith for me, because I did not know the mechanics of my message. I just didn't have the theological background. But God had spoken to me, and I knew that my response must be prompt obedience. After all, the truth of Proverbs had come to pass in me:

My son, give attention to my words; incline your ear to my sayings. Do not let them depart from your eyes; keep them in the midst of your heart; for they are life to those who find them, and health to all their flesh. Keep your heart with all diligence, for out of it spring the issues of life. Put away from you a deceitful mouth, and put perverse lips far from you (Proverbs 4:20-24).

Oral Roberts had been right. God's prophetic word, flowing from my spirit, had been medicine to me. It had saved my spiritual life, and I could waste no time in attending to it. So we began to book our meetings, scheduling the first one for February 1983.

I started to prepare for the initial event, devoting myself to fasting, prayer, and God's Word. I still had trouble connecting worship and healing theologically, and all my years of education weren't proving very helpful at the moment. But where class and curriculum had fallen short, experience took over. God, in fact, had been preparing me for years; I just hadn't recognized it.

I went through nearly two decades of ministry in my mind, re-living different events that I now began to realize were a series of lessons to prepare me for this new day. One of the most important had taken place ten years earlier in Poland.

DISCOVERING MY FUTURE IN THE PAST

During our 1970 tour of South Africa, the Lord had told me that He was going to send Living Sound into the closed countries of Eastern Europe: "You will do things that most people will believe impossible. If you obey and trust me, I will protect you." It was quite literally a jarring word, an audible voice that I heard with more than my ears. My entire body vibrated to the sound. Yet I fought it at first, knowing it would require a deeper level of commitment than any of us had ever made. The price could be high.

The word came while the team was onstage, singing their last couple of songs. I was in a prayer room just to the side of the platform. In about 15 minutes it would be time for me to preach. But now I was undone. I argued with the Lord, wrestled with him, despite—or perhaps because of—a promise I had once made to take the Gospel to the Soviet Union. I was stretched out on the floor, trembling, perspiring, and filled with fear.

The team sang their final song and walked offstage, while I slowly made my way to the pulpit, my heart pounding with every step. I looked like I had seen a ghost, one of them later said. My face was ashen, and my lips trembled when I tried to speak. I made several attempts to read my text, but I couldn't even put a sentence together. I stood there looking foolish for a while, several hundred onlookers no doubt bewildered by my mute rebellion. Finally I gave in and told the gasping crowd what God had said. Living Sound was going to minister behind the Iron Curtain.

When a preposterous, faith-stretching word is spoken it's important to refrain from "helping" God make it happen. I promised the Lord I would not solicit any invitations to Soviet Bloc countries. First Thessalonians 5:24 would have to hold true: "He who calls you is faithful, who also will do it." If God had called us, He would bring it to pass.

For two years nothing happened. Then in June 1972, a letter from Poland arrived while we were ministering in southern

California. It was from a group in Krakow, the home of Jagiellonian University. The seal on the letterhead looked official, but it was in Polish, so we weren't sure who had sent it. It appeared to have been written by students wanting us to sing for a special campus event, but the writer's broken English made it hard to decipher exactly what kind of event.

My heart leapt at the thought that this might be God's Word coming to pass. We were going to Europe in a few weeks, and the only clear part of the letter, the October dates it specified, would fit our schedule perfectly. That gave the whole situation the look of a big, divine fingerprint, and made it doubly intriguing.

We arrived in Krakow on the appointed October evening and made contact with our sponsors. The venue was not on campus after all, but in a nightclub near the old town square. We were booked for two concerts. But something seemed odd, strange beyond the culture shock experienced travelers take in stride.

For one thing, a few young people tried to buy drugs from us while we were setting up our equipment in the club. And they seemed not to know, or at least not respect, the fact that we were a Christian group. They treated us as if we were the stereotypical rock band for which America is infamous. Sex, drugs, rock 'n roll. That appeared to be what they were expecting.

The first concert was slated for five o'clock, the second for seven. By four-thirty the room was filled with young people, smoke, and the smell of beer. The nightclub's low ceiling made our audience of 200 feel like twice as many. The beer made them sound like it.

Larry Dalton had arranged some popular songs for the first part of the "show." Eventually the Fifth Dimension and Carpenters tunes would give way to contemporary Christian music with more meaningful, if not provocative, lyrics. I planned to deliver some culture-bridging remarks about Copernicus and other great Poles we Americans admired, before sharing what might accurately be called "Gospel lite." We were, after all, just testing the waters. This was Marx and Lenin country, the Communist world, and I thought we should be careful navigating it at first.

Two songs into the concert, the Holy Spirit wrecked our plans. The crowd was restive, upset, almost as if they knew we were holding something back. The group, not used to singing vapid top-40 songs, switched to more familiar territory, a rousing spiritual that featured my Jan. Still our young audience seemed agitated. Maybe they wanted a "harder" sound. If so, they soon got one, but not from the band.

I got up and walked to the microphone, praying silently on the way. My material on Copernicus and Chopin went out the window after the first couple of sentences fell flat, and suddenly I was preaching. "Marx and Lenin did not know the way," I heard myself saying. "There is only one way, and His name is Jesus."

Behind me I could hear the team muffling gasps and coughing nervously. *A few knees must be knocking,* I thought. And I was sure every heart was pounding like my own.

I told the now rapt crowd what Christ had done in the life of each Living Sound member standing onstage with me, and in particular how He had changed mine. I had been a drunken sinner, but Jesus had redeemed my life and made me a child of God. I explained how Christ could do the same thing for every one of them.

In my closing statement I challenged them to turn from communism and toward Jesus Christ. Then I walked offstage, my footsteps the only sound in a room as still as a picture.

As soon as I found the edge of the stage, two young men took me by the arms and escorted me down a flight of stairs a few steps away, into a predictably dank basement. They had not known who we were, they said. They were surprised that we were a Christian group, and were quite upset with the performance, especially with what I had just proclaimed. Then they told me who they were, and suddenly I realized the whole evening had been a set-up by none other than God Himself!

These men were the local leaders of the *Komsomols*, the Youth Communist Party of Poland. The nightclub was owned and operated by the Party, and every student upstairs was a card-carrying member. We were singing, they said, for a fundraising benefit for communism.

The team had finished the first concert by now, and one by one, several found the basement. They stood along the walls looking stunned, while I sat at a rickety card table, a bare light bulb hanging from the ceiling over me, angry men pacing the floor in front of me. They accused us of being from the CIA. It was a scene straight out of a bad spy movie, a cliché that would have been celluloid perfection in black and white.

A fund-raiser for the Communist Party. Living Sound was actually raising money for communism! What other Christian group could claim to have done something like that? "Yeah," one of the team members would later observe, "but what other group of communists ever sold tickets to a revival?"

Our young accusers were in a quandary now. It was almost seven o'clock, and a well-liquored audience upstairs would be in no mood for refunds. American groups were a rarity in Poland, and they wanted to hear this one. Not only that, but word was racing across town like a grass fire that the group was *Christian*, and that we were making some very bold statements. Now the place was packed far beyond what any fire marshal in his right mind would have allowed. Besides, the Party needed the money.

"OK, you can sing your songs," the boss said. "But *you*"—he pointed at me—"you will not speak. Don't even walk to the stage." Fine, I agreed, knowing that this was no compromise. Our songs were every bit as "dangerous" as my preaching. God was at work here. He had opened a door—an Iron Curtain—that no one could shut.

The team had already started singing by the time I made it back upstairs. They smiled when they saw me standing against the back wall, partly from relief, but mostly because they also knew by now that the Spirit was pulling off something bigger than any of us could have dreamed.

Halfway through the second concert I sensed a change in the spiritual power level in the room. The Holy Spirit was taking everything up a notch. Our singers were raising their hands in praise to God, a few of them crying as they stood in the presence of the Lord. I looked in awe around the room. Some of the students were crying too, but most sat motionless, their eyes and hearts transfixed. They were experiencing the presence of a God who dwells in the praises of His people. These young lives—and beyond them, Poland—would never be the same.

Larry ended the second concert with a count-off into a raucous choral rendition of a little song that had been popularized by the charismatic renewal. It wasn't an impressive lyric or some cleverly written Jesus jingle. It was just a simple chorus with a one-line prayer attached to the end:

God is moving by His Spirit, moving through all the earth.
Signs and wonders when God moveth.
Move, O Lord, in me.

The song ended with an enormous brass and percussion flourish, and the singers shouting "Hallelujah! Hallelujah! Amen!" Then there was dead silence. Joel Vesanen and I stood there leaning against the back wall, wondering what would happen next. "There's either going to be a revival or a riot," he whispered.

Fifteen seconds later we had our answer. Like soldiers leaping to attention at the sudden appearance of a general, the crowd jumped to their feet in thunderous ovation, yelling and clapping rhythmically for a reprise. Two encores and several hours later, dozens of young Polish communists had committed their lives to the same God they previously had claimed did not exist.

It was astounding, said trombonist Tom Hall afterward, to watch the words of a song come to pass before one's very eyes.

Now, years later, it was still astounding. But it was no longer a mystery. Now it made sense, so much so that I wondered why I had never made the connection before. We had worshiped God with abandon that night, and afterward many young people had been healed of the worst disease ever to plague the human race—sin.

Moreover, we had become so famous overnight that two years later, when we had returned at the invitation of a future pope, thousands of spiritually hungry Poles had filled halls and cathedrals around the country to hear us. And thousands had been healed. I began to see the connection. Praise had removed—*demolished*—spiritual barricades that diplomats and politicians gingerly danced around, barriers that kept needy people from their healing. ***Praising God had torn down strongholds.***

I had finally discovered the link between worshiping God and the healing of people—a thing called war.

ENDNOTE

1. In years to come, Palestinian-born evangelist Benny Hinn would build his worldwide healing ministry on this same mandate. As a result, millions have discovered the direct connection between the power of praise and worship and healing.

Chapter 3

War and Praise

Could it be that we live in two worlds, not just one? Could it be that the "mid-heaven," the arena of conflict, intersects with earth somewhere between our ears?

～

The terrorist attacks of September 11, 2001, plunged the United States into war. America did not choose to join this battle, but the nation was at war nonetheless, because she was under attack.

The same thing is true spiritually. Every human being on earth, including you, is under siege, although most of us have never fired a shot in self-defense. Whether we like it or not, life is war. The father of all terrorism hates us, and we must resist him or die.

But there is something different about spiritual war, about the *way* it is fought. In fact God has given us instructions that any military strategist would pronounce suicidal: you and I are called to march into the middle of the battlefield and then turn our focus *away* from the enemy. We are called to sing, to celebrate God while the enemy falls before us! Isaiah chapter 30 paints an incredible picture:

> *You shall have a song as in the night when a holy festival is kept, and gladness of heart as when one goes with a flute, to come into the mountain of the Lord, to the Mighty One of Israel. The Lord will cause His glorious voice to be heard, and show the descent of His arm, with the indignation of His anger and the flame of a devouring fire, with scattering, tempest, and hailstones. For through the voice of the Lord Assyria will be beaten down, as He strikes with the rod. And in every place where the staff of punishment passes, which the Lord lays on him, it will be with tambourines and harps; and in battles of brandishing He will fight with it* (Isaiah 30:29-32).

What an astounding scene! God calls His people to celebrate Him with singing and playing, and then He promises to do a little drumming of His own, *on the back of the enemy!*

Don't let the lesson be lost on you. This chapter, and those that follow, will show you how to overcome an enemy who for millennia has afflicted humankind with pain, heartache, and disease. And don't be misled; satan attacks you only because you bear the image of the One whom he truly loathes. He is waging a war to erase God's image wherever it is displayed, hence his hatred for you. And the best way you can fight back is to reflect that image, the blinding light of God's glory, right back at him. That is what happens when Christians praise the Lord.

Bible teacher and gifted violinist Steve Griffing points out that there were only two reasons for the men of ancient Israel to assemble in Jerusalem—to celebrate God in sacred festivals, and to gather for war. That is a key principle of this book: spiritually speaking, the two are one and the same. *The celebration of God is simultaneously an act of war.*

WAR AND PRAISE

Saint Peter said we were called "…out of darkness into His marvelous light" (1 Pet. 2:9). Are these two separate events? When you walk into a dark room, are there two switches, one to turn off the darkness and another to switch on the light? Of course not! Light automatically dispels darkness, as it has throughout the history of the universe. There has never been a single occasion, not even in the most remote corner of the cosmos, where light has co-existed for a single nanosecond with darkness.

After the death of my wife, Jan, and my subsequent deliverance from despair through praising God, He called me to minister healing and deliverance through the means of praise and worship. I have done my utmost to remain faithful to that calling, asking God not to bless my plans, but to show me His.

The believer's participation in the plan of God is called a "ministry of reconciliation" in Second Corinthians 5:18. Saint Peter explains in a later epistle that we are "a chosen generation, a royal priesthood, a holy nation, His own special people, that you may proclaim the praises of Him who called you out of darkness into His marvelous light" (1 Pet. 2:9). We reconcile people to God, bring them out of darkness into light, by proclaiming God's praises. In other words, we proclaim the same theme here on earth that the people of God sing before His throne in Revelation chapter 5:

And they sang a new song, saying: "You are worthy to take the scroll, and to open its seals; for You were slain, and have redeemed us to God by Your blood out of every tribe and tongue and people and nation, and have made us kings and priests to our God; and we shall reign on the earth" (Revelation 5:9-10).

We are kings who represent the King of kings to the people of the earth. That is our ministry of reconciliation. But we also are "priests to our God," representing the peoples of the earth to our High Priest. In other words, we "stand in the gap before [God] on behalf of the land" (Ezek. 22:30). We are the "go-betweens." In a word, we *intercede.*

There has been much discussion and teaching about "intercession" and its synonym "intercessory prayer" in Christian circles in recent years, especially as the 21st century made its explosive entrance onto history's stage. Unfortunately, sometimes we are prone to cast spiritual warfare in a wrong light. My friend Jim Gilbert puts a humorous touch on an ultimately serious point:

I was a Pentecostal preacher's kid, which I suppose sharpened my wit about some of the sacred cows of our movement. But I lacked grace as a teenager, and couldn't wait to barbecue as many of them as possible. In addition, my schoolmates already thought we "holy rollers" were weird, and the peer pressure made me desperate to be "normal." I especially recoiled at what some people called spiritual, but what I viewed as merely eccentric.

Intercession was an easy target for a smart aleck like me. I thought it meant locking yourself in a broom closet and wrestling with the devil. Then, after suffering three days of stomach cramps, you came out claiming to have had a good time! I figured the intercessors were the plain Janes who had no social life anyway, and were too dull to be interested in Sunday football. They had plenty of time to pray.

It's embarrassing as I look back on those days, of course, and I repented of my bad attitude years ago. But from the distance of several decades, I can also see that the stereotype often fit our ranks all too well. We made "spiritual" synonymous with "spooky." And we gave the devil a lot of airtime he didn't deserve.

I would like to paint a different picture of intercession for you in these pages. I'm not going to give you formulas for shutting down darkness. Of course we cannot ignore the enemy of our souls, but neither should we lavish attention on him. There is simply no need to expend great amounts of energy yelling at the devil when we are called to a higher way, a smarter strategy.

WINNING A WAR ALREADY WON

Spiritual wars are fought in five main stages:

- ❖ Identify the enemy.
- ❖ Assess the enemy's strongholds.
- ❖ Commit to a plan of resistance.
- ❖ Deploy tactics to carry out the plan and enforce the enemy's defeat.
- ❖ Maintain the peace.

The rest of this chapter is concerned with the first two stages of spiritual war. Just remember that "identify" does not mean "magnify." We shall not hold a lens to the devil and then marvel at how big he is, nor will we dramatize the battle of the ages as a "last-minute victory" for Christ and His Church. Instead, in the chapters that follow you will see how truly *small* your adversary became when your Deliverer bounded into the ring! And you'll see that, in every arena of the world, you and I have been commissioned as the announcers in that ring, lifting up the right hand of the Victor, and proclaiming His name to everyone in the seats. **The world awaits our proclamation.**

IDENTIFYING THE ENEMY

It is humanly impossible to identify an unseen enemy, and this is where most people—most *nations*—are blind. The very existence of tens of thousands of religions proves that sinful man has no idea how to defend himself from satan's onslaught, much less how to prevail. Saint Paul pointed out this innate blindness to a group of pagan philosophers in Acts 17:

> *Then Paul stood in the midst of the Areopagus and said, "Men of Athens, I perceive that in all things you are very religious; for as I was passing through and considering the objects of your worship, I even found an altar with this inscription: TO THE UNKNOWN GOD. Therefore, the One whom you worship without knowing, Him I proclaim to you: God, who made the world and everything in it, since He is Lord of heaven and earth, does not dwell in temples made with hands. Nor is He worshiped with men's hands, as though He needed anything, since He gives to all life, breath, and all things. And He has made from one blood every nation of men to dwell on all the face of the earth,*

*and has determined their preappointed times and the boundaries of their dwellings, **so that they should seek the Lord, in the hope that they might grope for Him and find Him,** though He is not far from each one of us (Acts 17:22-27).*

The Areopagus (Mars Hill) was the hilltop locale in Athens where Greece's philosopher-princes, who prided themselves on their religious diversity, gathered to discuss the latest spiritual trends. Paul made it clear that their search for God was commendable, and that in fact the true God had put this desire in their hearts.

But the Athenians' multitude of idols proved them blind on two fronts, first to the God who had created them, and second to satan, the enemy behind their blindness. The apostle told them they were groping about, spiritually sightless, and that their hope of a cure lay in coming to know the true God. "The One whom you worship without knowing, Him I proclaim to you" (Acts 17:23).

Satan doesn't care if you worship, as long as you don't *know* God. He doesn't even want you to *recognize* the true God, and it is to his further advantage if you don't recognize him (satan) either. But the Bible thoroughly exposes this fallen angel as the terrorist of the human soul. Moreover Ephesians 6:12 reveals that he does not act alone, but that we are also up against "principalities, against powers, against the rulers of the darkness of this age, against spiritual hosts of wickedness in the heavenly places." The devil has arrayed his entire house of hatred against Christ and His Church, in other words, against *you*.

ASSESSING ENEMY STRONGHOLDS

Unlike secularists, most Christians do not doubt the existence of satan, and are not surprised to hear that he hates them. Yet it isn't just sinners who suffer in the devil's murderous grip. Multiplied millions of believers are manhandled by him; tossed at will like rag dolls from sickness to sickness; battered by depression, divorce, and a host of addictions and other maladies. Worse, families seem to pass these curses, both genetic and habitual, from generation to generation.

Even more tragic, nations, and beyond them whole regions of the world, are held in demonic sway. They are as blind as the ancient Athenians; yet, far from being proud, they are utterly hopeless. From the murderous spirit that infects entire Middle Eastern societies to the genocidal rage of Rwanda, it is as if satan is operating spiritual fiefdoms.

In fact there is no "as if." Middle Eastern hatred, North African tribalism, communism, Western secularism, and other philosophies and worldviews are more than mere ideologies. Each one is a principality, governed by "rulers of the darkness of this age" (Eph. 6:12). Dictators (like the late Saddam Hussein) are both puppets and perpetrators; they "are of [their] father the devil, and the desires of [their] father [they] want to do." Jesus said those words in John 8:44, and then continued, "He was a murderer from the beginning, and does not stand in the truth, because there is no truth in him. When he speaks a lie, he speaks from his own resources, for he is a liar and the father of it."

I spent much time behind the Iron Curtain before the Soviet Bloc crumbled and was often interrogated by the notorious KGB. The motivating force behind that truly "evil empire" was easily recognizable—it was satan, still trying after 6,000 years to exalt his throne "above the stars of God" (Isa. 14:13).

Replacing God is impossible, of course, but that didn't stop a passel of aging pretenders in Moscow's Kremlin from trying.

The Soviet government, for example, attempted to be omnipresent, omniscient, and omnipotent, so they plastered the
USSR with propagandist billboards, policed every breath the
people took, and maintained more spies within their own borders than without.

The more I traveled there, and the more run-ins I had with
the system, the more I realized that I needed to understand Soviet communism at its core if I hoped to effectively overcome it.
After the Spirit's directive to me concerning praise and worship
in 1982, I began to reconsider our Iron Curtain outreach and
how to fulfill my mandate there. As I prayed, a single word kept
repeating in my mind—*strongholds*. I knew Paul had used the
term in one of his epistles, and I quickly found it in Second
Corinthians 10:3-5:

> *For though we walk in the flesh, we do not war according to*
> *the flesh. For the weapons of our warfare are not carnal but*
> *mighty in God for pulling down strongholds, casting down ar-*
> *guments and every high thing that exalts itself against the*
> *knowledge of God, bringing every thought into captivity to*
> *the obedience of Christ.*

That was *exactly* what had happened in Poland in the
Communist Youth Club! A newspaper report couldn't have
described the evening better. Through praise and worship we
had launched spiritual weapons, pulled down strongholds, and
cast down arguments. Now I saw that the same strategy, using
praise as a missile to deliver spiritual payloads, would work
elsewhere, not because it was a formula, but because the Lord
had ordained it.

Praise is a reversal of original sin, a direct rebuttal of satan's vow
to "be like the Most High" (Isa. 14:14). Psalm 22:3 says the Lord is

"enthroned in the praises" of His people. Our praises are the throne from which He chooses to exert His authority. Satan, and Adam after him, tried to dethrone God. Praise enthrones Him.

Satan's defeat is enforced when God is exalted. Yes, he fell "like lightning from heaven," according to Jesus (Luke 10:18), but the Bible speaks of more than one heaven. Paul said in Second Corinthians 12:2 that he (or someone close to him) had been "caught up to the third heaven." Whether the apostle was being literal or simply alluding to some aspect of the cosmic hierarchy, he was at least ascribing a multidimensional quality to the spiritual realm. Besides, Ephesians 6:12, cited earlier, speaks of "spiritual hosts of wickedness in the heavenly places," or to transliterate from the Greek, the "mid-heaven."

The scene in Revelation chapter 12, whether it is viewed as a past or future event in terms of prophecy, corroborates Paul's account of what goes on in the heavens:

> And war broke out in heaven: Michael and his angels fought with the dragon; and the dragon and his angels fought, but they did not prevail, nor was a place found for them in heaven any longer (Revelation 12:7-8).

Even though Jesus had seen satan plummet from Heaven, some years later both Paul and John were still describing the "heavenlies" as a scene of ongoing conflict. Taken in this light it becomes clear that strongholds are where the "rulers of darkness" establish their command centers. They are, specifically, *rebel strongholds.*

But what does all this mean to us in the "here and now" of life? After all, no matter what angels and dragons are doing in Heaven, right here on earth is where we suffer in our bodies, and equally so in our minds. Could it be that we live in two worlds, not just one?

Could it be that the "mid-heaven," the arena of conflict, intersects with earth somewhere between our ears?

THE PRIMARY BATTLEFIELD

Second Corinthians 10:4-5 is a description not only of spiritual victory, but also of the scene of battle:

> *For the weapons of our warfare are not carnal but mighty in God for pulling down strongholds, casting down arguments and every high thing that exalts itself against the knowledge of God, bringing every thought into captivity to the obedience of Christ.*

I had seen this passage prior to making my commitment regarding praise and worship, and would have acknowledged the existence of strongholds. I knew in general that they might include physical disease, spiritual oppression, temptation, financial bondage, and the like. But I had never really noticed verse 5; I had never really seen that *the mind is ground zero in spiritual warfare.*

The late psychoanalyst Viktor Frankl, a survivor of the Nazi Holocaust, vividly illustrated this fact with story after story in his acclaimed concentration camp memoir, *Man's Search for Meaning.* Frankl, a Jew, spoke the language of psychology rather than theology, but readily admitted that the battles he and his fellow prisoners fought were chiefly spiritual. In one story, Frankl tells of a man he called "F——," who had a dream that the camp would be liberated on March 30, 1945.

> When F—— told me about his dream, he was still full of hope and convinced that the voice of his dream would be right. But as the promised day drew nearer, the war news which reached our camp made it appear very unlikely that we would be free on the promised

date. On March twenty-ninth, F—— suddenly became ill and ran a high temperature. On March thirtieth, the day his prophecy had told him that the war and suffering would be over for him, he became delirious and lost consciousness. On March thirty-first, he was dead. To all outward appearances, he had died of typhus....The ultimate cause of my friend's death was that the expected liberation did not come, and he was severely disappointed. This suddenly lowered his body's resistance against the latent typhus infection. His faith in the future and his will to live had become paralyzed, and his body fell victim to illness.[1]

St. Paul makes it clear that, from individuals to entire cultures, *strongholds are primarily thought patterns*. In Acts 8:9-24 Peter and John encountered a former sorcerer named Simon. He held great sway over the minds of the Samaritans, who "heeded him because he had astonished them with his sorceries for a long time" (Acts 8:11). (In fact, his name means "hearkening.") But Peter turned the tables on this dominator of people's thoughts and told him to "pray God if perhaps the thought of your heart may be forgiven you. For I see that you are poisoned by bitterness and bound by iniquity" (Acts 8:22-23). Simon, himself, was caught in a stronghold; the perpetrator was a pawn.

Judas, the betrayer of Jesus, was also prisoner to a thought. John 13:2 says, "And supper being ended, the devil having already put it into the heart of Judas Iscariot, Simon's son, to betray Him...." Satan dropped a thought into Judas' mind, and he bought into it with his heart.

The reason it is possible to believe something with "all my heart" is because the mind and heart work together. In fact they form a two-way street. Thoughts are not only dropped into the heart via the mind, but according to Jesus, also come from the heart into the mind:

> *But those things which proceed out of the mouth come from the heart, and they defile a man. **For out of the heart proceed evil thoughts**, murders, adulteries, fornications, thefts, false witness, blasphemies* (Matthew 15:18-19).

When I read this passage my mind rewound two chapters to the Lord's parable about sowing, in which He said "some seed fell by the wayside; and the birds came and devoured them" (Matt. 13:4). The Savior went on to explain Himself in Matthew:

> *When anyone hears the word of the kingdom, and does not understand it, then the wicked one comes and snatches away what was sown in his heart. This is he who received seed by the wayside* (Matthew 13:19).

Satan has open access to the unrenewed mind. He sets up strongholds there by snatching the good seed of God's Word, leaving it barren, to be overwhelmed by weeds, the "evil thoughts, murders, adulteries," etc., about which we are warned two chapters later. Moreover, if the resulting ungodly mindset is shared with others, such strongholds can even become territorial.

A common example is the so-called "red-light district," the center of prostitution, pornography, and other criminal activity, that afflicts so many major cities around the world. One of them is Stockholm, Sweden, where my late wife, Jan, and I toured with Living Sound in the mid-1970s. The group of Christians hosting our concerts could not house the team with families, so they accommodated us in the one place they could afford—the downtown YMCA, which was situated in the seediest part of town. That meant, of course, being separated from Jan, and staying in a dormitory with our single men.

I grumbled myself to sleep that night, only to awaken at about 3 A.M. with an instant awareness that I was under spiritual attack. The most horrible, perverse sexual images I had ever known were filling—no, *invading*—my mind, with such realism that I felt as though I had just committed what I was imagining. *This might be a dream*, I thought, and instinctively fought to rouse myself.

"I've got you now, Terry Law," said an accusing whisper. "This is the real you. You're nothing but a pervert."

Oh, no, I'm not, I thought as I sat up in bed. *That's the voice of the devil, and those are his thoughts.*

I remembered from childhood days how Christians at my dad's church would sing about the blood of Jesus whenever evil spirits had been revealed. So, in a voice quiet enough not to wake the other guys, but loud enough for hell to hear, I began to sing an old hymn our team had revived:

> *Oh, the blood of Jesus*
> *Oh, the blood of Jesus*
> *Oh, the blood of Jesus*
> *It washes white as snow*

I repeated the chorus for several minutes, just sitting there in bed with my arms raised in worship. Then I decided to take my stand. "Satan, leave me alone, get out of my thoughts, and get out of this room, in Jesus' name," I whispered gruffly. I felt the evil spirit leave the room, and I got out of bed to pace and think. I was puzzled as to why such an odd attack had taken place.

Nothing like that had ever happened to me, and I certainly had never harbored such depraved desires.

I walked to the window and looked down at the street below, where a neon haze bathed the underworld red. There were prostitutes stationed not just on the corner, but all along the sidewalks. I saw movement in the shadows and realized that one of them had not even bothered to take her customer indoors. *This is the devil's territory,* I thought, and then it dawned on me that it really was. Satan had established a mindset in the people that this part of town belonged to him, and from prostitute to politician, everyone accepted it as fact. He called the shots here, and anyone entering was fair game for attack.

Your eyes are a gateway to your heart and mind. You must guard them, like King David, who said in Psalm 101:3: "I will set nothing wicked before my eyes." David learned this principle the hard way, through the biggest failure of his life. It happened the one time when he looked where he shouldn't have, and took a rooftop peek at another man's wife, the naked Bathsheba. Through David's "eye gate" satan was able to drop an "evil thought" into the king's unguarded mind. Later, after his sin had snowballed from lust to adultery to murder, and was exposed by the prophet Nathan, David publicly repented, going so far as to commission the song we know as Psalm 51. There he spoke of his thoughts in terms of his eyes, saying "my sin is always before me (Ps. 51:3). The resolution of David's song of repentance is of utmost importance here:

> *Restore to me the joy of Your salvation, and uphold me by Your generous Spirit. Then I will teach transgressors Your ways, and sinners shall be converted to You. Deliver me from the guilt of bloodshed, O God, the God of my salvation, and my tongue shall sing aloud of Your righteousness. O Lord,*

open my lips, and my mouth shall show forth Your praise (Psalm 51:12-15).

A song of praise on your lips is a safeguard for your mind. It causes you to see things from God's point of view, so that "the words of my mouth and the meditation of my heart [may] be acceptable in Your sight, O Lord, my strength and my Redeemer" (Ps. 19:14).

STRONG MEN

In Luke chapter 11, when Jesus' ministry of deliverance was absurdly attributed to demonic power, He likened a spiritual stronghold to a "strong man's house," and spoke of his ministry as "binding" the strong man (see Luke 11:14-23). And while the term "strong man" most often applies to demonic rulers, it can also aptly describe a prevalent mindset, such as Marxism, the philosophy of socialism that so thoroughly bound and impoverished the erstwhile Soviet Union.

Although the USSR collapsed politically in 1991, the spiritual principality behind it hung on. Thousands of statues of Vladimir Lenin, the USSR's founder, were torn down after that virtually bloodless revolution, but today millions of tiny "Lenins" still stubbornly stand in the minds of a generation that does not know how to topple them.

Russia, for example, made spasmodic economic progress after embracing some free market principles, but the nation still lags because of the habitual view that work is an unprofitable exercise to be avoided, and the assumption that the state is ultimately responsible to "take care of" people (an assumption more and more Americans are also starting to make).

New converts in the former Soviet Union often view Christian values in terms of lingering socialist ideals, naively dismissing a lifetime of oppression as a "good system run by bad people." Yet even a cursory understanding of Scripture reveals the incompatibility of biblical faith with the stronghold of socialism. Indeed as a friend of mine has observed, "Claiming that the USSR was a good system run by bad people is like saying hell is a nice place plagued with hot weather."

The nagging persistence of such mindsets is the reason Jesus commissioned us, in Matthew chapter 28, to make disciples by baptizing and teaching them "all things that I have commanded you" (Matt. 28:20). Paul, in Acts 20, described it as declaring "the whole counsel of God" (Acts 20:27).

This is the primary reason that my ministry, "World Compassion," always connects the provision of emergency aid to the long-term goal of making disciples. To feed people's bodies without giving them a future in Christ would be to deny our Lord's commission and leave millions in their sin, their inevitable slide into hell merely made more comfortable instead of being cancelled.

I wish I could tell you that this is a brilliant insight on my part, but the truth is, like King David, I had to learn the hard way. It was 1992, the year after Russia got her freedom, and my assistant, Joel, and I were in Maloyaroslavets, a little town two hours southwest of Moscow, distributing Bibles. A Russian pastor was translating for us as we passed out hundreds of copies of the Book that, for more than seventy years, had been denied these people.

At one point a delivery truck pulled up nearby. The driver got out, swung open the lift gate, and started handing out something. But after only a few minutes, he abruptly stopped, got back behind the wheel, and drove away, leaving dozens of frustrated people empty handed.

"What was that?" I asked the pastor.

"It was the bread truck, but he only had enough bread for twenty-five people," he replied.

Just then a little old lady, a *babushka*, as the Russian grannies are called, walked up and asked the pastor a question. He smiled and answered her, holding out a Bible, but she just waved him off and walked away, uttering a single, obviously bitter phrase.

"What did she say?" I asked him. He tried to dismiss it as nothing, but I insisted. "What did she say?"

"She asked me what we were giving away, and I offered her a Bible," he explained. Then, he looked at me downcast. "She said, 'We can't eat your Bibles.'"

I realized that day that I was like a boxer wearing only one glove. I could never defeat Russia's strong man by distributing spiritual bread alone. Marxism had impoverished not only Russian souls but Russian minds and stomachs as well. I needed to do what I had learned from Oral Roberts, to minister to the "whole" man—spirit, mind, and body.

That day World Compassion was born in my heart. And ever since then our ministry has endeavored to meet people at the point of their need, feeding, healing, and clothing their bodies, minds, and spirits. Isn't this the answer to the hottest question of the past few years: "What would Jesus do?" The Lord healed people, forgave them, ate dinner with them, and loved them exactly as the were. And He bound the strong man every time.

POISONED SOCIETIES

Marxism isn't the only poisonous mindset at work in the world. Satan has often poisoned the thinking of whole societies through the deceptive teaching and philosophies of prominent thinkers, dedicated revolutionaries, and socially influential personalities. We might also legitimately call these people "strong men," the kind Jesus described as "of your father the devil."

Most often the poisoning of a society begins with the gradual, subtle introduction of revolutionary ideas, and the legitimizing of previous taboos (euthanasia, for example). Eventually, however, these ideas prove to be veritable "thought-bombs," exploding at every level of society, giving proof to the saying that "the pen is mightier than the sword."

Immanuel Kant was a German philosopher who lived in Prussia from 1724 to 1804. His most potent "thought-bomb" was to dismiss belief in transcendent "absolute truth" in favor of the idea that knowledge is based purely on sensory experience; if you cannot not see, hear, touch, taste, or smell it, then you cannot *truly* know it.

Kant's work laid the foundation for *George Wilhelm Friedrich Hegel,* whose contributions to *German Idealism* were to lead in two influential directions. One the one hand he was followed philosophically by men like *Soren Kierkegaard, Friedrich Nietzsche, and Jean-Paul Sartre*, whose successive extension and refinement of Hegel's ideas led to the development and eventual dominance of a philosophy known as *Existentialism*, which posits an indifferent universe where individuals determine the meaning and purpose of their own lives.

Existentialism has become such a powerful stronghold that the typical college student today denies the existence of absolute truth. Relativistic thinking pervades our educational systems right down to the elementary level. It is a "thought-bomb" going off in kindergarten, yet many Christians are oblivious to it.

Karl Marx, on the other hand, liked Hegel's dialectical[2] *way* of thinking more than his actual content, and used it to develop an atheistic worldview called *Dialectical Materialism,* that comprehensively addressed education, religion, trade, economics, culture, and so forth. Marx held the view that the end justifies the means, drawing on the theories of his contemporary, British naturalist *Charles Darwin.*

In the mid-1800s, Darwin introduced theories that are taken as fact by today's public education establishment. He stated that all forms of life, including humans, evolved from lower forms— man is merely a higher animal. His theory of evolution, followed to its logical conclusion, breeds despair from classroom to boardroom, and has led multitudes to live meaningless lives, filled with immorality, and devoid of hope.

Sigmund Freud found Darwin fascinating. As the father of psychoanalysis, he claimed that humans, as mere evolved animals, have a single motivation: pleasure. Freud's ideas, like those of Kant, Hegel, Marx, and Darwin, were based on the belief that there is no purpose in man's existence. "Anything goes." Today's stronghold of sexual obsession is, at least in the West, traceable to Freud's influence.

Vladimir Lenin, who famously dismissed religion as the "opiate of the people," was the architect of the ultimate Darwinian conceit, modern communism. His political application of the concept of "survival of the fittest" rendered terror, torture, and murder quite justifiable. No wonder it proved to be the deadliest force of the 20th century.

Not all world-changers have been philosophers, politicians, and psychoanalysts. Some of the most profoundly effective ones, in fact, have been pop music stars.

When *The Beatles* burst onto the American scene in late 1963, they seemed harmless enough, a little rebellious perhaps, but ultimately just another fad. However, one of them, *John Lennon*, was an articulate pop-philosopher who in the long run became the Pied Piper of America's own cultural revolution. Ironically, Lennon's song "Imagine" is so atheistic in tone that it could easily have been penned by Vladimir Lenin himself.

There is one more strong man worth noting here. You are less likely to have heard of him than the others, yet he has been called the "most influential" philosopher alive by the *New Yorker* magazine. For this reason it will take a little longer to describe him.

Australian philosopher *Peter Singer* is, at the time of this writing, the Professor of Bioethics at Princeton University, and the world's foremost proponent of Preference-Utilitarianism, which, simply stated, says that the right thing to do is whatever produces the *preferred result* of the greatest number of persons. But Singer does not consider a baby a person, and among other things, has argued that parents should have 28 days *after* the birth of a baby (*any* baby) to decide whether it should live or die. He also believes that "fully consensual" sex involving any number of participants is ethically fine, including fully consensual animals (which Singer defines as "persons").

The reason *you need to know* about Peter Singer is that his many books are the "bibles" of various anti-Christian movements, among them militant environmentalism, homosexual activism, animal-rights activism, the pro-abortion movement, and of course, the increasingly vocal advocates of euthanasia. Most shocking of all, today's mainstream legal and medical professions openly welcome his views for consideration.

In every instance, these ideological giants have relied primarily on the power of ideas to change the world. Only one of them, the Soviet dictator Lenin, employed intimidation and physical violence, yet even he rose to power primarily with his pen, using guns later to retain that power.

On the face of it, you and I would appear to be the 90-pound weaklings getting sand kicked in our faces by the bullies of history. But God doesn't see it that way, and neither should we. According to Psalm 2, "He who sits in the heavens shall laugh; The Lord shall hold them in derision" (Ps. 2:4). And according to the apostle Paul, *we are sitting right there in the heavens with Him*:

> *But God, who is rich in mercy, because of His great love with which He loved us, even when we were dead in trespasses, made us alive together with Christ (by grace you have been saved), and raised us up together, and made us sit together in the heavenly places in Christ Jesus, that in the ages to come He might show the exceeding riches of His grace in His kindness toward us in Christ Jesus (Ephesians 2:4-7).*

To paraphrase the old comic strip, *Pogo*, we have seen the future, and it is us!

THE LIES HAVE IT

The mind is where spiritual warfare takes place from start to finish, even though the repercussions of the battle are felt everywhere else. Once the stronghold has been established—through buying into a lie, as Judas did—satan attempts to become entrenched in the mind of his captive. He does not want to give up ground, so he plants lying thought after lying thought, building new lies on the foundation of previous ones. Eventually it is impossible to distinguish truth from untruth. Reality itself becomes distorted.

I saw this kind of ruination on my first trip to Baghdad, Iraq, two months before the American military invasion. Saddam had done his best to convince the Iraqi populace that President George W. Bush was the devil incarnate. Even the lobby of my hotel, the Al Rashid, had a portrait of Mr. Bush on the floor, where Iraqis could walk on his face, the gravest of insults by their standards.

When I checked in, I respectfully walked around the President's image and asked for a high room that faced the city center. They gave me the same quarters where, in 1991, CNN reporter Peter Arnett had hunkered down for days as he broke the story of the first Gulf war.

I had heard the tragic report that a half million Iraqi children had died from disease in recent years, especially leukemia. So, the next day my assistant, Joel, and I went to the Saddam Hussein Children's Hospital to investigate for ourselves. What I saw was horrifying. Children were lying everywhere, some of them bandaged, the majority untreated. They looked utterly hopeless, as if they were just waiting to die.

Nabil, our translator, introduced us to the hospital administrator as concerned Americans, but instead of shaking our hands, the man began yelling at us. He called us murderers and told us how Saddam had exposed the USA's crimes. We Americans had purposely withheld food and medicine from the dying children of Iraq. He was so angry, yet so sincere in his rage. I stood there stunned, not knowing what to say, other than to promise that I would learn the truth and do my best to bring help.

In the weeks that followed I found out exactly what had taken place. Despite the United Nations' oil sanctions, the U.S. had purchased 39 billion dollars worth of oil from Iraq, paying for it with 29 billion dollars in food and another ten billion in medicines, the kinds of medicines that would save these children's lives. But Saddam had sold everything on the European black market, spending the profits on a military build-up, as well as constructing several of his 68 palaces. Not a penny had gone to the people of Iraq. This brutal dictator had allowed multitudes to die, blamed it all on America, and then audaciously billed himself as a hero, even naming the hospital after himself. And Iraq's medical community had bought the lie.

In early May, Joel and I, along with General Georges Sada and my two sons, Scot and Jason, found ourselves speeding across the Jordanian desert toward Iraq in a high-speed convoy of 15 white Chevy Suburbans. Having saddle tanks meant we could refuel without stopping. We drove in a wedge formation to foil potential bombers, covering more than 400 miles in a mere four hours, and flew through a border post left open for the same reason. Suddenly we were in Iraq, the first Western civilians on the ground there following President Bush's proclamation of victory the previous week.

Our first stop was the children's hospital in Baghdad, where I went directly to the administrator's office. He look astounded as I piled $80,000 worth—in wholesale value—of chemotherapy supplies on the floor in front of his desk. Then I stood and addressed him.

"We did not come to Iraq to kill your children, like Saddam told you on TV," I said quietly. "We've come to heal them in Jesus' name. Please accept these gifts from us as Christians who believe that Jesus is the Son of God."

I was exposing Saddam's lies, as well as binding the spiritual strong man behind him, with truth and love demonstrated in the name of Jesus.

A mixture of anger and grief settled across the administrator's face as I told him how Saddam had sold the food and medicine on the black market, and kept the profits. He looked away, cursing in Arabic as reality hit him. Then, turning back to me, he gratefully and humbly accepted our gifts.

THE GREATEST GIFT

I could have given the medicine to the Iraqi hospital administrator without mentioning the name of Jesus, but doing so would have left a lying spirit on the loose. In the long run, in fact, it is Jesus' name that will prove more valuable, more powerful, to that man, and to the nation of Iraq than all of the medicine in the world. I *had* to give our gifts in that name, **because without Jesus Iraq has no hope.** As a result, the young leukemia sufferers in that hospital received not only the chemotherapy they so desperately needed, but every child also received something of even greater, eternal value: a copy of my little *The Story of Jesus* booklet in Arabic.

The name of Jesus is one of three spiritual warheads that operate in tandem to defeat the devil and his devices. In Second Corinthians 10:4, St. Paul called them "mighty in God for pulling down strongholds." In the next three chapters we're going to take a look at these three warheads. They are the

* ❖ Word of God.
* ❖ Name of Jesus.
* ❖ Blood of Jesus.

Of course a warhead needs a rocket in order to deliver its payload to the target, and that's where praise comes in. *Praise is like a rocket launched from earth that breaks through the battleground of the "heavenlies," all the way to the throne.* Thus, in chapter seven, we'll see how the missile of praise launches these weapons into action against the enemy.

ENDNOTES

1. Viktor E. Frankl, *Man's Search for Meaning* (New York: Pocket Books, a division of Simon & Schuster, Inc., 1984), 96.

2. The word *dialectic* refers to the thought process of hypothesis, antithesis, and synthesis, that is, of posing an idea, testing it against completing ideas, and arriving at a conclusion.

Chapter 4

Spiritual Warhead: God's Word

The Bible ultimately challenges its reader not to accept, but to surrender to, the fact that it is God's Word.

～

When a Pashtun tribal elder, fleeing the war in Afghanistan, encountered the Lord Jesus in nearby Pakistan, it wasn't because someone told him about his sin, or the wages it brings. No one exposed the errors of Islam to him, or prayed a sinner's prayer with him. Nor did anyone explain that God "so loved" him that Jesus died for him. In fact it's doubtful that he even knew who Jesus was. Yet he met Him.

How did this happen? He saw a worship service, and it moved him. He frankly didn't understand what he was seeing, but the scene so gripped him that it drew him in. So he asked a friend of mine, Pakistani pastor David Nielson, for help.

"Sir, what is it about this Book?" he pleaded, holding up the Bible David had given him a week earlier. "Every time I open it, I see a vision of a Lamb standing by a glorious throne in front of millions and millions of people. When I close the Book, it goes away. When I open it up, it comes back. What is this?"

David turned to Revelation chapter 5 and showed the refugee in print what he had seen in the vision. He explained that Jesus was the Lamb who had been slain for him, and now stood at the right hand of God the Father, surrounded by millions of the redeemed worshiping him.

The Pashtun elder surrendered his life to Jesus on the spot. He had been convicted of his sin and saved to eternal life, not because someone had rebuked the darkness that imprisoned him, but because he had seen the shining light of God's glory in worship.[1]

Similar phenomena are taking place throughout the Muslim world. In fact today nine out of ten Muslim converts to Christ encounter Him in a dream or vision.[2]

The Holy Spirit could have given this Afghan man a vision of hell, or taken him on a Scrooge-like journey through his own past and shown him the horrors of his sin. But the Spirit did what Jesus had promised He would do: "But when the Helper comes, whom I shall send to you from the Father, the Spirit of truth who proceeds from the Father, He will testify of Me" (John 15:26).

This raises questions for us: What is our testimony? What do you and I reveal? If Jesus has called us "the light of the world" (Matt. 5:14), why do we develop techniques for cursing the darkness?

The Pashtun's story illustrates a recurring theme of these pages: *the celebration of God is simultaneously an act of war.* God gave him a peek into Heaven, where he saw a true worship cele-bration. And in that very moment a lifelong stronghold—the spirit of Islam—began to lose its grip on him.

When Pastor David subsequently opened the Bible to him, a spiritual sword pierced the man's heart (see Heb. 4:12). The grip of the Islamic mindset was broken because of the awesome power of the Word of God.

GOD'S WORD—A BIOLOGICAL WEAPON

Thoughts, as we have seen, are powerful for building strong-holds, *thought systems* that, once adopted, can hold sway over indi-viduals and families for generations. Entrenched mindsets can even reshape cultures, as Islam has done in the Middle East, and as Soviet communism tried, but ultimately failed to do in Eastern Europe. Russian writer Fyodor Dostoyevsky presaged the evils of commu-nism by several decades in his prophetic novel, *The Possessed*, calling the mindset of socialism a "fire…in the minds of men."[3]

But there are also good strongholds, desirable mindsets. United States President George W. Bush, in his second inaugural address, employed Dostoyevsky's phrase optimistically to de-scribe the mindset necessary to obtain freedom. "By our efforts, we have lit a fire as well—a fire in the minds of men. It warms those who feel its power, it burns those who fight its progress, and one day this untamed fire of freedom will reach the darkest corners of our world."[4]

When I minister healing and deliverance through praise and worship, I am tearing down evil strongholds and building godly ones. It is what Second Corinthians 10:5 means by "…bringing every thought into captivity to the obedience of Christ." As said in the previous chapter, satan wants to dethrone God, but praise and worship builds a throne for Him. Healing and deliverance flow from that throne.

Some Christians admirably attempt to prove the authenticity of God's Word by appealing to archaeological and historical facts, and certainly the testimony of history is always welcome. But God invariably exasperates men's attempts to measure Him, so He has made His Word self-attesting, both frustrating apologists and offending skeptics. *The Bible ultimately challenges its reader not to accept, but to surrender to, the fact that it is God's Word.*

Most American Christians never come to grips with this issue. *God's Word must become your final authority in all of life's decisions.* Mere mental assent is not enough. He wants to pierce you, to delve into the "thoughts and intents" of your heart (Heb. 4:12). Thoughts and intents are the battlefield of the spirit, and in terms of spiritual warfare, the issue of biblical authority is the "mother of all wars."

This conflict is vividly portrayed in the interwoven lives of two former best friends who at one time were probably the most famous preachers in the world: Billy Graham and Charles Templeton. Graham you undoubtedly already know, but unless you're a Canadian reader of the *Toronto Star* newspaper or *Maclean's Magazine*, both of which Mr. Templeton edited, you probably don't know him. Here's a glimpse of his life.[5]

Charles was a nineteen-year-old with a ninth-grade education when he accepted Christ as his Savior in 1936. Soon after, he left a budding career as a newspaper sports cartoonist to enter the ministry, first as an itinerant evangelist and then as a highly successful pastor in Toronto. By 1944, a mere eight years after becoming a Christian, Templeton's preaching was drawing huge crowds everywhere he went, and people were constantly comparing him to a young American firebrand, Billy Graham. So it was that together that year they founded Youth for Christ.

While Graham went on to preach to millions and counsel kings and presidents, Templeton faced a rockier road. He preached with enthusiasm, but his lack of grounding in the Scriptures caused him increasingly to doubt the authenticity of his experience with the Lord. His misgivings came to a head in 1948 in a discussion with Billy about whether the Bible was really God's Word. Graham said he had decided, "once and for all, to stop questioning and to accept the Bible as God's Word," a decision Templeton called "intellectual suicide."

When he left YFC after only four years to further his Christian education, Templeton chose—against the advice of Graham and a host of others—to attend Princeton Theological Seminary, a bastion of liberalism. Whatever embers of faith that remained when he entered Princeton were extinguished when he exited, a self-professed agnostic. In the decades that followed he pursued a varied career as a politician, newspaper editor, inventor, broadcaster, and author. The title of his twelfth and final book, published in 1995 when Charles Templeton was 80 years old, is both telling and tragic: *Farewell to God.*

God demands unconditional surrender, both to the written Word and to Jesus, the *living* Word. Charles Templeton saw the issue only as intellectual and not relational, and thought it would require him to stop thinking and, in his words, "begin to die."[6] But surrendering *to* Jesus isn't giving in to blindness; He's a real, knowable person. He is the standard by whom God will judge the whole world (see Acts 17:30-31), and it is only through surrendering to Him as *Lord* that the human spirit is recreated, "born again, not of corruptible seed but incorruptible, through the word of God which lives and abides forever" (1 Pet. 1:23).

Hebrews 4:12 speaks further about God's living Word. In fact, it classifies the Word as a genuine biological weapon:

> *For the word of God is living and powerful, and sharper than any two-edged sword, piercing even to the division of soul and spirit, and of joints and marrow, and is a discerner of the thoughts and intents of the heart.*

It's impossible to overemphasize the enormous power of God's Word in your life. It is also impossible to overstate its *importance.* That is why, in John 14:23, the Lord said, "If anyone loves Me, *he will keep My word*; and My Father will love him, and We will come to him and make Our home with him."

We cannot claim to love God if we do not love His Word. That is an indictment upon a generation of churchgoers for whom biblical illiteracy is the order of the day. But it is a fact: **God means only as much as His Word means to you.** "If you abide in Me, and *My words abide in you*," Jesus said in John 15:7, "you will ask what you desire, and it shall be done for you." Your love for God's Word is the measure of your love for Him.

Your mind is the treasury of your heart. It is where you store whatever is most important to you, whatever captures your affections. As we saw in the previous chapter, Judas bought into a lie that ultimately consumed him. That lie was the foundation upon which satan built a stronghold.

The only way you can tear down such a stronghold is to replace the evil "thoughts and intents of the heart" by letting "this mind be in you which was also in Christ Jesus" (Phil. 2:5). In other words, you "bind" the strong man by exalting the Stronger Man.

You defeat satan by exalting Jesus, by letting His words abide in your heart. Praise is, among other things, saying those words back to Him. Just as in football, your best defense is a good offense.

GOD'S WORD IS EFFECTIVE

No soldier marches into battle wearing a T-shirt and blue jeans; he needs a helmet, boots, body armor, and camouflage, as well as offensive munitions. Likewise God has equipped you to "fight the good fight of faith" (1 Tim. 6:12). Saint Paul listed your weaponry in Ephesians 6:

> *Stand therefore, having girded your waist with truth, having put on the breastplate of righteousness, and having shod your feet with the preparation of the gospel of peace; above all, taking the shield of faith with which you will be able to quench all the fiery darts of the wicked one. And take the helmet of salvation, and the sword of the Spirit, which is the word of God (Ephesians 6:14-17).*

The well-armed believer puts on the incredible defensive gear that the apostle terms "the whole armor of God." Then he straps on the most powerful offensive weapon ever devised—the Word of God, described in another passage as "mighty in God for pulling down strongholds." King David described it this way:

> *The law of the Lord is perfect, converting the soul; the testimony of the Lord is sure, making wise the simple; the statutes of the Lord are right, rejoicing the heart; the commandment of the Lord is pure, enlightening the eyes; the fear of the Lord is clean, enduring forever; the judgments of the Lord are true and righteous altogether. More to be desired are they than gold, yea, than much fine gold; sweeter also than honey and the*

honeycomb. Moreover by them Your servant is warned, and in keeping them there is great reward (Psalm 19:7-11).

Weapons have to work reliably or they are of no use, and, according to these verses, God's decrees are "sure." His Word never jams, rusts, or becomes obsolete. A soldier learns in basic training to take his rifle apart, clean it, and put it back together very quickly. Then he is taken to the firing range and taught to use it properly and to maximum effect.

The reason for all this preparation is so that he can rely on the weapon in battle, without second thoughts, or even first ones, since good training makes the weapon almost like an extension of his brain. The best fighters make the right moves on sheer impulse.

God's Word is utterly reliable in the mouth of the thoroughly trained. I don't mean the man who treats it like a candy vending machine to satisfy his latest craving, but the true lover of God who treasures it the way David did, whose mind is so interconnected with it that reliance on it becomes an impulse. Paul commended the Thessalonians for the way they "welcomed it not as the word of men, but as it is in truth, the word of God, which also effectively works in you who believe" (1 Thess. 2:13).

The Word of God is effective and will energize you in several specific, life-giving ways.[7] First, God's Word gives you *new birth*. According to First Peter 1:23, you were "born again, not of corruptible seed but incorruptible." More than being forgiven, you've been recreated, conceived by the very Word of God!

Second, God's Word produces *faith* in your heart. Romans 10:17 says, "So then faith comes by hearing, and hearing by the word of God." The three-stage sequence is always the same—first, God's Word is proclaimed; second, you hear; third, faith arises in your heart.

Third, God's Word provides you with **physical health and strength**, not only miraculous healing, but day-to-day health in your body. Bodily exercise is good, but God's Word is more basic to a healthy lifestyle than any exercise plan ever devised.

Fourth, God's Word gives you *light*. Psalm 119:130 says, "the entrance of Your words gives light; it gives understanding to the simple." James 1:22-23 says the Word is a mirror that brings spiritual revelation, which means looking at yourself the way God sees you (i.e., with much more hope than you see yourself).

Fifth, God's Word is your true spiritual *food*. In Matthew 4:4, Jesus declares, "It is written, 'Man shall not live by bread alone, but by every word that proceeds from the mouth of God.'" The Word is your daily bread; you're undernourished when you skip a day.

Sixth, the Word of God *cleanses* your mind and life. Jesus said in John 15:3, "You are already clean because of the word which I have spoken to you," and Ephesians 5:25-26 explains that "Christ also loved the church and gave Himself for her, that He might sanctify and cleanse her with the washing of the water by the word."

Seventh, God's Word brings you *victory*. Ephesians 6:17 calls it "the sword of the spirit." It is a powerful weapon in spiritual warfare. The devil will fight with all his might to keep you ignorant of its power. He knows that once you have God's words in your heart and on your lips that you will be able to withstand his attacks and topple his strongholds. *Satan fears this above all else. He fears you!*

The beloved apostle John said in First John 2:14 that "...the word of God abides in you, and you have overcome the wicked one." God's Word, abiding in you, enables you to stand strong in spiritual warfare, and makes satan flee.

WHEN GOD SPEAKS

No wonder Saint Paul told his spiritual son, Timothy, that God's Word makes the believer "complete, thoroughly equipped for every good work" (2 Tim. 3:17). His Word brings new birth, faith, healing, revelation, spiritual nourishment, cleansing, and victory over satan. Yet so many of us have never learned to enjoy these great benefits.

Jesus, on the other hand, used the Word of God very effectively, especially when the devil tempted Him in the wilderness. Satan came against Him with three temptations, and Jesus answered him with three quotations from the Word, defeating him then and there. Why was the Savior so powerful with His spiritual sword?

Luke 4:1 says He went into the wilderness *full* of the Holy Spirit, while verse 14 says He "returned *in the power* of the Spirit." It was in the interim that He faced temptation by wielding the Word. *God is taking you through a similar wilderness, on your own journey from potential to power, in order to teach you how to wield the sword of His living Word and defeat satan.*

The Greek New Testament uses two terms that are translated into English as "word." One is *logos*, and the other is *rhema*. Each has a distinct meaning. *Logos* refers to the unchanging, self-existent Word of God "which lives and abides forever" (1 Pet. 1:23). It refers to the whole Bible, the complete revelation of God in Scripture.

Rhema, however, is derived from the verb that means "to speak." In Romans 10:17 Paul says, "So then faith comes by hearing, and hearing by the word of God." The "word" in that verse is *rhema*. Faith comes by hearing the *rhema* of God. *Rhema* is a word God speaks especially to us, relating directly to our situation. *Logos* is vast; it is constant. *Rhema* is personal, a portion of the *logos* quickened in us for a given situation.

The power is in the Word; all you have to do is listen. But how can you hear the *rhema* of God? Proverbs tells you exactly how.

> *My son, give attention to my words; incline your ear to my sayings. Do not let them depart from your eyes; keep them in the midst of your heart; for they are life to those who find them, and health to all their flesh* (Proverbs 4:20-22).

If you give God's Word your undivided attention; if you "incline" your ear, i.e., listen attentively and submissively; if you take your eyes off other things and focus only on what it says to you; if you center your heart and constantly meditate on it until it penetrates every area of your being, then *there will be no room left for opposing strongholds.* This is how you hear God's Word.

Rhema always has something to do with the mouth. When Jesus answered the devil in the wilderness (Matt. 4:4), He said, "Man shall not live by bread alone, but by every word [*rhema*] that proceeds from the *mouth* of God." What an amazing statement! You need more than physical bread to survive. Your "daily bread" is every *rhema* that *proceeds* (Greek, present tense) from the mouth of God. *There is a word proceeding from God's mouth to you right now.*

Just as the Israelites gathered manna in the wilderness, I'm asking you to pick up the *rhema* as it comes. This is the Word of God that will produce faith in your heart to see miracles. It "effectively works" (1 Thess. 2:13) to pull down the strongholds of the devil.

You can be a hearer of the Word all of your life, but never become a doer. It is only when you *speak* the Word of God that its power is exerted in your behalf. *Then* you begin to see the manifestation of divine life that is inherent in it.

Some years ago my friend, Pastor John Bosman, described the difference between hearers and doers in terms of flies versus honey bees. John is a South African transplant to Louisiana, and, believe me, he's colorful enough to fit right in. The fact that his former church in Lake Charles swelled to 2,000 after he arrived is testament to that fact. John knew I was in the middle of writing my book, *The Truth About Angels*,[8] when I ministered with him, so he told me his story over lunch.

The church was about to have a special series of meetings, and in preparation Pastor John got out of bed one night to pray that God would do something wonderful. Suddenly an angel appeared in his bedroom and said, "I want to show you what is going to happen in the services."

"He took me into a meeting that actually took place five evenings later," said John. He saw the church full of people, mostly his own with a few visitors sprinkled amongst them. The angel told him to look closely at them, and to describe what he saw.

"I saw a fascinating phenomenon," he told me. "There were honey bees flying around some people's heads and flies buzzing around others."

The angel explained that honey bees feed on nectar from live plants, while flies feed on death and decay. Some people, explained the angel, are doers of the Word, always producing life, while others come and hear the Word every Sunday, but continue to live off their old religious experiences. They live with the deadness of the past.

Pastor Bosman's vision is intriguing to say the least, but I find it especially noteworthy that the bees and flies were buzzing around people's *heads*—near their ears, eyes, mouths, and minds—the same area addressed by Proverbs 4:20-22, which I quoted earlier. I've no doubt that the bees were drawn to those who were habitually attending to God's Word, inclining their ears to hear Him speaking through it, keeping it constantly before their eyes, and treasuring it in their hearts—in other words, the *doers*.

I also believe that the bees and flies represent people—your spouse, children, friends, and associates—who feed off the nectar or decay of your life, especially your speech. Solomon's wise observation that "death and life are in the power of the tongue" (Prov. 18:21) means that you have tremendous power not only to attract blessing, but also to invoke it in the lives of those you love.

THE STOCKHOLM STRATEGY

The devil does not flee the presence of God's Word in your mind. He's also not afraid of God's work in your past. He flees only when you resist, and you do so the same way Jesus did in the wilderness. He said, "Away with you, satan! For it is written…." He used God's Word against the devil. *There must come a time when you make a deliberate choice to launch the warhead of God's Word against the stronghold of the devil.*[9] This isn't automatic. You must actively resist.

Just because your car has a motor doesn't mean it's going to go anywhere. You have to start that motor with a key and put it into gear. In the same way, the power of Almighty God resides within you right now, while you're reading, but you have to turn the key and fire it up. You must fire God's Word at satan. *The Word that lives in your heart, spoken from your lips, will tear down the devil's strongholds.*

Better yet, why not use my "Stockholm Strategy" from Chapter 3? Why not *sing* God's Word right there in the middle of your battle? Just sing it right into the darkness, and set yourself to keep on singing it until the darkness starts to flee. That's what I did after Jan's death, when I was in the pit of despair. I quoted and sang Psalm 34:1 over and over: "I will bless the Lord at all times; His praise shall continually be in my mouth." This wasn't the vain repetition Jesus warned against in Matthew 6:7; it was warfare. I was shining the light of God on a dark lie sent to convince me that I couldn't praise Him anymore. That light exposed satan's stronghold for what it was. The light was already there, in my memory, but I had to aim it into the darkness.

When satan tries to heap the guilt of your past on you, remind him of Second Corinthians 5:17: "Therefore, if anyone is in Christ, he is a new creation; old things have passed away; behold, all things have become new." If you've never heard that verse set to song, *make up your own!*

If the devil has made you doubt your salvation, sing First John 5:11-12a: "And this is the testimony [i.e., the legal record]: that God has given us eternal life, and this life is in His Son. He who has the Son has life." Just sing it over and over: "I have the Son, and I have life. I have the Son, and I have life."

If you've been a worrier, sing the "do not worry" of Philippians 4:6. If he attacks you with sickness, sing First Peter 2:24 that says you *were* healed by His stripes. If he strikes at you with fear, taunt him with a melodic reminder that Jesus said, "My peace I give to you" (John 14:27). If he tries to convince you that you're defeated, just sing the facts: "We are more than conquerors through Him who loved us" (Rom. 8:37).

Too many Christians have known the agony of defeat without tasting the thrill of victory. *One of your great learning experiences will be to see how quickly satan flees when you fire God's Word at him.*

Galatians 5:19-21 runs down a list of strongholds, areas of weakness that plague humankind: lust, idolatry, hatred, judgmentalism, violent outbursts, gossip, lying, envy, drunkenness, and various other areas where satan will search for weak spots to attack. *Find a Scripture song for every weakness.* If you have a computer, search the Bible online to find multiple Scriptures for each stronghold on the list. Then, every time the enemy attacks you, launch the rocket of praise with the warhead of God's Word! "Away with you, satan! *For it is written....*"

Jesus has granted us "power of attorney" to use the Word of God in His name. It is *His* voice satan hears when we invoke this power against the strongholds that bind us. We counterattack the devil's thoughts—they were his before we bought into them—and they lose their grip on our minds.

As you will see in the next chapter, satan is absolutely terrified of the name of Jesus. That name is a constant reminder of his defeat at Calvary. He remembers the irreversible mistake he made in crucifying the Savior. He is haunted by the defeat he suffered at the Cross, as well as the humiliation that followed, when Jesus, "having disarmed principalities and powers...made a public spectacle of them, triumphing over them in it" (Col. 2:15).

The name of Jesus simply makes satan shudder.

ENDNOTES

1. Terry Law, *The Fight of Every Believer* (Tulsa, OK: Harrison House, 2006), 41.

2. The 90 percent figure is based upon consistent, widespread anecdotal evidence.

3. Fyodor Dostoyevsky, *Devils: The Possessed* (Oxford: Oxford UP, 2000).

4. http://www.whitehouse.gov/news/releases/2005/01/20050120-1.html; accessed 3/28/08.

5. Templeton's memoirs are available online at http://www.templetons.com/charles/memoir/.

   The information accessed from: http://www.templetons.com/charles/memoir/evang-graham.html: accessed on 4/17/08.

6. Ibid.

7. I am indebted to Bible teacher Derek Prince for these insights.

8. Terry Law, *The Truth About Angels* (Lake Mary, FL: Charisma House, 2006).

9. Watch for my upcoming book, *The Power of Choice*.

Chapter 5

Spiritual Warhead:
The Name of Jesus

First-century "political correctness" was as pointed as the modern version—then as now, the offense lay in the exclusiveness of that Name.

~

In October 2001, one month after the terrorist attacks of 9/11, the United States invaded Afghanistan and overthrew that nation's brutal Taliban regime. Days later I found myself touring makeshift refugee camps in the war zone, delivering several thousand coats and blankets to Afghan children already facing nighttime temperatures well below freezing. The situation was not only tragic but infuriating, because I had bought every item from a well-stocked market in a nearby town, where the locals obviously did not care that these people were dying. And dying they were, especially the children, as the camp's commandant showed me on a grim tote board. There were 11 hash marks, one for each little life lost to the previous night's cold.

In April 2002 we returned with a shipment of food and headed south to a camp near Kandahar. There I met a warlord named Haji, who wanted me to see firsthand the desperate straits of his hometown. I agreed to go with him, and soon we were speeding across the desert in a Toyota Land Cruiser, Haji's personal bounty from the battle for Kandahar a few weeks earlier. The sands were laced with landmines, so we maintained high speeds to stay ahead of any explosions we might trigger.

We were hurtling along at 70 miles per hour when Haji turned to me and said, "You know, I like you Christians, but I don't like Hindus." He went on to explain that Hindus have 300,000 gods, but that Muslims and Christians, "both have the same God." He was pleased by our perceived similarities.

I was tempted just to bite my lip and say nothing, an impulse heightened by the presence of three burly warriors in the back seat, holding AK-47s in their hands. But the Holy Spirit rose up in me and quietly I replied, "No, we don't have the same God."

Haji jerked his head toward me, his brow arched and his dark, piercing eyes as big as saucers. For a moment I wondered if he might shoot me, or just dump me out alive in the desert.

"My God has a Son," I continued in a friendly tone. "How about yours? I believe Jesus is the Son of God." Then I handed him a Pashtun copy of *The Story of Jesus*, our little 16-page booklet, and invited him to read it.

Haji pulled over and climbed into the back seat to read while one of his warriors took the wheel. He spent the next several hours thumbing the pages again and again, learning for the first time about the One whose Name makes all the difference.

I've learned in my travels that the name of Jesus is *the* stumbling block to non-Christians everywhere, from Afghan deserts to Western talk radio. Americans and Europeans both love to trumpet tolerance and religious diversity. But mention Jesus, and the polite smiles tighten. Say that you believe He is "the Way," and the limits on diversity suddenly become clear. Claim that "there is no other name under heaven given among men by which we must be saved" (Acts 4:12), and the tolerant become instantly intolerant.

They don't mind talking about the Jesus who cuddled children, healed the sick, and fed the multitudes. Just don't show them the One from *The Passion of the Christ* movie. Their problem is the "rock of offense" that Isaiah prophesied (Isa. 8:14), the One in whose Name the apostles raised the dead, yet for whose Name they themselves died.

Their problem is Jesus' *name.*

WHAT'S IN A NAME?

Names are powerful in several respects. In the most elemental sense they are formative—at least we hope they are—in the naming of children. An Oklahoma couple with the surname Fail knew that truth decades ago when they named their baby son Never. Never Fail grew up to be a successful businessman in our community.

Names are also influential. An aspiring Broadway producer some years ago tried to guarantee himself success in a novel way. He found ordinary New Yorkers whose names were identical to those of famous critics, and treated them to a sumptuous dinner and the best seats to his new show. Afterward he quoted their glowing "reviews" in a full-page newspaper ad, including a photo of each to protect himself legally. The ploy worked, at least at first, if only for the publicity his clever ruse generated. The producer had used the "power" of names.

Sometimes names are used in occult incantations, as though magical forces are released by their saying. The very name of Jesus, in fact, has been abused this way from time to time over the centuries, as corrupt church leaders, in efforts to grow the Church without true evangelization, allowed Christianity to be blended with pagan practices. Generations later the result is many lands where superstition, not the Holy Spirit, sets the religious pace.

Yet names are inherently powerful when they are used governmentally, i.e., when they represent some higher authority. When a man holds up his hand to stop traffic, he and all the drivers who see him know that he does not have the physical power to stop them. But when that man is a policeman, wearing a badge that represents the entire legal establishment of a city or state, the drivers all respond to the authority in the badge. They stop.

THE NAME IN THE EARLY CHURCH

Simon Peter has always fascinated me. How could such an impetuous, foul-mouthed fisherman turn, almost overnight, into such a powerful preacher and true apostle, not only astounding in his command of Scripture but mighty in spiritual power as well? Let's face it: Peter was a man with a good heart, but he was weak in character, and totally unarmed when it came to battles of the spirit.

"Before the rooster crows, you will deny Me three times," Jesus assured him as Calvary neared (Matt. 26:34). Sure enough, that night the fisherman's courage fled him faster than the evening chill, and in short order he had disavowed his Master three times, the last with an oath and a curse.

But flash forward seven weeks to the day of Pentecost, and it becomes clear that Peter has been utterly transformed, almost as though he himself has been resurrected along with Jesus. In terms of spiritual warfare, he is not only well armed, but has become a biblical sharpshooter. His sermon pierces the hearts of the thousands of Jews who have come from all over the known world to Jerusalem for the feast, and 3,000 surrender their lives to the Messiah, many becoming instant immigrants. A few days later he and John heal a man, lame from birth, and within minutes thousands more are added to the Church. (See Acts chapters 2-3.) What in the world—or out of it—has happened to this man? What is the secret of his transformation? Here it is:

> *And fixing his eyes on him, with John, Peter said, "Look at us."*
> *So he gave them his attention, expecting to receive something*
> *from them. Then Peter said, "Silver and gold I do not have, but*
> *what I do have I give you:* **In the name of Jesus Christ of**
> **Nazareth,** *rise up and walk"* (Acts 3:4-6).

Peter "had" something for the lame man, something that had been *given* to him. He had *the name of Jesus*. The locals readily associated Jesus with healing, of course; His astounding works had been the talk of the town for the previous three years. But now it appeared two fishermen had inherited the late rabbi's abilities! Peter saw the people's amazement and immediately explained the source behind the awesome display of power:

> *And His name, through faith in His name, has made this*
> *man strong, whom you see and know. Yes, the faith which*

comes through Him has given him this perfect soundness in the presence of you (Acts 3:16).

The apostle could not have made it clearer: The *name* of Jesus "has made this man strong." Thus, when he and John were interrogated by Annas, the high priest, the next morning, they were asked, "By what power or by what *name* have you done this?" (Acts 4:7). Annas was a man who understood authority. He knew that his problem wasn't Peter, but the name of Jesus. He also knew that he must be very cautious at this point, because the authenticity and sheer goodness of the man's healing were beyond dispute. So he released Peter and John with a warning that they should not "speak at all nor teach in the name of Jesus" (Acts 4:18). First-century "political correctness" was as pointed as the modern version—then as now, the offense lay in the exclusiveness of that Name.

But the two apostles made it clear that they were going to continue preaching in the Name. They went back to the other disciples, called all the believers together to report what God had done, and then prayed: "Lord…grant to Your servants that with all boldness they may speak Your word, by stretching out Your hand to heal, and that signs and wonders may be done through the name of Your holy Servant Jesus" (Acts 4:29-30).

Now the whole church understood. They had been given a potent weapon, to be used with the highest authority and power. They were even bold enough to pray, "that *signs and wonders* may be done through the name."

Acts chapter 5 records how the move of God's Spirit spread like fire not only throughout Jerusalem, but to surrounding cities as well. Predictably, the high priest and his cohorts were "filled with indignation" because "you have filled Jerusalem with your doctrine" (Acts 5:17,28). This was their persecutors' own estimate of what the early Church was doing with the name of Jesus. *The apostles had filled the city with the doctrine of the Name.*

Annas had the apostles flogged this time, but it was like throwing gasoline on the fire. Soon the Name was spreading amongst the nations, as Philip the evangelist preached to the people of Samaria. Before long, a fiery little rabbi named Saul had been transformed just as radically as Peter. And within a few years, as St. Paul, he had taken the power of the name of Jesus to Europe. Within two-and-a-half centuries, the Roman Empire, seat of all things pagan and impure, would become the *Holy* Roman Empire. The world would never be the same.

Peter, Philip, Paul, and every preacher in the early Church seemed to have but one sermon in their repertoire—the name of Jesus. They knew the Name was a weapon, and they *used* it to demonstrate God's power, with signs and wonders following.

THE NECESSITY OF THE NAME

Since 2006 World Compassion has distributed 120,000 Arabic-language Bibles in Iraq, half of them illustrated Bibles for children and youth. But the key to reaching the kids has been the 15,000 pairs of athletic shoes we have given them *with* the Bibles.[1] Iraq, you see, is soccer crazy, not to mention soccer savvy, as their 2007 Asian Cup championship attests.

For decades football (not the oblong pigskin we Americans throw with our hands, but the real, round, black and white *football*) has been the national obsession, even during the days when Saddam's son, Uday, tortured the team if they failed to bring home trophies. Everywhere you go, children play in the streets, kicking balls, sand bags, cans—if you can kick it, it's a football!

In April 2007 I decided to give 20 American pastors and businessmen a firsthand look at our Bible distribution project. We flew to the city of Irbil, in northern Iraq's Kurdish region, and set ourselves to the task of assembling 600 packages (one pair of shoes, a youth edition of the Bible, and five *Story of Jesus* booklets per sport bag). Then we headed 90 minutes west from Irbil into an area of frequent Al Qaeda violence.

Soon we came to the little town of Sufaya, where the mayor and village elders had prepared a reception for us at their community center. These Kurds were tough looking, leathery-skinned men, with heavy gray beards. They wore turbans that looked like they hadn't been washed for a decade, and sported pistols on their hips. Several carried AK-47 assault rifles at the ready. I hoped they weren't trigger-happy.

I sat at the head table with the mayor and elders, and for a few minutes we drank a strange green tea. Then his honor stood and in Kurdish welcomed us. The people of Sufaya had never seen Americans before, he said, and were overwhelmed to have us visit their village. Then he invited me to tell them why we had come.

I stood and greeted our hosts in solemn fashion, and told them we had brought 600 gift packages for their children, placing a package on the table in front of me as I spoke. Most of the kids I had seen outside were barefoot, so I pulled out a pair of athletic shoes first. There were smiles all around. Now it was time to take out a Bible.

"This is a Christian Bible," I explained, and then uttered what the Qur'an (5:017) calls a monstrous blasphemy. I looked around the room full of armed men and spoke clearly: "I believe that Jesus Christ is the Son of God." This was sacrilege, but I knew that without the Name our gifts were worthless, and that I would forever lose the opportunity to evangelize the region.

I steeled myself for a violent reaction, but there were no wails or moans, and no guns were drawn. Instead the mayor just kept smiling. "Thank you very much," he said. "We would love to receive your gifts. Now, let us go to where the orphans and widows of our village live."

Iraq has lost a multitude of men to violence, so it came as no surprise that widows and orphans would occupy an entire neighborhood. We boarded our SUVs and drove through the narrow streets, eventually stopping in an area that looked poor and run-down even for this little backwater. The mayor sent messengers out to gather orphans, and soon we were surrounded by sweet, smiling, dirty little faces. For a moment it was a postcard come to life. Then some kids caught a glimpse of a pair of bright new shoes and a near riot ensued. One of the pastors is a former linebacker who weighs about 250 pounds, but he looked like a puppet, tossed one way and then another as he tried to stay on his feet. We finished our give-away in minutes and ran for our trucks, laughing for joy at our adventure with the delightful little mob.

With the mayor's cooperation, we soon sent Kurdish pastors back to Sufaya, to give away more Bibles and shoes, and to preach to the people. Today a local church has been established, and the name of Jesus Christ is being preached in the region. In a land of widows and orphans, a land that has seen so much death, the Name is bringing life.

THE GREATNESS OF THE NAME

Names are never meaningless, but their import was far greater in Bible times. In fact, names often were prophetically given, describing the traits their bearers would manifest throughout life. For example, *Isaac*, whose name means "laughter," was born to aged parents, Abraham and Sarah, who chuckled in disbelief before he was born, and laughed with indescribable joy afterward. Moreover, Isaac was a living reminder that God Himself had gotten the last laugh on the doubting couple.

History's most important name, Jesus, comes from the Hebrew *Yeshua*, which means "Yahweh saves." Fittingly, the Son of God was named after His Father. And just as Almighty God had more than a hundred names in Scripture, so Jesus' name encompasses all that those names represent. In fact, the late Watchman Nee often referred to Christ as "the sum of all spiritual things." Nee, the legendary Chinese Bible teacher who died in prison in 1972, loved pointing out that Jesus does not show the way, reveal the truth, or give life, but that He is all three. Likewise, the Lord Himself claimed not to give the bread of life, but to be the Bread of Life (John 6:35), and not merely to shine light to the world, but to be the Light of the world (John 8:12).

Yet of the more than one hundred names for God, there was one that the Lord used more than all the others combined—*Father*. Jesus constantly called God His Father, a scandalous provocation that ultimately led to His crucifixion. Moses had taught that, "the Lord our God, the Lord is one" (Deut. 6:4). In Israel's eyes, just as we have seen with Islam, the idea of a "Son of God" was unthinkable, because it implied that Jehovah was *more than one*. Only pagans worshiped multiple gods.

If anyone in history could have used the various names of God most appropriately, surely it would have been Jesus. Certainly, all the others were acceptable. Yet *Father*, the one name that caused the greatest consternation among the religious authorities, invariably overruled all others both in His prayer and preaching. In fact, of all the prayers Jesus prayed, He addressed God as Father in all but one. When He hung on the Cross, and sin separated Them, He cried out, "My God, My God." But in every other instance He prayed, "Father."

According to John 17:26, the real "Lord's prayer," the crux of Jesus' mission was to reveal the Father's name to His disciples: "*I have declared to them Your name, and will declare it, that the love with which You loved Me may be in them, and I in them.*" Even if it cost Him His life, there could be no other way.

Jesus' purpose was—and is—to fully reveal God's manifold name to His disciples, and in the Gospels He did so, but not just through His amazing teaching. He actually put flesh to the theological terms that referred to the Father, displaying God's names with signs and wonders performed before His followers' very eyes, from the tender touch that raised a dead girl to life, to the radiant glory of His transfiguration on the mountain.

The Fatherhood of God and Sonship of Jesus constituted the most important aspect of the Savior's mission to humankind. He could have come as a warrior, a king, or an entrepreneur. But Jesus came to model Sonship, and to reveal God's Fatherhood, to a world of spiritual orphans. Even today, this is the revelation most sorely lacking. My coauthor Jim Gilbert says it well:

> Check the statistics of any nation in decline, or of one trying to rise from the pit, and you will see the common characteristic that (a) marriage is in trouble, and

(b) manhood, especially head-of-the-house father-hood, has withered. Take away fatherhood, and you kill womanhood, childhood, brotherhood—the entire neighborhood. Shoot the head, and you've killed the whole body.[2]

This is why satan approached Eve. If he could undermine Adam's headship, he would subvert the headship of God as well. But Jesus, the "second Man" (1 Cor. 15:47) came "to seek and to save that which was lost" (Luke 19:10). His mission was to seek out sons and daughters for His Father. That's why He said in John 4:23 that "true worshipers will worship the Father." He could have simply said they would worship "God," but He tied true worship to a relationship with a Father. And just as some children bear a striking resemblance to their parents, Jesus Himself so perfectly personified divine Sonship that He could say, "He who has seen Me has seen the Father."

THE WEAPON OF JESUS' NAME

Matthew 28:18-19 says, "And Jesus came and spoke to them, saying, 'All authority has been given to Me in heaven and on earth. Go therefore and make disciples of all the nations....'"

What a profound command. The Lord essentially said, "I have been given total authority; therefore, I'm commissioning you to use My name!" In this single act, Jesus granted the *power of attorney* to His disciples, the legal authority to invoke His power through the use of His name.

Mark's passage backs this up: "Go into all the world and preach the gospel to every creature," adding, "And these signs will follow those who believe: In My name they will cast out demons; they will speak with new tongues…they will lay hands on the sick, and they will recover" (see Mark 16:15-18).

Supernatural ability to cast out devils, to speak with new tongues, and to heal the sick is committed to you and me through the authority of the name of Jesus. In other words, the Church has been "licensed" to use the Name with power.

With that in mind, here is a key: ***When God delegates something to us, we are made responsible for it.*** The name of Jesus has been given to the Church, and the Church therefore is responsible for its use. ***We are also held responsible if we do not use it:*** The sick will not recover. Spiritual prisoners will not go free. However, if we do use the Name, with an awareness that it carries the awesome power of God, then we will see the miracles of the early Church repeated in our time.

This makes many common prayers redundant, like asking God to do something we have been commissioned to do. ***God waits for us to do something about the devil.*** He waits for us to cast out demons. Nowhere in the epistles is there any verse that encourages us to pray to God about satan. Jesus did everything there was to do about the evil one and his works, and then He sent the Holy Spirit to empower us to continue on to greater works.

Well-meaning opponents of crime are wont to warn us that "guns kill." But that is like saying pencils commit spelling errors— it's impossible. A weapon is perfectly pointless until someone with intent picks it up. Likewise, the name of Jesus is a weapon that God has placed in our hands. It is up to us to use it.

Look at these verses for proof:

First Peter 5:8-9 says, "Be sober, be vigilant; because your adversary the devil walks about like a roaring lion, seeking whom he may devour. Resist him, steadfast in the faith, knowing that the same sufferings are experienced by your brotherhood in the world." Got that? You are commanded to resist the devil, not to pray to God to do something about him. *You are to resist satan through the authority resident in the name of Jesus.* James 4:7 adds that when you resist the devil, "he will flee from you." That word *flee* means "to run from as in terror." When you resist him, you terrorize him.

Saint Paul backs up Peter and James by simply saying in Ephesians 4:27, "nor give place to the devil." He doesn't make it complicated, doesn't teach sophisticated techniques of spiritual warfare, because the truth is simple and wonderful: You do not have to give satan a place in your life. You have the power to *not* sin, because you have been given the name of Jesus to successfully resist the devil.

Over the past four decades I have learned that Jesus' name carries great power when dealing with evil spirits. In one instance, I was conducting a church meeting on the West Coast of the United States. During the first service a man in the congregation stood and requested prayer for the pastor. "Every time I get on my knees to pray for our pastor," he said, "I feel that he is in great danger, that there is going to be an attack made on his life." We prayed in response to the request, and I put the matter out of my mind.

Two days later we held a meeting for deliverance from evil spirits. When the main service had ended, I continued ministering to people in another room for about two hours, and God graced us with an awesome display of His power.

Later, as I walked back through the half-lit sanctuary toward the exit, I noticed a woman sitting near the aisle in the otherwise empty building. She grabbed my sleeve as I passed by and implored me: "You must pray with me *now*!" I was worn out, and encouraged her to come back the following night, when I would be happy to pray for her. But as I spoke, I saw torment in her eyes and knew she should not be made to wait.

Since I knew the source of her misery, I explained to the woman that I was going to cast out the evil spirit that was oppressing her. Then I permitted the spirit to identify itself. Its name was anger, and it left her without any problem. Then to my surprise, a second spirit spoke, not in the woman's voice, but in a male voice. It said it was going to murder the pastor.

I had never encountered anything quite like this before, but I knew my authority. I informed the evil spirit that it could not murder the pastor, and commanded it to come out in the name of Jesus. As soon as I uttered the Name, the woman began to tremble. For a short time, in fact, the spirit shook her with real force, but finally left. She was free.

I discovered only later that the woman had been sitting there with a loaded .22 caliber pistol in her purse. She fully intended to shoot the pastor when he walked through to lock the doors, which would have been within the next five minutes. But the Holy Spirit led me across her path at precisely the right time, and the deliverance of God was there for her.

TO THE END OF THE EARTH

For years I read Jesus' prophecy in Acts 1:8 that His followers would carry His name "to the end of the earth," but I never dreamed quite how far that Word would take my colleagues and me. Yes, we had taken the Gospel into a wide variety of places, from the expanse of Vatican Square to the forbidden hills of North Korea. Yes, I had preached Christ's name in diverse locales like South African high schools, Russian forests, Chinese homes, and Polish nightclubs. But in 2004 I received word that our "printed preachers," *The Story of Jesus* booklets that we've published in over 70 languages, were making an impact at the very "top of the world," in the Himalayan Mountains of Nepal.

Soon my elder son, Scot, and his wife, Kathy, were on their way to one of the remotest cities in the world, the Nepalese capital of Kathmandu. From there they flew northward by private plane to a tiny kingdom called Mustang, near the Tibetan border. Their "airport" was a dirt strip carved into a mountainside at 11,000 feet above sea level.

"Our left wing tip was 8 feet from the rock face, and on the right you looked down thousands of feet," recalls Scot. "There was no room for error. We descended rapidly, banked left…and landed in less than 15 seconds on the front wheel."

Scot and Kathy were greeted by a team of horsemen, who led them 90 minutes further into the mountains, where they met a former Tibetan Buddhist who had translated *The Story of Jesus* into Lhoba, the language of the kingdom. He had traveled by horse for two days to meet them and tell his story.

In 2001 the King of Mustang had invited a Nepalese Christian named Pran[3] to be his houseguest. It was customary to bring a gift to the King, so Pran, knowing how prized the printed world is in that part of the world, gave him the recently translated *The Story of Jesus*. (World Compassion paid for the printing of 5,000 copies.) The booklet might never have been rendered in that obscure language had it not been for a local prisoner named Daniel, who had been serving a seven-year sentence for drunkenness and vandalism when Pran met him and ministered to him. Daniel was a highly educated man who spoke several languages, but his life had been aimless enough to land him in jail. He agreed to read and translate the little book his Christian visitor gave him, and soon found himself immersed in its strange and wonderful story.

Eventually he came to the part about Jesus' crucifixion. Daniel read it over and over, and wracked with guilt, stopped translating altogether. But he couldn't stay away from the story, and eventually decided that he had to serve this "Son of God" who came and demonstrated His Father's love to mankind. Right there in jail he became the first known Christian amongst the previously unreached Lhoba tribe of some 45,000 people.

Shortly after finishing the translation, Daniel was released from prison. Today he, like Pran, travels the rooftop of the world, preaching the name of Jesus. As for Pran, the Prince came to him on the second day of his visit. He had read the little book Pran gave to his father and was deeply touched. Then he asked if he could personally distribute the rest of the booklets to the Lhoba people.

Before Scot and Kathy left the region, they met another Lhoba, John, who had been born again after reading *The Story of Jesus*. That man, once an adulterous drunkard, had become a Christian and a wonderful husband to his astonished wife. He also had led 25 other Lhobas to the Lord.

Popular opinion would frown on taking the Name to a remote little enclave like Mustang, with its centuries of Buddhist tradition. "The don't need your foreign religion," folks would say. Americans mistakenly, almost romantically, perceive all Himalayan kingdoms as peaceful and wise, when in reality they are in the grip of deception, bound by strongholds like Daniel's alcoholism and John's adultery. And only the name of Jesus, His blood, and His Word, can make them free.

The stories of a prisoner and a prince are proof.

STRONG TOWER

So many people use Jesus' name as a signature on their prayers, but it is so much more. King Solomon called it, "a strong tower; the righteous run to it and are saved" (Prov. 18:10). The Name is where your protection lies, and there is not another in the world like it.

My Pashtun driver, Haji, was sure that he and I worshiped the same God, that we both saw the same truth, only through different windows. And he wasn't the first to make that mistake. From Hollywood to the Himalayas, billions of people are ensnared by the same deception. "Allah, Jesus, Buddha—it doesn't matter what name you use," they say. "We're all on a journey to find our own truth."

But it does matter. Truth is not relative, and the name of Jesus is not merely the name of a great man who spoke his version of it. He said, "I am...the truth" (John 14:6). *"Jesus" is truth's real name.*

Only that Name can free Haji and a billion other Muslims from the deception and destruction that are their way of life. Only that Name can bring lasting freedom to Iraq and Afghanistan. Only that Name was worth praising when death had taken my wife from me. *Only that Name, the name of Jesus, is worth praising in the middle of your situation.*

ENDNOTES

1. Quoted from Jim Gilbert's weblog, *@Large*: http://jimgilbertatlarge.blogspot.com/2005/04/genticide.html.

2. At this writing another 10,000 Arabic-language illustrated Bibles are on order.

3. Names of all locals changed for their protection.

Chapter 6

Spiritual Warhead: Jesus' Blood

Even when the crowd outside had swollen to 10,000 angry Afghans armed with rocks, I knew God would keep us from death because we had applied, with the "hyssop" of our testimony, the power of Jesus' blood.

~

The San Francisco Bay area of California is known for its quirky landmarks, from the pyramidal Transamerica Building, to snaky Lombard Street, proudly advertised as the "crookedest street in the world." But no area attraction is stranger than the Winchester Mystery House in San Jose.[1]

Sarah Winchester started building her mansion in 1884, shortly after the deaths of her husband, William, principal owner of the Winchester Repeating Arms Company, and their only child, the infant Annie. The widowed heiress moved from

Connecticut to California and undertook construction at the direction of a psychic, who told her that the Winchester family was under a curse, brought on by the thousands of deaths caused by their invention, the repeating rifle. The spirits of the dead were seeking vengeance, the medium said, and Sarah's only relief would come from building them a home. But once started, the project must never stop.

So the Widow Winchester bought a home already under construction, and then built and built and rebuilt. She added dozens of rooms and included features that no human could use, such as stairways leading into ceilings, closet doors that opened to blank walls, and upstairs portals that opened precipitously onto the lawn below. She also built mazelike hallways to confuse the haunts, and if a room's construction went wrong, she simply stopped building it and erected a new one around it. Surely the ghosts would know she was doing it all for them.

With a $20 million fortune that would be worth twenty times as much today, plus a tax-free income of a staggering $1,000 per day, Sarah Winchester eventually wasted a quarter of her wealth trying to appease her haunts and assuage her guilt. But the tortured woman never found relief, and the 38-year project came to its end only after she died in 1922. Now a tourist attraction on San Jose's Winchester Boulevard, the 160-room mansion is a sad monument to the ravages of one of satan's favorite weapons—guilt.

ACCUSER OF THE BRETHREN

All of us are troubled by recurring guilt problems of some sort, though probably not to the same degree as Sarah Winchester. For centuries, Christians have thought—and sometimes have even been *taught*—that guilt feelings are the voice of God. Yes, if I'm feeling miserable God must be dealing with me. But a clear conscience? That's just the devil lulling me into a spirit of complacency.

Don't confuse guilt feelings with a spirit of conviction. True conviction takes place when God clearly shows you your sins and *invites* you to repentance. Guilt, on the other hand, is satan's weapon to keep you from learning to live consistently as a Christian. *Guilt drives you away from God, not toward Him.*

Revelation 12:10 calls satan your "accuser" for a very good reason: *accusation is the devil's primary weapon against you.* You've probably heard a voice inside you saying things like:

❖ You didn't give enough in that offering;

❖ You're *always* late;

❖ You never do anything right.

Well, it wasn't your voice! Satan wants to keep you as aware as possible of your shortcomings. In fact, he wants sin, not innocence, to be the light in which you see yourself. And you're not alone. *Sin consciousness* holds millions of Christians in bondage. They never really come into a revelation of their right standing with God and the reality that they are new creations. They are at war within themselves. They don't really like who they are, and they focus continually on their weaknesses. It never occurs to them that an outside force is involved.

If I'm describing you, then it's time to break that curse and come to peace with who you *really* are: a child of God, and the very "apple of His eye." That's a phrase, from Psalm 17:8 and Zechariah 2:8, describing your pupil, that little black dot through which you see the world. You can move your eyes up and down and from side to side, but the dot stays right there, in the middle of your eye. You cannot make it otherwise. Likewise, you are never out of God's gaze, but always the center of His attention!

Humankind as a whole is dominated by a spiritual inferiority complex, a profound sense of unworthiness. This is plainly evidenced by the sheer number of the world's thousands of religions. People know there's a God, and that they are estranged from Him. Saint Paul alluded to this sin consciousness in Acts chapter 17, when he pointed to the myriad idols that dotted the Athenian landscape as evidence that the people of Greece knew they were alienated from the true God, but couldn't figure out how to find Him.

The word *gospel* is an old English contraction for words meaning "good news." Saint Paul knew that evangelism doesn't consist of telling people they are sinners. They already know it, as proven by their efforts to justify themselves, from ritual sacrifices to "alternative lifestyle" activism. Rather, Jesus came (and commissioned us) to "heal the brokenhearted, to proclaim liberty to the captives and recovery of sight to the blind, to set at liberty those who are oppressed" (Luke 4:18). That is why Paul designed his message to erase people's shame, not compound it. He turned the bad news that they did not know God into the good news that they *could* know Him. And several people on Mars Hill came to Christ that very day.

Guilt is one of the most powerful psychological forces in the human race. Satan, master strategist that he is, knows how to manipulate us with guilt feelings. My major problems as a young man growing into adulthood were problems of overwhelming guilt. It was as if the devil knew me better than I knew myself.

He repeatedly triggered a sense of sin in me that constantly robbed me of spiritual victory.

I felt like the sparrow in one of my father's sermon illustrations. A pastor had a friend who was the caretaker of a zoo. An imported snake was arriving from Africa, so the caretaker invited his minister friend over at feeding time to watch a fascinating phenomenon.

The caretaker opened the door of the snake's cage and threw a live sparrow in. When the little bird saw the snake, it was terrified, and fluttered wildly to the corner of the coop farthest from the reptile. But the snake did not chase the bird, and in fact didn't move. It simply sat coiled in the corner, eyes fastened upon its prey. The rapt pastor watched as after awhile the bird stopped fluttering and began to stare back at the snake. Then, to his amazement, the sparrow loosened its claws from the metal grid, hopped down to the floor and toward its enemy. The snake slowly opened its mouth, and its hypnotized victim simply jumped in.

Saint Paul referred to the "mystery of iniquity" (see 2 Thess. 2:7). Sin and guilt, like the hungry snake, have a certain hypnotic quality to them; as long as your attention is fastened upon them, you're powerless to break away. In fact, you're likely to remain spellbound by the very habits you're trying to conquer, even though you are searching inside for the willpower to say no.

Sin's Treadmill

Let me play mind reader for a moment: A voice has been telling you that you're a spiritual failure. You're never going to break that bad habit. In fact, you gave in to it yesterday, and you probably will again today. You also didn't work hard enough last week, and let's see…God won't bless you because of your past. You disappointed your parents. Your marriage doesn't have a chance, *and* you've done a lousy job raising your kids.

How am I doing? If that kind of thinking describes you, then welcome to the devil's workout club. You're officially stuck on a treadmill of sin. Here's how it works.

You hear the preaching of the Gospel, and you're cut to the heart with guilt. So you confess it to God, sometimes with strong tears, saying, "Lord, forgive me this one time, and I promise you I'll never do it again." Afterward, everything seems fine for a couple of weeks, maybe a month. But it's only a matter of time until you're blindsided. You stumble and fall...again. Now back at square one, you feel absolutely worthless. So you get up and run a little faster. "Lord, forgive me just one more time," you say, wheezing a little. But the accuser is at work, drilling away at your mind, so your prayer comes out in hopeless, helpless tones. Before your knees leave the floor, you're set up for more failure. Eventually you're so disgusted with yourself that the tears come less and less often. What's the point, you ask yourself, but it's really more of a statement than a question. After all that running, you haven't moved an inch.

I once read a survey in which 500 people were asked the question, "What do you experience when you're feeling guilty?" Their answers fell into three categories. First, they were overtaken by a fear of punishment. Second, they experienced depression, and feelings of worthlessness and lowered self-esteem. Third, they felt isolated and rejected.[2]

Where do such feelings come from? Think back to your childhood for the answer. What did your parents do when you fell short of their standards, especially for the second or third time? They probably expressed anger or frustration, or shamed you for your misbehavior. Or they might have subtly rejected you—at least that's how you saw it—by sending you to your room.

As we grow up we tend to project these reactions onto our heavenly Father. We think God is saying to us, "Shame on you! You know better than that. After all I've done for you, how could you treat Me this way?" Or we expect Him to withdraw His presence from us, much like when we were sent to our room.

You're running even faster now. Satan is capitalizing on your feelings of guilt, and now you've got two problems: sin *and* guilt. Now it's doubly difficult to exercise strong faith in God. First John 3:21 says, "Beloved, if our heart does not condemn us, we have confidence toward God." But you've turned that verse on its head: your heart *does* condemn you, and you do *not* have confidence toward God. Praying is pointless, you huff and puff to yourself.

Now you find yourself utterly unable to praise the Lord. *It's all my fault*, you think. *How can I possibly offer up praise to God? I make the same dumb mistake over and over again. He won't want to hear a hypocrite like me.* The treadmill is at full speed now, and you're exhausting yourself in cycle after cycle of sin, guilt, repentance—sin, guilt, repentance. You know you're running a race to nowhere, but you can't jump off.

UNIFORM OF GUILT

People's reactions to guilt are fairly uniform. In fact, in contrast to a garment of praise, guilt is the uniform. It's a straitjacket called *fatalism*. Some people simply put it on and give up. They accept the devil's accusations as truth. Spiritually and emotionally drained, they settle for the "fact" that they're just no good. So they plod through life, their lowered sense of spiritual self-esteem weighing on them like storm-soaked clothes that never dry out.

Other folks get *angry*. They decide the rules are unrealistic and unfair, and that they're going to fight back. That's how I reacted as a teenager. I was so bound by a sense of inferiority that I started flailing at God and anyone who represented Him, especially my parents and the leaders of our church. *I'll show you that you can't shove God down my throat,* I thought. Then I would do something extreme to underline my anger, like blowing up our neighbors' outhouses with pipe bombs I made with materials I had stolen from my high school chemistry lab.

This was essentially Adam and Eve's rebellion. They wanted to be their own source of "the knowledge of good and evil." So they took God's law—that's what the fruit represented—into their own hands. But their "religion of revolution" failed, just as mine did. So they turned to the alternative false religion of escape. They covered their nakedness behind fig leaf excuses.

Escapism is a third reaction to guilt. When rebellion doesn't work, some people turn to rationalizing their guilt. "I'm not really a bad person. There are lots of people who do worse things than I." But philosophical fig leaves are as unacceptable to God as Eden's real ones were. Just as He covered original man's nakedness with the skin of slain, innocent animals, so He arranged for the blood of His own innocent Son to cover our sin. Nothing else will do.

A fourth common reaction to guilt is to **pass the buck**. That's what Adam did when he pointed his finger at his wife and blamed his sin on "the woman You gave me." Of course Eve performed an equally quick handoff, blaming the serpent for deceiving her. (See Genesis chapter 3.) Generations of that first couple's offspring have been following suit ever since.

There is yet a fifth reaction to guilt, and it is perhaps the most dangerous of all. Some people realize they can relieve the psychological pressure of guilt by asking God for forgiveness, like the mafia godfather who knocks off the competition and then heads for confession. He hopes a little holy water will wash the blood off his hands, but he fully intends to continue his killing ways. What such people really want is relief from the pressure, not the sin. Like the child nabbed with his hand in the cookie jar, they're sorry not for what they've done, but simply that they got caught. So they ask for forgiveness, without really intending to change their behavior. They're after what I call spiritual cosmetic surgery, something to make them look good, but leave the inner person untouched. That is not repentance; it is *manipulation.*

The sixth, and right, reaction is *constructive sorrow.* Paul describes it best:

> *Now I rejoice, not that you were made sorry, but that your sorrow led to repentance. For you were made sorry in a godly manner, that you might suffer loss from us in nothing. For godly sorrow produces repentance leading to salvation, not to be regretted; but the sorrow of the world produces death* (2 Corinthians 7:9-10).

This is sorrow that produces lasting change. That's why the apostle called it "godly sorrow...not to be regretted." In other words, the result is worth the suffering!

Chuck Colson, former chief counsel to President Richard Nixon, is a prime example of someone who experienced godly sorrow leading to repentance. Although technically innocent of crimes related to the Watergate scandal that led to Nixon's resignation, the crisis itself had helped bring Colson to Christ. Realizing that he was indeed guilty of obstructing justice in an unrelated

Nixon "dirty trick," the once-powerful White House official confessed his crime and served seven months in prison.

Shortly after his release from prison in January 1975, Colson and I were appearing at the same conference, so I picked him up at the airport. As we walked through the baggage claim area and out to my car, people stared, some sneering and making snide remarks. He had been on television virtually every night for months, and as far as most people were concerned, he was guilty on all counts, his conversion nothing more than jailhouse religion and a publicity ruse. They hated him as they hated Nixon.

That evening, as I listened to Chuck give his testimony, I was transfixed. There was no regret in him, no lingering sorrow, only thanksgiving. He was thankful to have been brought low by God, no matter what it took; thankful to know peace with God in Christ for the first time in his life; thankful that his time in prison had been the greatest reeducation of his life.

Chuck Colson went on the next year to establish Prison Fellowship Ministries, which today is the most highly respected and effective prison ministry in the world. He has also authored 20 books, several of them bestsellers, and is considered one of his generation's most able Christian apologists.

The Greek word for *repentance* actually means to change one's mind, to do an about-face, like Chuck Colson did. Yet you are powerless in yourself to make such a change. So the question is: How can you be not just forgiven, but also permanently transformed?

THE DIVINE EXCHANGE

The answer to guilt is found in the very first chapter of Romans:

For I am not ashamed of the gospel of Christ, for it is the power of God to salvation for everyone who believes, for the Jew first and also for the Greek. For in it the righteousness of God is revealed from faith to faith; as it is written, "The just shall live by faith" (Romans 1:16-17).

Paul makes a fundamental truth very clear. **The good news of Christ is essentially a revelation of righteousness.** It is first a revelation of God's righteousness in Christ, and second a revelation of your righteousness in Him. Understand that truth, and you will realize the power of God over sin.

If you have not understood the righteousness imputed to you through the Gospel, then you have not understood the Gospel. Many Christians sadly have believed a half-Gospel for years. They know righteousness was revealed in Christ, but not that it actually has been imputed to them. Consequently they refuse to take their stand in the truth of God's Word, that the righteous, the just, "shall live by his faith." Yet Christian living is grounded in righteousness, not in keeping a set of rules. You need to repeat this to yourself every day by faith: *"I am righteous."*

Second Corinthians 5:21 makes it crystal clear: "For he hath made him to be sin for us, who knew no sin; that we might be made the righteousness of God in him" (KJV). This verse is really describing a divine exchange. God by nature is righteous and holy, while people by nature are sinful. Fellowship between the two would seem impossible.

The innate challenge of redemption is this: *God legally must make you as righteous as He Himself is in order to have fellowship with you.* But He has met the challenge and has done the impossible! He made Jesus to be sin by imputing your sin to Him, so that you might be made righteous concurrently with Him. *God has given you His righteousness as a gift, and it is yours no matter how you feel: guilty, depressed, rejected, or worthless.* It is yours the moment you place faith in Christ as Savior. It cannot be added to or improved upon by God or man. You receive it strictly on the basis of faith alone. God has made you righteous in spite of how you perform. *You are as righteous as Jesus Himself!*

Believe it or not, God wants you to feel good about yourself, to feel secure. He wants you to have a healthy self-image, the kind that comes not from self-help books, but from a revelation of your righteousness in Christ Jesus!

A friend of mine has an acquaintance who has asked God to forgive him of the same sin some 350 times—yes, he actually kept count. But he obviously didn't believe God forgave him the very first time he asked, and proved it 349 more times. You can—no, you *must* choose to stop feeling bad about yourself in order to break such a cycle. The feeling that you're not worthy comes straight from the devil. *Sure, grace sounds too good to be true, but it's true anyway! The fact that you don't deserve it is exactly what qualifies you for it.*

The time has come for you to stand and declare, "I am righteous." God does not grade us on a curve. This is no such thing as being 67 percent righteous. You either are completely righteous or not righteous at all. The fact that God has imputed *His* righteousness to you means that He no longer views you in terms of your own, which falls far short of His perfection. Instead He sees you through the "prism" of Jesus' righteousness. Therefore, you are as acceptable to Him as Jesus, regardless of your daily performance.

Few believers really understand the true meaning, the sheer completeness, of righteousness. They mistake condemnation from *satan, fellow believers, and their own conscience* as being from God. They think accusation is God's conviction.

Moreover the dagger cuts two ways. If you condemn myself for a weak Christian life, you're likely to make the same assumption about others. One of my favorite teachers in Bible school, a fiery little Scotsman named John Cooke, first taught me this truth. "When a preacher rides a hobby horse of sin in his preaching," he said one day, "he's actually telegraphing his own obsession." Sadly, the accuracy of that observation has been proven time and again, especially in recent years through the scandals that have plagued celebrity ministers. The fact is, we hate most in others what we hate about ourselves.

An understanding of righteousness is foundational to every aspect of Christian living. If you aren't clear on this critical subject, then nothing else will "work" right for you as a Christian.

Romans 10:10 says, "For with the heart one believes unto righteousness...." Believing takes place in the heart more than in the mind. Satan will try to convince you that you are a liar. He will use every psychological guilt trick from your past. He will say that you are inwardly rotten, that God is going to judge you severely for your sin and hypocrisy. He will tell you that you're just not good enough to serve the Lord.

That's why you must declare it: "I am righteous. Right now, for real. And it's not because of me, but because of Him." Tell yourself, "I know I'm the apple of God's eye, and right now I'm putting on the breastplate of His approval (see Zech. 2:8; Eph. 6:14). He is pleased with me and accepts me the way I am, warts and all. He knows everything about me, yet He's *still* head over heels in love with me."

That's not conceit—it's a fact! You've got to stick with it, continually confessing it with your lips until the reality of it grips you. And as you do, God will honor your faith and open your spiritual eyes to the *real* truth about you: you are the righteousness of God in Christ Jesus! Then satan will have lost his foothold of accusation. He is defeated when you understand what your righteousness really means.

You probably have a few questions at this point: "Will saying these kinds of things about myself really help me? How can I reinforce them in my life until they're a permanent frame of mind? Is it possible to live with a continual awareness of my right standing before God?"

JUSTIFIED BY BLOOD

The answers to these questions are found in the blood of Jesus Christ. It is your spiritual weapon, your source of victory. Romans 5:9 says, "Much more then, having now been justified [made righteous] by His blood, we shall be saved from wrath through Him." *It is the blood of Jesus that has made you righteous.*

This is a fundamental truth. In order to understand the reality of your right standing with God, you must understand the meaning of Jesus' blood. This is the point where you move into spiritual warfare, where you learn to resist the accuser of your soul. It is a daily battle, but it is one that God assures you that you have already won. Revelation 12 says:

> *Then I heard a loud voice saying in heaven, "Now salvation, and strength, and the kingdom of our God, and the power of His Christ have come, for the accuser of our brethren, who accused them before our God day and night, has been cast*

down. And they overcame him by the blood of the Lamb and by the word of their testimony, and they did not love their lives to the death" (Revelation 12:10-11).

This Scripture is commonly used about the end times, but its truth is ageless. Look at the way the believers in this passage used their spiritual weapons to cast down their accuser. Their weapon in this case was the blood of the Lamb. And they launched that weapon "by the word of their testimony." **You must testify to what the Word says the blood of Jesus does for you.** And since the enemy constantly attacks you, the counterattack of your testimony must be constant as well. Understanding the blood of Jesus is the key to your realization of righteousness.

Instead of allowing your "self-talk" to be full of accusation and condemnation, learn to talk to yourself about the Blood. "Because of the Blood, God totally accepts me. He has great plans for me and He is pleased with me." That is what God's Word says about you. It's God-talk, and you need to make it yours.

THE BLOOD OF GOD

We have been presumptuous about the term, "the blood of Jesus." I'd like to explain what I believe it really means. When a baby is conceived, neither the male spermatozoon nor the female ovum contains blood. But as soon as the two come together in conception, the microscopic new life begins manufacturing its own blood cells. The baby's blood type may, in fact, differ from that of its mother, and in any case the placenta guards the unborn child from any flow of her blood.

When Jesus was conceived, the Holy Spirit planted divine Life directly into Mary's womb. Conception did not occur in her fallopian tube. Hence Mary's Adamic DNA was never transmitted to the spotless Lamb of God she now carried. The blood type of God's Son was pure and perfect, free from the stain of Adam's sin. Jesus' veins flowed with—as it were—the very blood of God.

This is why the truth of Hebrews 9:12 is so powerful: "Not with the blood of goats and calves, but with His own blood He entered the Most Holy Place once for all, having obtained eternal redemption."

After Jesus died, this verse says He ascended to God's "Most Holy Place." Since His blood was that of a truly innocent Man, completely unaffected by Adam's sin, Jesus could offer His blood to atone for man's sin. And remember, this act occurred in the eternal "now" of God's throne room. Thus it is there today, as freshly shed as it was 2,000 years ago at the Cross.

Of course it's one thing to accept this as an objective theological fact, but there is still a subjective problem: How is this saving blood applied to your life? You need to appropriate the truth that His blood has made and *continues* to make you righteous *right now*.

THE POWER OF TESTIMONY

Exodus 12 paints a beautiful analogy of how you can "apply" the blood of Jesus in your life. Israel had been in bondage to Egypt for 400 years, and now Moses had gone to Pharaoh with God's command to "let My people go." When Pharaoh refused, Moses commanded a variety of ten plagues that subsequently afflicted the nation of Egypt, the final one being the most severe. The death angel would move across the land, and every house that was not covered by the blood of an innocent lamb would be smitten in a specific way: The oldest boy child in the home would be slain by the angel of death.

God gave Moses a plan to protect the sons of Israel. They were to slay a lamb for each family, collecting the animal's blood in a basin. Then they were to take the blood and sprinkle it on the side posts of the door, and on the lintel over the door.

Furthermore, the lamb's blood had to be applied in the prescribed way. Each family must take a weed-like herb called hyssop, dip it into the blood, and then fling it at the doorposts, sprinkling them in the process. This hyssop is symbolic of how believers overcome the devil "by the blood of the Lamb and by the word of their testimony" (Rev. 12:11). *Your testimony is the hyssop that applies the blood of Jesus to your life.* It is how you daily "dip" into the truth of what God's Word says about the blood, and effectively apply it to the spiritual doorways of your mind.

Remember, your conscience is where the battle takes place. It is where you declare before the devil, before God, and to yourself, what the Blood does for you. This daily confession is the perpetual application of Jesus' eternally fresh blood that empowers you to live in Him. It is also what terrifies satan, the accuser, because it effectively renders him mute. *He cannot point to offenses that have been washed away.*

Take Aim

Just as the Israelites had to fling the lamb's blood at their doorposts, you also have to take aim in applying the blood of Jesus to every "doorway" on your conscience. Satan makes constant, unrelenting assaults on your mind, not only with overt accusations, but with a flood of subtle smears and temptations that Song of Solomon 2:15 called "little foxes that spoil the vines."

I know about little foxes, as well as coyotes, wolves, and other varmints, from watching my father hunt them down in Canada when I was a boy. Bert Law was a true "pioneer" pastor. He and Mom established churches in villages on the western plains, places like Meadow Lake, Saskatchewan, where I was born in the local Indian hospital.

When I was six years old, Dad accepted a call to the town of Parkside, about 80 miles north of the city of Saskatoon. The parsonage was small and primitive, with an outdoor toilet I still find far too memorable because of frigid winter nights. Since Dad needed a study, and Mom needed a place for canning and storing food, he decided to dig a basement under that little house that would meet both needs.

Digging under an existing house was a daunting engineering proposition, but Dad took it on. He and some friends from the church dug a starter hole near one wall, then hitched a big scoop—sort of an upside-down backhoe—to a horse, and the serious excavation began. Once the hole was deep enough, the men took spades and crawled down under the house to dig out the big rectangle that would become a basement. They dug for days down there, while up above Mom cooked their meals.

One day Dad came up out of the hole carrying something rusted and clogged with dirt. It was a Winchester Model 1876 hunting rifle, and he recognized its value at once, even in its present condition. Although introduced to celebrate the American Centennial, the Canadian Mounties had once used this rifle as their standard long arm. Now, when he wasn't digging, Dad was repairing that rifle. He straightened the bent sights, unplugged the barrel, made his own stock, and transformed the rusted throwaway into a well-oiled firearm that would repay his labors many times over in food on our table.

Until now Dad's only gun was the .22 rifle that he used to supplement his meager salary by shooting squirrels and selling the skins. But the "new" gun would enable us to eat well, not only during hunting season, but all winter long, thanks to Mom's sausage making and our new, naturally refrigerated underground cannery.

My father was also the best shot in the area—he once dropped a charging moose at 25 feet—so neighbors began hiring him to shoot wolves that preyed on their sheep and young cattle. One day he took me to a nearby town for a reason I don't remember, and on the way slammed on his brakes and pulled to the side of the road. "Look at that," he said, pointing to a wolf sprinting across the prairie about 300 yards away. "I've been looking for that one for weeks." The animal had been killing local livestock, and thus far had eluded him.

Dad pulled me out of the car, grabbed the rifle, and told me to keep quiet. Then he laid the barrel across the hood of the car, and tested the wind with his finger. The wolf was at full speed and very far away, so he would have to aim above and ahead of it. "Watch this," he snickered as he beaded down on the four-legged rustler. Suddenly I saw the barrel move quickly and smoothly to the left and *bam!* With a single shot the wolf flew head over heels, a slug through its heart. I already knew Dad was a good shot, but on that day, in my eyes, he was the best in the whole wide world!

If I had to trace my sense of adventure to its beginnings, I'd probably point back to that day, to the dirt where I stood on the side of the road, watching my hero take aim at the impossible and then somehow hit it. Times like that awaken something within a child; they take the blinders off his vision for the future. Suddenly anything seems possible. And although I never learned to shoot a gun like my father, I learned a lot about aiming like him when it comes to firing the weapons of spiritual warfare.

The Word, the Name, and the blood of Jesus are every bit as real as Dad's old rifle, and infinitely more powerful. How much more important is it, then, for you to practice your skills in handling, aiming, and firing them at the wolves of hell that would devour you? I'm talking about the skills of prayer, praise, and testimony. *Your testimony is the rifle that fires the bullet of Jesus' blood.* Keep it by your side, always at the ready. Fire it often. *Declare your testimony every day.*

TURNING GOD-TALK INTO SELF-TALK

You've got at least one thing to be very optimistic about at this point. The fact that you're investing your time to read this book shows a certain amount of sincerity on your part. Even if you've despised yourself, you have to give yourself credit for that. So why not go the rest of the way? Why not make God's testimony about you your testimony about yourself? Why not make God-talk your self-talk? There are many Scriptures I could list, but here are six I recommend declaring on a regular basis.[3]

One of my favorites is Ephesians 1:7: "In Him we have redemption through His blood, the forgiveness of sins, according to the riches of His grace."

Forgiveness is more than God canceling your sins; it also means that He has remitted them—forever blotted them out of His memory. *They will never be brought up against you again, because*

NOT SO!

— 138 —

there is nothing to remember. Remind yourself that God keeps no record of your sin, because it has been blotted out by the Blood. *The blood of Jesus is all he sees!*

Redemption goes even further than forgiveness, not just dealing with what you've done, but with who you are. Redemption is the work of Jesus Christ on your behalf, not only canceling your debt, but also releasing you from slavery to sin, and to sin consciousness. Redemption makes true *transformation* possible. Nothing that you've ever done is too much for the mercy of God. Sorry, but you're not *that* good at sinning! So remind yourself that God is not angry with you, and He doesn't keep a running tally of your mistakes. *BuT HE DoES!*

On the basis of Ephesians 1:7, you can regularly make these two declarations:

1. "According to Ephesians 1:7, by the blood of Jesus I am redeemed, bought back out of the hand of the devil."

2. "According to Ephesians 1:7, by the blood of Jesus all my sins are remitted. God has no memory of them. He wants me to accept the *new* me. I'm forgiven, and I believe it!"

Another of my favorite verses is First John 1:7, to which I alluded earlier. Here is the entire verse: "But if we walk in the light as He is in the light, we have fellowship with one another, and the blood of Jesus Christ His Son cleanses us from all sin." The word *cleanses* is in the continuing present tense in the Greek. It means that the blood of Jesus is *continually* cleansing you. You may have failed to do the right thing *again* yesterday. Ask for forgiveness *again* and believe that you're cleansed. You may have lost your temper *again*, or tossed your common sense right out the window. Maybe you really blew it...*again*. On the basis of this verse, you can make the following declaration:

3. "According to First John 1:7, the blood of Jesus Christ, God's Son, continually cleanses me from all sin. No matter how many times I fail, His blood keeps washing me clean." *"fail" not sin, did not choose*

The next verse is Romans 5:9: "Much more then, having now been justified by His blood, we shall be saved from wrath through Him." Here is your declaration:

4. "According to Romans 5:9, by the blood of Jesus, I am justified, made righteous just as if I had never sinned. This means I am 100 percent righteous, not 50 percent or 99 percent. God sees me through the blood of Jesus. I am forever acceptable to Him. Who can separate me from God's love?"

Hebrews 13:12 takes you from righteousness to sanctification—holiness. Whereas righteous is the opposite of sinful, holy is the opposite of common. This doesn't mean that God "de-chromes" your personality and paints you basic black. To the contrary, He makes you holy the way a master artist can turn a piece of driftwood into a unique, expensive work of art. God has taken your bent and twisted life and turned you into a one-of-a-kind (i.e., holy) treasure for His trophy case. *You are His child, and He's proud of you!* Here is the verse: "Therefore Jesus also, that He might sanctify the people with His own blood, suffered outside the gate." In light of this verse, make the following declaration:

5. "According to Hebrews 13:12, by the blood of Jesus, I am sanctified, made holy, set apart unto God. He has turned my throw-away life into a priceless treasure, and put me on display before the world."

A sixth declaration is taken from First Corinthians 6:19-20: "Or do you not know that your body is the temple of the Holy Spirit who is in you, whom you have from God, and you are not your own? For you were bought at a price; therefore glorify God in your body and in your spirit, which are God's." You may have formerly abused your body in many ways, but Paul makes it clear that an outrageously high price, the very blood of God's Son, was paid to turn your condemned property into God's temple.

Here is a sixth, grand declaration that encompasses the first five as well:

6. "According to First Corinthians 6:19-20, my body is the temple of the Holy Spirit, redeemed, forgiven, cleansed, made righteous, and sanctified. Therefore, satan has no place in me and no power over me. I renounce him and loose myself from him by the blood of Jesus."

If you have stopped reading long enough to make these six declarations aloud, you more than likely felt a spirit of praise welling up within you. That's because praise to God is the natural, if not inevitable, release that comes with a sense of righteousness. *When you truly understand your righteousness in Christ Jesus, praise will become your daily frame of mind.* It will finally dawn on you once and for all that God isn't mad at you, but has redeemed you by the blood of Jesus. You'll actually be able to look the person in the mirror right in the eyes and smile because they're clear.

I have found it very helpful to sing choruses that declare my righteousness through the blood of Jesus.

What can wash away my sin?
Nothing but the blood of Jesus;

What can make me whole again?
Nothing but the blood of Jesus.
Oh! precious is the flow…

As I sing such melodies daily, I reinforce my testimony to myself—and particularly to the accuser—that I truly am righteous.

Such reinforcement saved my life not long ago in Afghanistan. World Compassion had been asked to deliver several truckloads of food to Mohammed Khail, an Afghan camp where 90,000 refugees were barely subsisting in the heat of the desert bordering Pakistan. My associate Joel, my elder son Scot, and I followed our nine trucks into the camp early one morning, only to be met by a stone-throwing mob intent on killing us.

We would learn only later that Taliban fighters were hiding out in the camp at night, and had convinced the people that all Americans were their oppressors. Adding fuel to the fire was a huge "World Compassion USA" banner on the side of one of our trucks, put there without my knowledge by a well-meaning but naïve aid worker. We were attacked almost as soon as we arrived.

One of the stones hit my driver in the nose, bloodying his face and shirt. Another took out one of our windshields. "How do we get out of here?" I shouted. One of the drivers yelled back that there was a United Nations headquarters about three miles away, so we headed through the center of the camp, a mob of about 3,000 people throwing rocks, chasing us, and blocking our path. We had to drive slowly to keep from running over them, so by the time our convoy reached the UN compound we had lost six windshields and windows.

The fort's massive gates had barely slammed shut when hundreds from the mob began pouring over the 9-foot-tall green fence, intent on killing us. The hail of rocks continued, one smashing the Jeep window beside Joel, who thought it was a grenade. With that the Pakistani soldier sitting next to me opened the door and began firing his AK-47 into the air, scaring people back over the wall.

"You're going to die today," one of the UN workers yelled to me, as more rocks flew at us from beyond the wall.

"No, I'm not going to die," I yelled back.

"Yes, you are," he insisted. "You'll never get out of here alive."

"No," I said loudly. "I'm not going to die today. I'm protected by the blood of Jesus." He probably thought I was crazy, but I didn't care. Even when the crowd outside had swollen to 10,000 angry Afghans armed with rocks, I knew God would keep us from death because we had applied the power of Jesus' blood with the "hyssop" of our testimony.

Eventually I remembered that Scot was carrying a brand-new satellite phone that we had never used. One phone call and an hour later, we were being escorted to safety by a convoy of heavily armed soldiers from a nearby base. But most important, we had overcome the enemy of our souls "by the blood of the Lamb and the word of [our] testimony." The devil had thrown rocks at us, but we had launched a missile in return.

As for the relief supplies, we left everything in the UN compound, with the understanding that it would be kept until we could return. One week later, Pakistani Pastor David Nielson was back there, not only giving out the food and blankets, but also preaching the Gospel and distributing several thousand *The Story of Jesus* booklets to the very same people who had tried to kill us.

ENDNOTES

1. www.winchestermysteryhouse.com.

2. Bruce Narramore and Bill Counts, *Guilt and Freedom* (Santa Ana, CA: Vision House Publishers, 1994), 19.

3. I am thankful to have learned the habit of making scriptural declarations from one of my mentors, Bible teacher Derek Prince.

Chapter 7

Spiritual Rockets

That's the nature of praise. It draws our attention away from our problems, no matter how overwhelming they are, and lifts our gaze to God.

~

Adjacent to the zoo in Atlanta, Georgia, is a tourist attraction called the "Cyclorama." It's a 360-degree painting of the 1864 Battle of Atlanta, fought during the American Civil War. Visitors to the Cyclorama are seated in a slowly revolving theater while a narrator describes the passing scenes—sounds of gunfire both near and distant add to the feeling of history come to life.

I've taken you through a cyclorama that depicts spiritual warfare. *First*, I have shown you scenes from my own life's battles, and how I initially discovered the power of praise and worship.

Second, you've seen strongholds, rebel outposts set up in the mind by satan, the accuser of every Christian. This is the battlefield where he attempts to pull us down, make us sick, and bind us with oppression. Strongholds exist to destroy marriages and families, and to put believers into any type of bondage, financial or otherwise, that stops God's will from being done "on earth as it is in heaven."[1]

Third, we've examined the awesome power of the three great spiritual warheads that the Bible calls the "weapons of our warfare" (2 Cor. 10:4)—God's Word; Jesus' Name; Jesus' Blood. We have discovered that the Word of God is a hammer (Jer. 23:29) that smashes strongholds, brick by ugly brick. We have learned that even though strongholds may dominate our thoughts, the name of Jesus is a "strong tower" (Prov. 18:10) that tears them down. And we've seen that the blood of Jesus, brought to bear against a stronghold by the word of our testimony (Rev. 12:11), washes our consciences clean, sweeping away guilt and all of the other debris from our pasts, leaving the accuser of our souls completely unarmed against us.

Warheads are useless without a delivery system. Therefore, we need to learn how to launch our weapons into enemy territory by putting spiritual rockets under them.

LAUNCHING OUR WEAPONS

I believe the most awesome manmade weapon in history is the intercontinental ballistic missile (ICBM), armed with a nuclear warhead. An ICBM can travel thousands of miles in minutes, and then destroy its target with pinpoint accuracy.

But there's something even faster and more powerful: the name of Jesus beamed via satellite television at the speed of light.

Reza Safa knows firsthand. The Iranian-born Oklahoma pastor has a passion to evangelize his native country, and is teaming with the Trinity Broadcasting Network to beam Gospel preaching in the Farsi language into Iran by satellite.

The importance of Reza's efforts cannot be overstated, because Iran currently poses the biggest danger to the entire Middle East. "Forget everyone else," says my friend, Iraqi General Georges Sada. "Iran is the major player in the region."

The prime minister of Iraq's northern province of Kurdistan, Nechirvan Barzani, agrees. He recently told me that if America withdraws all of its troops from Iraq, "within seven days Iran will be on my doorstep here in Irbil, on their way to Israel." Certainly it's no secret that Iran harbors a deep and ancient hatred for Israel. Their president, Mahmoud Ahmadinejad, has stated many times that his nation's greatest desire is "to wipe Israel from the face of the map." And as I write, my sources tell me that Iran is purchasing large numbers of surface-to-surface missiles, ostensibly to arm them with nuclear warheads for an attack against Israel. No wonder, then, that the Iranians are working so feverishly to develop their nuclear capabilities.

Meanwhile God Himself is conducting a counterinvasion of Iran, with spiritual weapons that are far faster and more powerful than anything man could ever devise, as I discovered recently when I was in Iraq. Before leaving the U.S., I had preached on several of Reza's programs. Ten days later I flew to Iraq, where I stayed at the Prime Minister's guest house in Irbil. Shortly after my arrival a Kurdish man from Kirkuk walked into my room and stopped dead in his tracks, a shocked look on his face.

"What are *you* doing here?" he blurted out.

I replied that I had no idea what he was talking about.

"I just saw you on television last night in my living room," he explained. "You are being broadcast all across Iraq and Iran."

Only then did I realize the potential of satellite television for reaching Iran, the modern world's first self-proclaimed Islamic republic. In a land where Christians are persecuted and martyred in large numbers, conservative estimates indicate that 850,000 Iranians have been brought to Jesus as a result of satellite television.

But let's get back to earthly warfare for a moment. Imagine if Iran were to launch a thousand rockets, but without arming them with nuclear warheads. They would just make a thousand small craters in the ground, and maybe destroy a few cars or houses in the process. Likewise, they could possess the most powerful warheads on earth, but without missiles to carry them, their only power would be to wipe themselves off the map.

Now think of a nuclear Iran, with armed warheads sitting on ships a couple of hundred miles off the east coast of America. With a range of more than a thousand miles, they could destroy Washington, D.C., or New York, or even an inland city like Chicago. Now place those ships in the Mediterranean, and you'll understand why Israel will never allow Mr. Ahmadinejad's fantasy to take place. Nonetheless the Iranians are stockpiling rockets from Russia, and working feverishly to develop their nuclear program.

The rocket and the warhead are both essential, aren't they? Each is much less useful without the other. So it is in spiritual warfare. God's power lies in His three warheads: the Word, the Name, and the Blood. But even that awesome power is useless without the spiritual ICBMs that He has designed to carry these weapons to their targets. There are four primary spiritual rockets: *prayer, preaching, testimony,* and *praise* and *worship.*

ICBM OF PRAYER

There is no question that *prayer* has great power when armed with a spiritual weapon. But it's also true that prayer in itself is useless, amounting to nothing more than what the Bible calls "vain repetitions" (Matt. 6:7).

The prophet Elijah knew this when he challenged the 450 prophets of the Canaanite god, Baal (see 1 Kings 18:22-39). The pagan priests cried out and cut themselves until they bled profusely, but "there was no voice; no one answered, no one paid attention" (v. 29).

Elijah, on the other hand, "built an altar in the name of the Lord," offered a sacrifice, and then prayed to the "Lord God of Abraham, Isaac, and Israel" (1 Kings 18:32,36). The prophet launched the ICBM of prayer, armed with the warheads of the Name and—through the prophetic symbol of a slain bull—the Blood. His enemies, though there were 450 of them, didn't stand a chance. Nor would they if they had numbered 450,000 or even a million. Elijah's weapons were unbeatable, and the altar of Baal, a stronghold, was torn down.

Jeremiah 33:3 says, "Call to Me, and I will answer you, and show you great and mighty things, which you do not know." That's a powerful promise and an astounding truth. Yet more amazing is the corollary: If we do *not* call to Him, those great and mighty things will never occur. In other words, God has sovereignly chosen, in certain instances, to limit His work to our prayers. If we will not pray, He will not work.

God wants us to ask Him, to consult and cooperate with Him in carrying out His will in the earth. The prophet Amos bore eloquent witness to this fact: "Surely the Lord God does nothing, unless He reveals His secret to His servants the prophets" (Amos 3:7). We may not all be prophets, but nonetheless God refuses to do an "end run" around His Church. *His government is real, and as His sons and daughters, we are agents of His will on earth.*

I owe my life to the truth of that statement. In 2005 I was in northern Iraq yet again, and needed to fly back home to America, but the airport in Irbil was closed. Kurdish President Massoud Barzani offered me three armored cars and bodyguards if I wanted to fly out of Baghdad, and I had accepted his offer when an even bigger problem arose. Our new church in Irbil had just concluded a conference that drew news coverage from all four Arab TV networks. Abu Musab al-Zarqawi, the Al Qaeda founder (who would be killed just a few months later) had seen the reports and issued an order to kill me on the road back to Baghdad. Kurdish intelligence had learned of the plot and sent word to President Barzani the night before my intended departure. I would have to leave some other way.

The airport in Diyarbakir, Turkey was my best alternative, so the next morning the President sent a car, and we headed toward the Turkish border about a hundred miles to the north. After several stop-and-go hours, we arrived at the checkpoint, where I was to hire a taxi to take me north and west to Diyarbakir. But which one? There were at least 50 cabs waiting for fares, among them a dour looking Turk who spoke three or four words I could understand. We agreed that he would drive me to Diyarbakir for $125.

Iraqi customs checked us thoroughly for contraband and then admitted us across the river, where we cleared Turkish customs easily. At the first town I signaled that I needed to stop for the restroom, so the driver pulled over and pointed me up some steps into a run-down hotel. A couple of minutes later I trotted back down the stairs, only to surprise my driver, who was pulling green bags full of white powder from under my seat. I knew it must be either heroin or cocaine, either of which would have landed me in a Turkish prison for life.

The driver looked like a rat caught in a trap, and I saw by his expression that I was in trouble. As I got back into the car, I checked my cell phone and saw that I was picking up a signal from nearby Syria, so I called my office in Tulsa. My business manager, Ben, answered the phone.

"Ben, I'm in the Turkish desert with a driver I just found out is smuggling drugs. If I don't call you again within five hours, call Interpol and the Turkish national police." I saw a mile marker and told him exactly where we were. Ben immediately started calling prayer groups around the country to pray for me.

By now I had moved to the front seat, in case I needed to defend myself. There was no time to contemplate, "What would Jesus do?" My adrenalin had decided to stick with what Terry Law would do! "If he pulls off the highway, it means he's going to try and kill me," I thought. I made a plan to jam my left elbow into his neck, open the door with my right hand, and push him out. Sure enough, he soon pulled off the highway at a bend in the road, and I sat forward to make my move. Then suddenly we were back on the road, and I realized he had merely taken a shortcut.

I sat back with a sigh of relief, asking the Lord what to do. Just then the Turk's cell phone rang, and he handed it to me. A woman with a thick accent wanted to know if I'd like to buy an airline ticket. "No, my ticket is already prepaid from America," I answered, and handed the phone back to the driver, who listened for a moment and then became visibly irate. He glared at me.

"Lord, what now?" I prayed with eloquent brevity. "Pay him now, and pay him well," a Voice inside me said. I pulled out three, crisp one-hundred dollar notes and held them out to him.

"Change?" he said, with a suspicious tone. I smiled and said no change, that it was all for him. His frown became a toothy grin, and he gave me a thumbs up. For the first time, I knew I'd make it to the airport.

I made my flight from Diyarbakir to Istanbul, and headed for a hotel near the airport. It was nearly 4 A.M. when I collapsed into bed, only to be awakened by my cell phone. It was Don Moen calling me from his home in Alabama.

"Terry, what were you doing eight hours ago?" he asked, getting straight to the point.

"Why?" I asked, intrigued but still groggy.

"Just tell me, what were you doing eight hours ago?" he insisted.

I told Don he wouldn't believe what I was about to tell him, and then unfolded the whole adventure. He began laughing uproariously, and then with great satisfaction explained why he had called.

"Laura and I here having breakfast with Laura's sister and her husband when they asked about you. As soon as I heard your name, something told me we had to pray for you right then." The four of them stopped eating and got on their knees right there by the table, and Don led a prayer of intercession for my safety.

Don and Laura invoked the government of God, just as surely as Elijah had, launching a missile of prayer that carried the name of Jesus into the "heavenlies," where the principalities assigned to kill me were stopped in their celestial tracks.

When you pray, you leverage the very power of Heaven. On your knees in prayer you can assist missionaries in the most remote corners of the world. You can dispatch help to prisoners behind bars, invoke peace in troubled neighborhoods, and seed the clouds over arid lands. And because there is no barrier of time or space with God, He sometimes answers such prayers even before we learn that there is a need to pray. That is why Isaiah 65:24 says, "It shall come to pass that before they call, I will answer; and while they are still speaking, I will hear."

Just as Moses stretched his rod over Egypt on God's behalf, so the church in prayer stretches forth Christ's authority over the nations and their rulers. In fact, though most Christians rarely pray for civil government, that is our first call to prayer:

> *Therefore I exhort first of all that supplications, prayers, intercessions, and giving of thanks be made for all men, for kings and all who are in authority, that we may lead a quiet and peaceable life in all godliness and reverence. For this is good and acceptable in the sight of God our Savior, who desires all men to be saved and to come to the knowledge of the truth* (1 Timothy 2:1-4).

We are to pray for civil rulers, Paul says, "that we may lead a quiet and peaceable life." What exactly does that mean? One commentator only half humorously says it means that we should pray for them to leave us alone! In fact, the connection between good civil government and the freedom to preach the Gospel is obvious, as the First Amendment to America's Constitution demonstrates. No wonder a man like Paul, consumed with spreading the Good News, would make praying for civil government a top priority for the Church.

ICBM OF *PREACHING*

A second spiritual rocket is **preaching**. I have proclaimed God's Word, the name of Jesus, and the power of His blood throughout dozens of nations for more than four decades, and I can attest to the fact that preaching is a powerful and precise way to launch spiritual weapons. When I preach I expect to pull down strongholds and see captives set free.

When I preached the Gospel with Living Sound in the Communist nightclub in Poland (see Chapter 2), I launched the Word and the Name. Dozens of Polish youth were set free, and in fact the effect of that proclamation reverberated throughout Eastern Europe, making our team famous almost overnight.

When I prophesied the Word of God at my wife's funeral in 1982, the stronghold of despair that had towered over my soul was struck at its base. Later, through prayer and praise and worship, I repeatedly launched my spiritual weapons, and the stronghold in my mind was demolished once and for all.

This book, in fact, is an extension of my call to preach, a long-range missile of sorts, carrying a powerful spiritual payload. And I know my readers worldwide are being set free by the power of God that is delivered via these pages.

The Bible dramatically illustrates how the disciple Peter went from total failure to spiritual marksman, launching the Name, the Word, and the Blood, with such effectiveness that the early church exploded in growth. Likewise Saint Paul was commissioned to preach the name of Jesus to the Gentiles and before kings. The former Saul was highly educated in the Scriptures, even before being transformed on the road to Damascus, but had never known the power of Jesus' name and blood. Yet afterward, having himself been overpowered by the Name, the Bible says, "Immediately he preached the Christ in the synagogues, that He is the Son of God. Then all who heard were amazed, and said, 'Is this not he who destroyed those who called on this name in Jerusalem, and has come here for that purpose, so that he might bring them bound to the chief priests?'" (Acts 9:20-21). The great apostle's preaching focused from the beginning on the name of Jesus.

Notice also how the weapon of the Word, apparently useless in the Pharisee's former life, now came alive in Paul. He interpreted with ease that which he previously had studied but never recognized, that the name of the child Isaiah foresaw, the name of the Lord in Jeremiah's visions, and the Name that David praised so often, was the name of Jesus. He preached that righteousness came to anyone willing to believe Christ's resurrection and to confess Him as Lord (see Rom. 10:9-10). He understood right away that righteousness came through confessing the Name and being cleansed by Jesus' blood (see Rom. 5:9).

Within three days of his own salvation, Paul was preaching the Word, the Name, and the Blood. From that day on, for the rest of his life, the apostle never stopped. And the world has never been the same.

ICBM OF TESTIMONY

As we saw in Chapter 6, Revelation 12:11 depicts believers who overcame the devil "by the blood of the Lamb and by the word of their testimony." Here we have a warhead, the blood of Jesus, transported by a third spiritual rocket, *testimony*.

The Greek word for *testimony* in the Bible is also translated as "witness." When you appear as a witness in a court of law, you are directed to tell only what you saw and clearly heard. You speak from personal experience, not from opinion or presumption. Legal testimony is a basic element of our justice system, and it is equally foundational to the government of God. It is a spiritual rocket, and properly armed, it helps to establish God's Kingdom in the earth.

So many Christians think that somehow God is on trial and that they have to defend Him, convincing skeptics with undeniable proofs that Jesus really is Lord. But God doesn't need a lawyer; He wants a witness, and has equipped every believer to be exactly that: "But you shall receive power when the Holy Spirit has come upon you; and you shall be witnesses to Me in Jerusalem, and in all Judea and Samaria, and to the end of the earth" (Acts 1:8).

Think about the Day of Pentecost, when the 120 believers spoke with other tongues. Was this gift just for their private edification? No! God wanted His praises understood by the thousands of foreigners in Jerusalem for the Passover. (See Acts chapter 2:1-11.) Preaching and the working of miracles are wonderful, but it is the testimonies of believers that will bring worldwide revival. The Holy Spirit did not empower us with gifts so that we might play with them like so many swimming pool toys, splashing about from one charismatic meeting to another. *The Spirit's power was given to make us witnesses, to launch our spiritual weapons and win a war.*

In this respect the explosive growth of the Chinese church is worth noting. When I was there recently I was amazed at the repression and current tightening of restraints on Christians by the Chinese government. Persecution of pastors is routine. Stadium-based evangelistic meetings are against the law. Nor are churches permitted to televise their services. In fact all forms of evangelistic outreach are illegal. Yet even by the most conservative estimates, there are multiple thousands of Chinese citizens coming to Christ every day. And since 1950 the number of believers has jumped from a few hundred thousand to nearly 100 million. This amazing growth is almost exclusively testimony driven.

In one instance a few years ago, a medical missions team had gone to a remote area in China for a week to conduct a free clinic. They typically would have used the opportunity of ministering to people's souls while treating their bodies, but this time the Chinese authorities were watching them closely. So the week came and went without a single chance to minister, not even to say a simple prayer over a patient. The foreign doctor in charge of the mission told Jim Gilbert[2] that in the weeks following that fruitless mission he had begun to question his call to China. Everything began to seem so pointless that he found himself sinking further and further into depression. He began to think about giving up medical missions altogether, but eventually decided to keep going. Unfortunately, the depression stayed with him.

Two years later, a peasant from the countryside came knocking at the doctor's door. He had been searching for him for a long time, he said, because he wanted to say thanks.

"Before you left our village," he explained, "you gave my daughter a small card that simply read, 'May you come to know the God who created you.' When I read those words I didn't know what they meant, but somehow they grabbed me. I began to show the card to everyone I met, asking them if they knew about this God who created us. After a long while I met a Christian who explained its meaning to me. He told me about Jesus, and I gave my life to Him.

"Jesus changed my life, and I was so happy that I began telling everyone around me about Him. He changed them too, and soon we decided to start meeting together at my house to talk about the wonderful things He was doing in our lives. We would share one by one, and some people were even composing songs about Him and how they loved Him. We would all learn the songs and sing them together.

"Then one day one of our group brought a foreign Christian to a meeting. This person asked me how long we had been a church and when I became a pastor. I didn't know what a church was and what he meant about being a pastor. He also asked me if we had Bibles, and I told him I didn't know what a Bible was. So he gave me a Bible, and we were all so happy to discover that God had given us such a wonderful book of His own Words! From the Bible we learned that what we had been doing together was the same thing as the people in the first church.

"We have now been a church for two years and our numbers have grown to more than two hundred believers. I have been looking for you for a long time, because I wanted to say thank you for the sentence you wrote on that card."

Today that medical team continues to serve God in China, and stories like this one continue to be written all over Asia's "Middle Kingdom."

Christians in some circles are given to debate whether miracles still happen today, but the believers in China are too busy experiencing them to argue about such nonsense. In the end, a simple true story beats a sophisticated theory; a testimony trumps an argument! Yet many believers are cheated out of their personal testimony because they don't think their story is as sensational as someone else's. What a devilish lie. Every testimony is a witness to God's power.

Saint Paul gave his personal testimony on several occasions throughout the Book of Acts and elsewhere in the New Testament. He knew that repeating one's own story of God's grace is a powerful way to launch spiritual weapons. After all, the second bullet from a gun packs just as much punch as the first.

There is nothing more vital in all the world than to recount what God has done for you, because it builds both your listeners and yourself in faith, and it overcomes the devil. It's your story. Stick to it!

ICBM of Praise and Worship

The fourth spiritual rocket, and the primary focus of this book, is *praise and worship*. Each of the other rockets is launched by individuals: preaching, testimony, and prayer are offered one speaker at a time. Even corporate prayer, while it may include agreement on a petition, is primarily comprised of many individual expressions of that petition.

Praise and worship are also very personal, of course, yet in musical form they afford us unparalleled opportunity for unified expression. When people sing together they express the same ideas at the same time with the same intensity. This was the secret of Living

Sound's praise services. We used the means of musical praise to corporately launch spiritual weapons and resist the devil. And he had to flee because—as the saying goes—God showed up.

I'm not sure congregations realize the firepower of corporate praise. As I said in Chapter 3, praise constitutes spiritual warfare. In Isaiah chapter 30 the Lord promises to lash the backs of His enemies to the music of His peoples' praises. The experience of Jehoshaphat, King of Judah, further illustrates this principle.

Second Chronicles 20 tells how three nations conspired to attack the little kingdom during Jehoshaphat's reign, and how this godly ruler gathered the entire population to petition God for guidance, and remind Him that they were faithfully keeping the covenant He had made with them. The best part of the story, of course, took place when the king assigned singers and musicians to the front lines, and sent his army into battle with a song instead of a sword. They launched a corporate ICBM of praise and worship that invoked the most powerful force in the universe: the very presence of God. This spiritual "combined aerial assault" caused confusion to reign amongst Judah's attackers, and they wiped one another out to the last man. Then it took three days for the people of God to gather the spoils of victory.

Such is the power of a congregation in worship. Our front line may be a young man with a guitar, or a few young ladies standing across the platform, but we are a people whose God promises to indwell our praises (Ps. 22:3). And when God walks in, satan and his minions cannot stay any more than darkness can resist the rising sun.

Confusion in the enemy ranks was exactly what happened when Living Sound sang in the communist nightclub in Krakow, Poland (see chapter 2). What's more, collecting the "spoils" of our victory took not three days but several years! First, we were invited to return to Poland by the *real* power in that nation, the Roman Catholic Church, to sing at a festival in the sacred city of Czestochowa. We accepted the invitation and in 1975 found ourselves ministering to 150,000 spiritually hungry Poles attending the festival. Their response was overwhelming, and in 1976, we returned to find the audience had doubled to 300,000.

In 1978 our Polish patron, Cardinal Wojtyla, moved to Rome and became Pope John Paul II. And although we subsequently were invited to minister at the Vatican and throughout the entire Roman Catholic world, the memory I savor most took place when the new Pontiff returned to Poland in 1979, to the city of Katowice, and led a crowd of one million worshiping Poles in a little melody we had taught him: "Hallelujah, hallelujah, hallelujah, hallelujah."

It was a moment of phenomenal victory for the cause of Christ in a communist nation, and no doubt a pivotal one on their path to freedom, which came a decade later. But the power released that day into the heavens to tear down strongholds was not in the melody or the chord progression, nor even in the considerable emotion of the moment. No, the real power at work that day in Katowice was in the weapon being launched from a sea of praise: Hallelujah, "praise to Yahweh," praise to the Name!

Every time you gather with God's people, whether there are ten of you or a million, you face the golden opportunity of uniting your voice with theirs in praise to the King of Heaven and earth. Together you and I can join our hearts and merge our wills with the very will of God, as His name flows from our lips.

We can develop a synergy, a divine knockout punch that strikes down satan's strongholds with a mighty blow.

THE WAR IS REAL

By now you've noticed that all four spiritual rockets—prayer, preaching, testimony, and praise and worship—have something to do with the mouth. *Your mouth is the launch pad from which you fire the weapons of God's Word, Jesus' Name, and the Blood.* Your tongue, therefore, is very valuable territory, and satan would love to destroy it, or better yet, capture and use it for launching his own weapons of mass destruction.

You can gossip, backbite, criticize, and unjustly judge others, and turn your mouth into the devil's launch pad. Or you can choose to launch the Word, the Name, and the Blood through prayer, preaching, testimony, and praise and worship, and unleash the very power of Almighty God. But you cannot have it both ways. Unlike political parties, heaven and hell do not work out power-sharing arrangements. That is why it is so important to recognize the place of the tongue. (For a more comprehensive treatment of this subject, see chapter 12, "The Confession of Praise.")

James, the senior pastor of the first Jerusalem church, gave this profound teaching on the subject:

> *If anyone does not stumble in word, he is a perfect man, able also to bridle the whole body. Indeed, we put bits in horses' mouths that they may obey us, and we turn their whole body. Look also at ships: although they are so large and are driven by fierce winds, they are turned by a very small rudder wherever the pilot desires. Even so the tongue is a little member and boasts great things. See how great a forest a little fire kindles! And the*

tongue is a fire, a world of iniquity. The tongue is so set among our members that it defiles the whole body, and sets on fire the course of nature; and it is set on fire by hell. For every kind of beast and bird, of reptile and creature of the sea, is tamed and has been tamed by mankind. But no man can tame the tongue. It is an unruly evil, full of deadly poison. With it we bless our God and Father, and with it we curse men, who have been made in the similitude of God. Out of the same mouth proceed blessing and cursing. My brethren, these things ought not to be so (James 3:2b-10).

Although he was instructing the church, the apostle could easily have been describing the spirit of modern Islam. From turning men into human bombs to turning heaven into eternal debauchery, the Muslim mind has so confused and intertwined virtue and evil that love can turn to murderous rage in a flash. And what is behind it all? One man's words, taught for centuries, increasingly were put into practice, until they became a demonic cultural stronghold. To use the apostle James' ship analogy, Islam is a destroyer steered by the 14-centuries-old rudder of a false prophet's tongue.

In Matthew 28 Jesus gave us His "great commission," to disciple the nations by baptizing and teaching His commandments to those who respond to His grace. That grace is based upon the fact that He sacrificed His life for us, in order to raise us up to live with Him.

The Islamic great commission, on the other hand, is to conquer the world by coercion rather than conversion, to establish dominion by literally destroying all resistance. "Salvation" involves taking innocent lives rather than saving guilty ones. And while we know that the *jihad* (holy war) against the West is spiritually motivated, its casualties are often flesh and blood.

When a friend of mine—let's call him Ali[3]—traveled to Baghdad, Iraq, in the fall of 2006, he took with him several children's Bibles in Arabic, picture books that I commissioned which present the story of creation, the Old Testament fathers, and the Gospel.

When Ali entered the Customs department at the Baghdad airport, the agent inspecting his bags held up one of the Bibles and asked what it was. "An Arabic Bible for children," Ali replied forthrightly.

"Come with me," said the agent, leading him down a hallway to a nearby room.

After checking the hallway for other personnel, the agent closed the door, and began talking freely. He said he had lost his previous job, and had taken the very dangerous position of working at the airport—considered collusion by Al Qaeda because it involves working with Americans—in order to support his family.

"We live in a poor neighborhood," the man told Ali. "One day my son came home with some food, and when I asked him where he got it, he pointed to the church down the street." Ali remembered the church because we had left a supply of Bibles there.

"I thought I should go and thank them for giving us food, and when I got there they gave me one of these children's Bibles," the agent explained. "As a result I gave my life to Jesus, as did my wife and son. He has changed everything! My name is Ahmed, and you must remember from now on that you have a brother working at the airport."

Before Ali left Ahmed asked him for a complete Bible, which Ali quickly agreed to supply. "I want to share Jesus with my family," he told him a little later by phone. Ali warned Ahmed to be careful, because conversion can be very dangerous, since Sharia law requires a convert's family to execute him if he doesn't recant right away.

"I cannot be silent," Ahmed replied. "I have to share Jesus. Jesus changed my life. Jesus changed my wife's life. I send my son to Sunday school. I'm a Christian. I want to share Jesus with people."

In the weeks that followed Ahmed and Ali began exchanging frequent emails, and Ali was enjoying the prospect of seeing his new brother in Christ as often as possible. But in December, when a week passed with no emails from Ahmed, Ali began to worry.

"After a couple of weeks, my telephone rang in the middle of the night. On the other end I heard a woman sobbing." It was Ahmed's wife, Sana. "Ahmed is dead," she cried into the receiver. "His family killed him because he lived for Jesus."

In January 2007 Ali received a letter from Sana. Here is his translation, word for word:

> *Hi Ali. Good morning. It is me, Sana, Ahmed's wife. Thank you very much for taking care of us.*
>
> *I don't know what to say, for only God Himself knows about us since Ahmed left. I miss him a lot, and believe me, my eyes are not drying off tears. I have no one left but you. Ahmed left me the two most important things for him: Our son and his Bible.*
>
> *I miss him a lot, as we used to read that Bible together and pray in secret. I need your prayers, and I am sure that Jesus will not let us down.*
>
> *Your sister,*
> *Sana*

Ahmed will receive a martyr's crown when he stands before Christ in the resurrection. But he did not have to strap bombs to himself and blow up innocent women and children in order to earn his reward. Instead he gave life to one woman and one child. For that he died. And for that he lives!

You see, Ahmed understood that *the only way to stop the Islamists from fulfilling their great commission is for us Christ-followers to fulfill ours.* The only way you and I can overcome the language of death is to speak the language of life, that is, to launch God's Word into the heavenlies and around the world with our tongues, and then watch demonic principalities fall like lightning (see Luke 10:18).

King David understood the real nature of our warfare and wrote a song about it:

> *Let the saints be joyful in glory; let them sing aloud on their beds. Let the high praises of God be in their mouth, and a two-edged sword in their hand, to execute vengeance on the nations, and punishments on the peoples; to bind their kings with chains, and their nobles with fetters of iron; to execute on them the written judgment—this honor have all His saints. Praise the Lord! (Psalm 149:5-9).*

No wonder Jesus called us the salt of the earth and the light of the world. You and I have the honor—the *honor*—of singing God's praises and carrying His Word to the nations, in order to bind spiritual strong men like Allah, and loose more than a billion lost sons of Abraham he holds captive in the Muslim world.

ENDNOTES

1. See also Terry Law, *The Fight of Every Believer* (Tulsa, OK: Harrison House, Inc., 2006), available at www. worldcompassion.tv, and at bookstores.

2. The conversational part of this story has been recon-structed for readability.
3. All names in this story have been changed to protect identities.

Chapter 8

Thanksgiving, Praise, and Worship

Just as the old Rodgers and Hammerstein tune claims that "a song is no song 'til you sing it," so praise is not praise until we give it.

~

Many Christians use the words thanksgiving, praise, and worship interchangeably. And of course the three are closely related, but they are also distinct. Thanksgiving and praise, for example, both relate to God's deeds, but praise goes further to focus on His character. And worship, although it is inclusive of thanksgiving and praise (and for that matter every aspect of the Christian life), also surpasses them. It takes us beyond thanking God for what He has done, beyond praising Him "according to His excellent greatness," to a place of sheer awe at His presence. Worship, in other words, relates directly to God's holiness.

Let's take a closer look at the meanings and purposes of thanksgiving, praise, and worship.

THANKSGIVING

Thanksgiving as an inward offering—something that may or may not be expressed publicly—first appears in the New Testament. By contrast, all of the Hebrew terms translated "thanksgiving" in the Old Testament are *vocal* expressions of one sort or another, and frequently are also translated as "praise." The Hebrew word, *yadah*, for example, means to thank or praise by lifting the hand, and comes from the term, *yad*, for hand. Likewise the word, *towdah*, which is derived from *yadah*, is translated in some instances as a "sacrifice of thanksgiving," and in others as a "sacrifice of praise."

The New Testament, however, makes distinctions between the two. It regularly speaks of thanksgiving as something that may be given privately, even silently in one's heart. Praise, on the other hand, is vocal and public; it includes the concept of giving witness to God's goodness.

In New Testament Greek, the word for "thanks" is the word *charis*. It is the root for our English word, "charismatic," and is related to the word for grace. In other words, **thanksgiving is the appropriate response to God's grace.** In fact it is the *commanded* response: "Rejoice always, pray without ceasing, in everything give thanks; for this is the will of God in Christ Jesus for you. Do not quench the Spirit" (1 Thess. 5:16-19).

If thanksgiving "in everything" is God's will for us, then it follows that if we do not give thanks in everything, we are out of God's will. But how is this possible? Are we supposed to give thanks when a friend is killed, or when someone dies of cancer? Should a woman thank God when her husband leaves the faith, or when their marriage falls apart? At face value this passage appears to say just that. But let's face it, regardless of one's views on the sovereignty of God, it is simply nonsensical to thank God when an unsaved friend dies and goes to hell.

So what is the truth? How do we give thanks in everything, when everything isn't good? Let's start with simple logic.

First John 3:8b states flatly, "For this purpose the Son of God was manifested, that He might destroy the works of the devil." Logic dictates that if Jesus came to destroy satan's works, then satan must have been working. Indeed, Jesus described those works in John 10:10, calling the devil a thief who comes only "to steal, and to kill, and to destroy," while "I have come that they may have life, and that they may have it more abundantly."

Logic also says that if satan were somehow strangely fulfilling the will of God, then Jesus would be working against His Father's will in destroying satan's works. That would make God's own house a house divided, and according to Jesus, Himself, such a house will not stand.

The Bible in fact does not command us to thank God *for* the devil's work. Rather, we are encouraged to thank God *in the midst* of whatever is happening, no matter how dreadful it may be.

We give thanks in the midst of disease because according to First Peter 2:24, Jesus "bore our sins in His own body on the tree, that we, having died to sins, might live for righteousness—by whose stripes you were healed." We give thanks that "…He Himself took our infirmities and bore our sicknesses" (Matt. 8:17), and that He says in Exodus 15:26, "...I am the Lord who heals you." In other words, *we give thanks for God's answer to satan's attack.*

The simplest explanation is that we can always give thanks to God, because unlike us, He is never left without a response to what the devil does. His Word makes us "complete, thoroughly equipped for every good work" (2 Tim. 3:17). Thanksgiving simply launches that Word in our spirits, lifts our faith, and aligns us with God's perspective. It opens our eyes to see His hand at work, and then cooperate with His will.

There are three characteristics of thanksgiving that deepen our understanding of its purpose. First, *thanksgiving is an expression of the fullness of the Holy Spirit.* Look at Ephesians 5:17-20:

> *Therefore do not be unwise, but understand what the will of the Lord is. And do not be drunk with wine, in which is dissipation; but be filled with the Spirit, speaking to one another in psalms and hymns and spiritual songs, singing and making melody in your heart to the Lord, giving thanks always for all things to God the Father in the name of our Lord Jesus Christ.*

In verse 17, Paul instructs us to understand the will of God, and then proceeds to spell it out: We are to satisfy our soul's thirst with the Holy Spirit rather than getting drunk on wine. Most Christians readily agree that drunkenness is not the will of God, but there is something more we should acknowledge, namely, that *it is equally wrong to refrain from being filled with the Spirit.* Christians may disagree from denomination to denomination about what constitutes that infilling, but one thing is clear—we are *commanded* to actively drink, not passively wait.

Then the apostle explains, in verses 19 and 20 that the natural overflow of the Spirit is to encourage one another with psalms, hymns, and spiritual songs, to sing and make melody in our hearts, and to perpetually give thanks. Jesus alluded to such expression in Matthew 12:34b, when He said, "out of the abundance of the heart the mouth speaks." Thanksgiving is one of the manifestations of the infilling of the Holy Spirit.

If we are to give thanks to God in the midst of everything, then an unthankful person, even someone who exercises various spiritual gifts, simply is not full of the Holy Spirit. Saint Paul complimented the church at Corinth for the way they excelled in spiritual gifts (see 1 Cor. 1:7), yet lamented their continued carnality and spiritual immaturity a mere two chapters later (see 1 Cor. 3). No, *the real mark of the Spirit-filled life is continual thanksgiving flowing from the lips.*

Moreover, when thanksgiving is no longer an exercise, but becomes a mark of character, then we move from the lifestyle of crisis-to-crisis Christianity that plagues so many modern "Corinthians," into a place where obedience becomes our *first* response to the Spirit, and we can go about fulfilling the will of God for our lives.

Psalm 100:4-5 summons us to…

> *Enter into His gates **with thanksgiving**, and into His courts with praise. Be thankful to Him, and bless His name. For the Lord is good; His mercy is everlasting, and His truth endures to all generations.*

The first stage of our approach to God involves thanksgiving, not because of what we feel, but because of who He is. Note that this passage does not prescribe a rigid formula—thanksgiving before praise. As worship leader Don Moen wryly observes, if such were the case, then there are a few psalms where David violated his own protocol and backed out of God's presence. Nonetheless, the truth is clear—thanksgiving gets us through the palace gate!

The constancy of thanksgiving is made clear yet again in Philippians 4:6-7:

> *Be anxious for nothing, but in everything by prayer and supplication, **with thanksgiving**, let your requests be made known to God; and the peace of God, which surpasses all understanding, will guard your hearts and minds through Christ Jesus.*

Supplication simply refers to making a request, a petition, to God. Most of us are accustomed to asking the Lord to meet our needs. But according to the Scriptures, *this kind of prayer must be accompanied by thanksgiving.*

Here's a second characteristic: ***Thanksgiving cultivates faith.*** Therefore, it must permeate all that we do, especially our praying. We should *soak* our prayers in thanks, never asking God for something without first gratefully recalling what He has already done. Thanksgiving for God's past faithfulness overcomes inertia in our present faith; it gets the wheels moving in our spirits, like a starter on the engine of faith.

In fact, if we were to list just the recent events in our lives for which we can thank the Lord, and then regularly enumerate them before Him in our prayers, most of us would see far more answers to prayer than we currently do.[1] Our faith would surge, and we would find ourselves more and more often walking head-on into blessing.

Thanksgiving helps us focus on the answer rather than the problem. It lifts our eyes to God and reminds us that we really are victors. Satan hates this, of course, because he wants us to focus on the complicated mess of the present and give in to thoughts of fear and discouragement. But thanksgiving turns fear on its heel and gets us moving in God's direction.

Paul's prayers for the churches invariably began with thanks. In Romans 1:8 he said, "First, I thank my God through Jesus Christ for you all...." In Ephesians 1:16 he wrote, "[I] do not cease to give thanks for you." In Philippians 1:3 he said, "I thank my God upon every remembrance of you." Likewise, in Colossians 1:3 he said, "We give thanks to the God and Father of our Lord Jesus Christ, praying always for you." He opened First Thessalonians the same way in verse 2: "We give thanks to God always for you all, making mention of you in our prayers." And in Second Timothy 1:3, he told his spiritual son that he thanked God and prayed for him without ceasing, night and day.

Jesus also constantly gave thanks, and one instance in His ministry is especially noteworthy. In John chapter 6 we have the account of the Savior miraculously feeding a multitude with just a little boy's lunch. The story is well known, of course, but it contains one fascinating, overlooked fact—Jesus did not pray for that miracle. He simply gave thanks to the Father and started breaking bread! His thanksgiving led to an immediate miracle that provided enough food to feed at least 5,000 people.

This leads us to a third truth: *Thanksgiving triggers faith for miracles.* In musical terms, we might call it a prelude to the faith march. Remember, even though Jesus was the Son of God, He nonetheless ministered strictly as a Spirit-filled man, *just like you and me.* Acts 10:38 says that "God anointed Jesus of Nazareth with the Holy Spirit and with power...." It was the Holy Spirit working through Jesus Who performed this miracle, and it was thanksgiving on Jesus' part that invoked the Spirit's power. *Thanksgiving, therefore, triggers faith for the miracle-working power of God.*

This principle was powerfully illustrated when Living Sound and I made our first foray into the Soviet Union in 1978. We had bought an old bus from a touring company in England, and simply left the company's name on the side. The bus logo, a cargo hold full of musical instruments, and our passports stamped with ordinary tourist visas, combined to make the Soviet border guards assume we were an American band on holiday.

We took the Georg Ots ferry from Helsinki, Finland, to the Soviet port of Tallinn, Estonia, a city I had visited briefly as a college student on a summer tour with Oral Roberts ten years earlier. On that trip I had attended an underground prayer meeting, where I met a young man named Jaanus Karner. Jaanus had paid a big price for his work as a Christian youth leader. Three times the KGB, the Soviet secret police, had invaded his home. He had been expelled from university, and was even beaten, for following Christ. That night in 1968 I had seen a fire burning in Jaanus' eyes that hadn't even flickered in mine, and I prayed a silent prayer: "Lord, if you ever call me to bring the gospel to these people, I promise that I will do it, no matter what the cost."

Now, after ten years, I was back to fulfill that promise. But, seeing as the KGB was probably following us already, where and how could I find Jaanus? We checked in to the Viru Hotel, the only place in Tallinn where Western tourists were allowed to stay, then headed on foot to the city's "old town," a maze of narrow cobblestone streets and tall, old buildings with red-slate roofs. When we got to the market square, I recognized St. Olaf's Church, a 12th-century landmark, atop whose giant spire the Soviets had mounted equipment that jammed "Voice of America" and similar broadcasts from across the Baltic Sea. I knew the church still held services; maybe there were some believers inside. We scaled an iron fence and started pounding on a big steel door, but no one answered. (Only later did I learn that we had been banging away on the door of a KGB office at the bottom of the bell tower.)

At length we made contact with some local Christians and asked if they knew Jaanus. Their startled, slightly frightened looks said they did, and within hours I stood, once again, face to face with this living, breathing hero of the faith. He had remembered me too, he said, and always hoped I would return. We made plans to hold an "impromptu" concert at Jaanus' church the next day. That way the event would be over before the police even found out about it. But such was not to be the case.

Back at the hotel that night we dined in the one and only restaurant for tourists, and discovered a local band playing some pretty decent jazz. A tourist-hotel gig, it seemed, was the Soviet counterpart to a Las Vegas booking, so only the USSR's best would be performing. During a break in the music our guys decided to introduce themselves to the band. "Drums," said our drummer, pointing to himself. "Guitar," he said, pointing to his buddy. "Americanskis!" he smiled, hoping he'd pronounced it right.

Within minutes we were onstage, playing a couple of instrumental tunes to establish our credibility. Then our singers clustered around the jazz singer's microphone and began to sing worship songs they had learned in the local language. By midnight we were the talk of the town, and both the restaurant manager and hotel boss were an inch away from losing their jobs.

When we arrived at Jaanus' church the next evening the place was jammed with hundreds of young people from all over

Tallinn and beyond. The word was out. Even the famous jazz singer, Marju, was there.[2] By the end of the concert I was really feeling my oats, so happy that we hadn't given up that first day when we couldn't find anyone, happy that we hadn't given up on getting here in the first place, that we had pierced the mighty Iron Curtain with the Gospel of Jesus Christ.

The moment of pride was short lived. As I stood near the sound booth, I saw a young woman with tears in her eyes. I recognized her as Ulle, one of Jaanus' friends I'd met the day before.

"Why are you crying?" I whispered to her while the band played.

"We heard you sing three years ago on a Polish radio station we receive here in Tallinn. We were amazed to hear Christian music being played on the radio in a communist nation, and we began thanking God for this miracle every day. In fact, it inspired us to start praying that God would bring you here as well. We've been praying constantly ever since then, and now…here you are."

I was simultaneously humiliated and overjoyed. We hadn't broken through the Iron Curtain because of our great faith, but because this young girl and her friends had humbly, wholeheartedly poured out their thanks and praise to God in our behalf. Their thanksgiving had triggered faith that emboldened them to pray for a miracle: God bring that group to us! And of all the places that the Lord could have taken us across the USSR's vast expanse, there we were, in *that* city, in *that* young woman's church. "Prayer and supplication, with thanksgiving" had brought it to pass.

PRAISE

The Psalms of David can be divided into two types: psalms of *descriptive* praise and psalms of *declarative* praise. The latter emphasize what God has done for His people. They declare the glory of God's mighty works. But the psalms of descriptive praise exalt *the person of God* and His attributes. They praise Him for who He is.

There can be no relationship with God without praise. Furthermore, praise is never impersonal or even objective. In fact, although God is objectively glorious—His glory is complete whether we worship Him or not—praise is always personal and subjective. Just as the old Rodgers and Hammerstein tune claims that "a song is no song 'til you sing it," so praise is not praise until you give it.

The English word *psalms* is a transliteration of the Greek title of the biblical book, which simply refers to it as a collection of "songs with stringed accompaniment." But in Hebrew the Psalms are called a book of *tehillim*, which means spiritual or prophetic songs. The longest book in the Bible is a book of prophetic songs!

The Psalms have it all—music, beauty, wisdom, theology, experience, as well as complaint, lament, mourning, and repentance. Yet even the saddest of the composers' laments resolve with praise, because they understood that no matter how broken their hearts, or how egregious their sins, *God's mercy belonged to them and their praise belonged to Him*. The covenant demanded both.

So they sang joyful songs—whether they felt like it or not—because God is worthy. In fact, First Chronicles 25 says they did so "according to the order of the king." They were *appointed to praise*. So are you!

Thanksgiving may be expressed in thought, but praise is never silent; it is always vocal. It extols and magnifies the Lord's virtues, much in the same way a real estate appraiser attaches value to a house by examining its various features. And while praise need not be boisterous, it is definitely public.

The best way to understand praise is to examine the various Hebrew words for it in the Old Testament, particularly in the Psalms, where a variety of acts and expressions constituted praise to God. We have already seen that *tehillah* (plural *tehillim*), the actual Hebrew title of the Psalms, means "to sing a spiritual song." It is used in Psalm 22:3, where God inhabits (sits enthroned upon) the praises of His people. More than visiting us, "inhabits" means He dwells—takes up residence—in the spiritual songs of His people.

A second Hebrew word for praise is *halal*, the root for "hallelujah" in Psalm 150, et al. *Halal* connotes a boastful, almost riotous celebration of God. *Shabach*, on the other hand, is a bit more dignified. It means to speak in a "high" manner—both loudly and with lofty speech, the way in which a monarch or head of state is announced. It can also describe the battle cry of a charging army.

Barak, in contrast to *halal* and *shabach*, carries the sense of kneeling before the Lord in quiet adoration (see Psalm 34:1). Then there is *yadah*, which means to lift or thrust the hands up in a public expression of praise, as in Psalm 138:1, where David vowed to "praise You with my whole heart; before the gods I will sing praises to You." A sixth word for praise, *zamar* (see Psalm 33:2, et al), means "to skillfully play a stringed instrument." Note that the idea of playing *skillfully* is intrinsic here.

Finally there is *towdah*, mentioned previously in connection with thanksgiving, but also frequently translated as a sacrifice of praise. In Psalm 50:23, David said, "Whoever offers praise [*towdah*] glorifies Me; and to him who orders his conduct aright I will show the salvation of God." *Towdah* means rejoicing in something that is promised in the Word, but which has not yet taken place. It is a powerful concept, one that carries over into the New Testament, where Hebrews 13:15 exhorts us to "continually offer the sacrifice of praise to God, that is, the fruit of our lips, giving thanks to His name."

Although most of my ministry thus far in the new century has focused on reaching into the Middle East, I have continued conducting praise and healing rallies here in the USA from time to time. In these meetings, I encourage people to praise the Lord before there has been any manifestation of healing from God. Such praise involves a sacrifice, especially if people are very sick in their bodies. A carnal mind would chafe at the very idea. Yet a *towdah*, a sacrifice of thanksgiving and praise, delights the Lord, who honors it by performing miracles.

The most notable characteristic of all these verbs for praise is that they are words of *sound*. Biblical praise is always audible and public, and in my experience, often excited.

Once, when Don Moen and I were ministering at Oberlin College in Ohio, Don was leading the audience in praise to God. I had just preached and was standing onstage, looking out over the crowd, when I noticed a man near the back of the auditorium jumping up and down, shouting, and repeatedly flexing his right hand. Obviously something good had happened, so I called him to the front to interview him. He was a carpenter, he said, and while on the job, he had fallen from the second story of a building *through* the first floor and landed in the basement. The middle three fingers of his "hammer hand," as he called it, were completely severed in the fall. Thanks to quick-thinking coworkers, however, he was rushed to the hospital, where doctors reattached his fingers. Unfortunately, he had suffered severe nerve damage, and the injured fingers quickly atrophied.

During the time of praise I had encouraged people to physically test their areas of affliction, so he lifted his right arm and tried to move the dead fingers. To his shock and delight, the fingers worked perfectly, hence his shouting and jumping. The next day I saw the man and wife again, and he told me he hadn't slept all night, because he was so excited, picking things up and testing his hand. His groggy wife confirmed her husband's story!

WORSHIP

The word *worship* comes from the Old English word "weorthscipe," which was later shortened to "worthship." It is still used as a noun in British courts, where the judge is referred to as "your worship." As a verb, *worship* means to pay homage or respect. Yet when we speak of worshiping God, the word encompasses much more, including the ideas of adoring, magnifying, esteeming, revering, venerating, and exalting the Lord.

The Old Testament Hebrew word for worship is **shachah**. It means "to bow down, to reverence, to prostrate, to beseech humbly." Whereas praise is vocal, worship invariably involves an attitude of the body. Sometimes it refers to a stretching out of the hands toward God, sometimes to a bending of the knee, and sometimes (see Lev. 9:24) falling down on one's face before the Lord.

The most common New Testament term for worship is **proskuneo**, a combination of two Greek words that taken together mean "to kiss toward." Used more than 50 times in Scripture, *proskuneo* is a lavishing of affection. It was perfectly depicted in Luke chapter 7 by the woman who washed Jesus' feet with her tears and then repeatedly kissed them, to such an extreme that the Lord's hosts were offended by the display. Perceiving their attitude, Jesus was quick to point out not only that He accepted her worship, but that He had forgiven her sins and extended salvation to her.

We have been created to worship God; it is in our nature. (There are no true atheists; see Romans 1:20.) Thus the choice is not whether we will worship, but simply *whom* we will worship. God, of course, demands man's worship; He will not share it with anyone or anything else.

When satan tempted Jesus in the wilderness, he offered Him all the kingdoms of the world, "if you will fall down and worship me." Jesus answered with a rebuttal: "Away with you, Satan! For it is written, 'You shall worship the Lord your God, and Him only you shall serve'" (Matt. 4:9-10).

This illustrates a profound principle of worship: whatever we worship we eventually will wind up serving. That's because the more we worship something or someone, the more we increase our level of commitment, and the more we become like the thing we worship. Jim Gilbert recalls seeing this principle in the flesh in Calcutta, India:

> I was riding down the street in a taxi, and noticed a cow on the sidewalk, grazing on offerings left there for it by Hindu worshipers. Then, not two blocks later, I saw a man pulling a large, two-wheeled hay wagon. What a scene! The cow was a well-fed god. The man was a gaunt beast of burden. And I thought to myself, *he has become like what he worships.*

Worship is the ultimate act of submission. Our nature demands that we worship, and in fact everything within us longs to bow down. As Saint Augustine said, "Our hearts are restless until they find their rest in Thee."[3] We were made to worship and are incomplete if we do not. Our only choice is whether we will bow to God or something else. And in fulfillment of Romans 8:7, which says, "the carnal mind is enmity against

God...," rebellious hearts throughout history have chosen to worship wooden idols, animals, physical desires, money, power, and even other people. Worshiping all these false gods, of course, is tantamount to worshiping satan.

The story of the woman at the well in John chapter 4 provides a classic illustration of humanity's inner drive to worship. Jesus was traveling from Judea to Galilee, and had stopped in Samaria to rest by a famous landmark, Jacob's well, while His disciples went into town to buy food. Soon a woman approached the well to draw water, an unusual event in the heat of the afternoon, since the women in the city customarily drew their water early in the morning. The Lord began a conversation with her, and it soon became clear that she was a social outcast.

The woman's past, as the story unfolded, had included five husbands, and now she was just living with a man. There obviously was a deep craving in her spirit, and the Lord knew that immorality would not satiate such profound spiritual thirst. She had gone from one man's arms to another, unquenched, because the craving in her spirit was actually a craving for the arms of God. So Jesus engaged her at that level, telling her that He possessed "water" so satisfying that she would never thirst again.

The woman asked the Lord for a drink of His water, not even realizing that she was inviting Him to speak to her spiritual thirst. But He was gracious and did indeed speak to her true appetite, by telling her to go and get her husband. When she feigned innocence by replying that she was unmarried, Jesus spoke a word of knowledge, gently exposing her life for the lie it really was. He knew, after all, that rebuking her immoral conduct would only compound her hopelessness. He wanted to satisfy the need that such a lifestyle advertised, the need to know God and worship Him.

Suddenly the woman's perception sharpened, and although she did not yet recognize that she was face to Face with the Messiah, she did realize that she was speaking with a true Man of God. And immediately she began to question the Lord about worship! How significant that she, not Jesus, broached the real subject of her soul.

Our unsaved neighbors' lives also show, in various ways, their hunger and thirst to worship. In fact, such displays are universal. That is why Paul, when he preached in Athens (see Chapter 3), pointed the Greek philosophers to their idol that paid homage to "the unknown god." That idol, just like the Samaritan woman's lifestyle, advertised their thirst for God.

Paul's instruction in Ephesians 5:18 perfectly concurs: "And do not be drunk with wine, in which is dissipation; but be filled with the Spirit." All are thirsty for God. And the same thirst that drives one person to drink drives another person to God.

Jesus went on to tell the woman that not only had she been seeking God, but that God was seeking her! "But the hour is coming, and now is, when the true worshipers will worship the Father in spirit and truth; for the Father is seeking such to worship Him" (John 4:23). What an amazing fact! *God is seeking people to worship Him.* He does not need our worship to be complete; God is perfectly glorious in Himself. Yet He desires, even seeks, a relationship with us.

Take note of the phrase "in spirit and truth." These words are reminiscent of Paul's confession in First Corinthians 14:15 that he prayed "with the spirit" and also "with the understanding." True worship involves both spiritual experience and down-to-earth reality. Those who truly worship God flow toward Him in their spirits, but are also careful to worship according to the truth of His

Word. Their worship is authenticated both by the subjective witness of experience and the objective witness of the Word.

We have been describing what worship *does*—bowing, kneeling, lying prostrate on our faces. But it is very difficult to describe what worship *is*, because it is a mystery. We Westerners love to categorize and quantify; we want tidy definitions. "This is thanksgiving; this is praise; this is worship." But sometimes explanations merely profane the sacred.

Sexual expression is a good example (although it is by no means the only analogy for worship). Young people entering marriage need a certain amount of instruction as to what to expect and how to handle their new conjugal privileges. Yet there sometimes is a fine line between a helpful marriage manual and a lurid book. So it is with worship.

When Don Moen and I visited Christ for the Nations Institute in Dallas, Texas, the students worshiped the way college students do everything else: radically. We were there for five days, and all week long they were passionate, raucous, and fervent. In fact, at times I wondered if Don was leading them or simply trying to catch up! But one evening, as the meeting drew to a close, everyone present sensed that something different was happening. We had called upon God, but now He was calling us, inviting us to a place more sacred than we had been thus far.

Don stopped playing, as one song turned to hundreds. Nothing was happening, yet everything was happening. There were no requests to make, no proclamations or exhortations. A genuine "joyful noise" filled the room, as 1,500 young people bowed 3,000 knees before the throne of God. The King was walking amongst us, and nobody needed anything more than that.

Second Chronicles 5 is the record of King Solomon's dedication of the temple he built to fulfill the vision of his father, David. Far beyond my simple two-hour rally in Dallas, it was a massive celebration. Hundreds of priests assisted thousands of worshipers in "sacrificing sheep and oxen that could not be counted or numbered for multitude" (v. 6). And in keeping with David's precedent, there were hundreds of musicians and singers as well. In fact, there were 120 trumpeters alone!

But as usual, God was looking at Solomon's and the people's hearts, and the love their extravagance represented, rather than the material expenditure in itself. Thus, in Jerusalem, just as in Dallas more than two millennia later, the Presence of God settled on the people.

> *Indeed it came to pass, when the trumpeters and singers were as one, to make one sound to be heard in praising and thanking the Lord, and when they lifted up their voice with the trumpets and cymbals and instruments of music, and praised the Lord, saying: "For He is good, for His mercy endures forever," that the house, the house of the Lord, was filled with a cloud, so that the priests could not continue ministering because of the cloud; for the glory of the Lord filled the house of God* (2 Chronicles 5:13-14).

Perhaps we could teach and write and discuss worship until we had it unraveled. Maybe we could examine it under the bright light of human analysis until the last shadow disappeared. But why? What is the point in trying to write lyrics to a song that is more beautiful left unsung? Saint Peter talked about "joy unspeakable" (1 Pet. 1:8 KJV). *Let's leave it that way.*

ENDNOTES

1. Even the world of professional psychology has begun to understand this, especially University of Pennsylvania psychologist Martin Seligman, former president of the American Psychological Association. According to a *TIME* magazine cover story entitled "The New Science of Happiness" (*TIME*, January 17, 2005), "extensive testing in controlled trials has convinced Dr. Seligman that 'the single most effective way to turbocharge your joy...is to make a 'gratitude visit.' That means writing a testimonial thanking a teacher, pastor or grandparent—anyone to whom you owe a debt of gratitude—and then visiting that person to read him or her the letter of appreciation. 'The remarkable thing,' says Seligman, 'is that people who do this just once are measurably happier and less depressed a month later. But it's gone by three months.' Less powerful but more lasting, he says, is an exercise he calls three blessings—taking time each day to write down a trio of things that went well and why. 'People are less depressed and happier three months later and six months later.'"

2. Marju Kuut's subsequent conversion caused such a sensation across the entire USSR that she was eventually expelled to the West. Today she is back in Estonia, appearing as Maryn Coote.

3. Saint Augustine, *Confessions* (New York, NY: Oxford UP USA, 1998).

PART II

Introduction

by Jim Gilbert

My coauthor Jim Gilbert has already written about one of the two most painful episodes of my life, the death of my first wife, Jan. Yet even in the midst of that tragedy, the seeds of my future were planted.

We had left the church and now stood at the graveside. After we had prayed and committed her body to the earth, Jan's older brother, Al, took me aside. He knew how much I had loved his sister, he said, and that I would need to wait awhile before thinking about marrying again. But he also believed that my three young children needed a mother.

"After a year or two, you'll need to start thinking about this, for their sakes," he said. I knew he was right, and for some reason the phrase "two years" stuck in my mind.

In September 1984, almost two years later to the day, I met Shirley, a young widow with two children. We were married the next January. Shirley adopted my three children, Misty, Scot, and Rebecca, and I adopted her two, Shawna and Jason. Fourteen months into our marriage we were blessed with a baby girl, Laurie.

I could never have conceived of the pain that would come 11 years later, nor of a sorrow worse than death. But it happened, and I am at a loss for words to describe it. That is why once again I have asked my friend, Jim, to tell the story for me.

Terry Law

~

Filmmaker M. Night Shyamalan's eerie 2004 movie, *The Village*, depicts a tiny isolated enclave whose residents live in fear of nameless creatures in the surrounding woods, beast-like beings they refer to as "Those We Don't Speak Of." Eventually the viewer learns that Those We Don't Speak Of do not actually exist, but are a fiction of the village elders to guarantee their continued isolation from society. And though the plot takes Shyamalan's signature twists and turns, eventually the lie works. The truth will not be told. After all, if it were, the village itself would be no more.

The following chapter faces facts many Christian leaders have long avoided. They fear, perhaps rightly, that it would cost them readers, viewers, and other faithful constituents of their ministries. It is the beast in our woods, something "that we don't speak of," but that the rest of the world lives with. Unlike the movie, however, this taboo is all too real. It is divorce.

The monster of divorce has terrorized millions of Christians' lives, including those of many well-known preachers and teachers, among them Terry Law. Yet there has been scant teaching on the subject, perfunctory at best, and usually from pastors personally untouched by it. Fear has silenced those best qualified—servants of God whose wisdom has been leavened by experience—to speak out. So the Body of Christ continues to suffer, not only from past wounds unhealed, but also from a divorce rate every bit as high as that of the unredeemed.[1] This is tragic, especially since forgiveness and healing are readily available from a heavenly Father whose grace remains sufficient when ours has been exhausted.

The death of a spouse is a horrid, almost indescribable experience, but the death of a marriage from divorce is worse by degrees, because it begs the assignment of blame and automatically arouses a thousand suspicions, especially when it involves someone who carries moral authority.

The Terry Law I came to know in 1969 never dreamed he would be widowed in his thirties, much less divorced by his early 50s. He is a steadfast, upright man, after all, who considered "'til death do us part" a literal commitment. Divorce was never an option; to him marriage has no back door, no emergency exit. Yet both death and divorce—the unthinkable and the unspeakable—happened to him.

"It's time to open up," he told me when we undertook this project. "Half the Body of Christ bears the scars of divorce, and I know what they've been through. I've kept silent for ten years, but I can't any longer. We've got to help them."

So here we are. Now you know. Oh, you don't know everything, but at least you know the One Thing, the secret that, like the proverbial finger in the dam, holds back a tide of healing until it is released.

The chapter that follows is written for three types of people. First, if you have been through divorce, then Christian or not, you've probably had to seal off parts of your heart and soul like a house condemned. Second, you may fear that your marriage is headed for divorce, and you don't want it. In fact you don't believe in it, but so many walls have gone up between you and your spouse that they seem insurmountable. Third—and almost everyone qualifies here—you probably know someone in the first two categories.

This isn't about blame, about vilifying one person and vindicating another. Nor is it a puff job, the kind that so often smoothes over the sins of men of God. It is about shining the light of God's glory deep into the darkest rooms of our hearts, those places in ourselves where even we are afraid to look, much less to let someone else rummage around in.

The writing is mine of course, but the story is Terry's. It is a costly one to be sure, an alabaster box of sorts, kept private for years but finally broken upon these pages. Its value will be found in the lives of readers who discover in it healing from the past and new hope for the future.

There are several other stories as well, but they will not be told. I am, for example, largely excluding Terry's and Shirley's six children from the chapter. But make no mistake: Divorce conscripts the whole family. It is a war without deferment.

At first it may seem odd to include a story of divorce in a book about praise and worship. But remember, we are concerned with spiritual warfare, and the *power* of praise and worship to win it.

Without doubt, the biggest reason for divorce—and the frequent, continuing acrimony afterward—is that *divorce is a spiritual mindset*. Couples break their indissoluble bonds because satan has convinced them that *they* are enemies, and that peace is impossible. At least one party, if not both, has forgotten that "we do not wrestle against flesh and blood, but against principalities, against powers, against the rulers of the darkness of this age, against spiritual hosts of wickedness in the heavenly places" (Eph. 6:12).

Terry Law learned the principles of spiritual warfare in the aftermath of widowhood. They were written on his heart, if not etched into his flesh. Thus when trouble arose in his second marriage, he vowed to remember them again. And since it is the nature of insecurity to display itself, some of that trouble was impossible to conceal from friends. We did not want to watch, but love and loyalty to both parties demanded it.

My wife and I love Terry and Shirley, and I am not interested in exploring either's flaws. Since this chapter is about his struggle, both fairness and continuing affection lead me to mention her only as necessary. In that regard I sometimes refer to "the Plaintiff," not to avoid using Shirley's name, but because *the term is inclusive of others* who inspired and conducted a courtroom attack on Terry's ministry.

Any soldier can tell you that in warfare character is as important as knowledge. Moreover, the battlefield of divorce has a way of testing the moral fiber of not only the contestants, but also those around them. I have watched Terry under fire, watched him endure both the sting of accusation and the ache of desertion by "friends" citing Scripture with all the sincerity of a newsstand tabloid.

There is a certain public loneliness that comes when you are not free to answer unavoidable questions or squelch inevitable rumors. "What can you say?" Terry once asked me rhetorically. "There are no good answers to bad questions, Jim. You just wear the muzzle, keep practicing what you preach, and wait for hell's next broadside."

I saw that loneliness in Terry, as well as his loyalty when I wished we could talk—wished I could speak for him—but knew his marriage covenant demanded silent fidelity. And I never saw him surrender his integrity, even when romance had fled and only the will to love remained.

God's Word says there is "a time to keep silence, and a time to speak" (Eccl. 3:7). Now it is time to speak.

ENDNOTE

1. http://www.barna.org/FlexPage.aspx?Page=BarnaUpdate&BarnaUpdateID=170; the Barna Group, accessed 3/29/08.

Chapter 9

That Which We Don't Speak Of

---

by Jim Gilbert

His marriage was a lie still spreading itself. For a man who had given his life to delivering Truth to the world, it was almost too much to take.

~

Terry Law and his elder son, Scot, sat in the blue and burgundy high-back chairs that fronted the master-suite fireplace of the Laws' Tulsa home. A student at Oral Roberts University, the young man had chosen to commute rather than live on campus. It seemed a sensible, temporary arrangement to both men, but not to Scot's step mom, who thought the 22-year-old should be living on his own. That was the immediate problem, and the reason for the father-son talk.

"We were sitting there discussing my dilemma when I heard the front door open," Scot recalls. "A few seconds later my step mom and a stranger walked into the room. The man asked Dad, 'Are you Terry Law?' As soon as Dad's identity had been confirmed, the man handed him some papers and said, 'You have been served.' Then they left."

His father's face turned ashen, Scot remembers. "He fell back into the chair and said, 'What is this?' We read through the first couple of pages to confirm that it really was a petition for divorce."

There were also orders to vacate the house, and sheriff's deputies would arrive soon to enforce them. "I decided to leave right away," says Terry. "I wasn't going to allow anyone to kick me out of my own home."

Father and son decided to meet up later at the Grandview Hotel, across the street from ORU. They would get a room for the night, and then plan their immediate future by checkout time the following morning.

The stunned husband quickly cobbled together a few belongings and walked to the garage. It was late afternoon, and Shawna, Jason, and Laurie—the other three of the Laws' six kids still living at home—were out. At least they would not have to witness the awful scene of their dad leaving them. Yet it would be just as traumatic when they discovered he was gone. Terry was so torn. Part of him wished they were there after all, so he could tell them how badly he did not want to leave, and then just hug them one more time.

He had tried so hard to keep the family together. After Misty and Rebecca had both left home, Scot was the only one of the children from his first marriage still there. He had fought to keep the six united, to prevent a split between "Shirley's kids" and "Jan's kids." But here it was. With Scot's exit, the division would be complete.

FAILURE

Terry pulled out of the garage slowly, forcing himself to overcome the urge to stay. His every instinct was to find a solution, to make peace if only for one more day. But there wasn't one more day, or one more anything really. A nightmare was coming true: Terry and Shirley Law had come to The End.

"Suddenly I was swamped with feelings of being a total failure," he recalls. "First, I obviously had failed my wife in our marriage, because she had come to the point of breaking it up. Second, I had failed my family—that was clear because I was driving away from three of my children and didn't even know what they had been told.

"Finally, I had also failed in my ministry. Here was one more scandal, one more high-profile evangelist going through a divorce. I was overwhelmed. Sitting there in the car, with a simple turn of the ignition key, the world blew up in my face. A sense of abject failure thudded onto my shoulders. It was like being torn away from your life, having your own body ripped to shreds. Shirley and I were dividing my family—bang—with that single act of my driving down the driveway."

The word "failure" had long been banished from the vocabulary of Terry's faith. The tough kid from western Canada had always been a person of total commitment, first as a teen prodigal, and later as a budding evangelist. As a student at ORU he had immersed himself in the teachings of the school's namesake, Oral Roberts, and the dozens of little "faith" books published by another well-known Tulsa minister, Kenneth Hagin.

Terry had also fed on "positive thinking" books in his early training and could quote them with a preacher's zeal. He especially loved the sayings of Napoleon Hill and often echoed the legendary motivator in Living Sound's early days: "Whatever the mind of man can conceive and believe, it can achieve." Such words might have been mind-over-matter malarkey coming from someone else, but the redheaded firebrand spoke them with such genuine conviction that it somehow sanctified their meaning to the rest of us.

The evangelist had also taken to heart another of Hill's famous lines: "The majority of men meet with failure because of their lack of persistence in creating new plans to take the place of those which fail." If the quote weren't racing through his mind as he exited the neighborhood, the sentiment surely was.

"I drove away refusing to give up, yet hopeless, saying, 'what in the world is the use of it, but I've got to hold this thing together anyway.' I had to come back; I couldn't let go like that. Everything inside of me said it's *got* to be redeemable."

Such tenacity came from more than books. It arose, in fact, from the confluence of several factors. First, there was his Pentecostal upbringing, where divorce was never an option. "My father pastored in the Pentecostal Assemblies of Canada, and I was raised with the mentality that every marriage can be healed. So I just kept telling myself there's a silver lining here somewhere, and if you just do the right things you can get back together again."

Forming a bond with Oral Roberts, himself, had reinforced such thinking. Roberts was known for his healing ministry, of course, but he had become equally famous for his signature line: "Something *good* is going to *happen* to you!" He greeted television audiences with those eight words, capped sermon after sermon with them, and drummed them into the ORU student body at every campus gathering. More importantly, he truly believed them, and spoke them just as fervently in private. Like any faithful spiritual son, Terry had embraced them with all his heart.

His Pentecostal upbringing, friendships with Oral Roberts and Kenneth Hagin, positive mental attitude, and a track record of achieving the impossible in missions work—all those influences had distilled in Terry an instinct of perseverance. It didn't matter how bad things looked; he would believe for something good.

To that end he immediately retained the services of two family counselors, arranging one-on-one appointments for not only Shirley and himself, but for each of the children as well. Countless tears and multiplied thousands of dollars later the cold, hard truth had only crystallized. Something good would not happen this time. The marriage was over.

BANISHED

There is something indescribably awful about being barred from home. It is your place in the world, your own private everywhere. Being locked out of it, oddly enough, is like being locked in. The rest of the world is a jail when you can't go home.

Yet Terry could not return home, not even to retrieve his briefcase and phonebook. That presented an immediate problem, since by now he had realized the need to call family members and certain colleagues. Then a solution came to mind, one that surprised even him.

Shortly after Terry had arrived at ORU in 1968, Oral Roberts had invited the new student to lead the song services in his West Palm Beach crusade in Florida. The organist for that event was a fellow junior, a music major and keyboard phenomenon named

Larry Dalton. The two men soon discovered they shared a common passion for evangelism, and their resulting friendship had given rise the following year to our innovative missionary group, Living Sound.

Larry had left Living Sound in the 1970s to arrange orchestral music for Oral Roberts' television ministry, but the friendship continued, and eventually he provided the music for Terry's and Shirley's wedding in 1985. But shortly thereafter all contact simply stopped. Trouble in the marriage already was leading the couple into insular, restricted lives. One by one old associations atrophied.

Yet on this night, December 11, 1995—less than two months before what would have been his eleventh wedding anniversary—Terry found himself parking the car at his old friend's front door. Though he lived a mere five minutes away, he had not been there in ten years.

On the surface he needed phone numbers for Oral and Richard Roberts, and some other ORU contacts. He knew Larry would have them. But far deeper was a need for the company of an old buddy whose friendship had been forged in days less complicated. "The doorbell rang and there was Terry," Larry remembers. "We wound up talking for three hours, mostly about the failure of his marriage, but also about our missed opportunities to work together."

The unexpected respite had been welcome, but it was getting late. Terry hurried down 81st Street to the Grandview Hotel. He needed to settle into his room and make those unpleasant but necessary telephone calls. He would notify the family in Canada, of course, as well as a handful of friends, among them Oral Roberts, a mentor both professionally and in private life. Such calls had to be made, but they were emotionally wracking. Scot remembers the ensuing hours vividly.

"When Dad opened the hotel room door to let me in, I could see his eyes were swollen from crying. That was a jolt because I had only seen him cry once, years earlier when mom died. It was obvious that he had shed a lot of tears since our goodbye at the house."

Scot's father admitted him, and then ran back to the phone to continue a conversation with ORU President Richard Roberts. "After the last call he was totally spent, and so shocked he could barely talk," says Scot. "He kept saying, 'How could this happen? How could this happen to me? First Jan, now this—what am I going to do?'"

That last question was fraught with implications far weightier than finding a place to live. Oral and Evelyn Roberts were in California for the month, and had already offered their vacant Tulsa home through the end of the year. No, this question came from somewhere deeper, from down in his depths, where he had fought for his life and won 13 years earlier. It was an old scene of battle he since had filled with "psalms, hymns, and spiritual songs," with melodies to the Lord.

But now a familiar pain was back, flooding his gut, drowning out the music. And though it was of a different sort, this agony was every bit as foul and appalling as before. "What am I going to do?" The question was the same, but the possibilities were all different, and all ugly.

"Jan's death had been a smashing blow to the heart," Terry explains. "There was a sudden finality to it that said, 'It's over. She's gone.' And even when satan had attacked me with the accusation that some unknown sin of mine had caused her to die, I at least had theological arguments to refute it.

"But divorce brought a different attack, and with it a sense of failure that far surpassed the previous battle. This time the devil had more than accusations to throw at me. It was plainly evident that I had failed in my marriage. Somehow I had caused this."

Terry's sense of blame was no doubt heightened by the influence of a popular Christian "marriage maintenance" book that had profoundly affected him.[1] The author made no bones about where the familial buck stops. When a marriage fails, the husband must stand before God to give account, regardless of how blameless he may seem in the eyes of the world. In other words—and to be fair, the author may not have intended this interpretation—husbands ultimately are to blame for marriages gone wrong.

The book had helped Terry to stand firm in his commitment to his wife when their marriage had hit rough seas. But the same principles that once strengthened him now rang in his conscience like an indictment. *This is entirely your fault.*

ONCE UPON A TIME…

Winter was still officially ten days away, but tonight it had come early to the top floor of the Grandview. The biting, bitter wind of separation blew through Terry's soul, made colder still by the dying embers of a real-life fairy tale.

Fourteen million *Guideposts* magazine readers knew the story of how Terry had met Shirley at a McDonald's restaurant on a sunny Saturday morning in September 1984. The widower with three kids in tow, smitten by the beautiful young widow with her two.

They had read how a few days earlier, sitting on an airplane with Terry, Don Moen had prayed for his friend to find a wife, someone widowed who had a heart for ministry, and that Shirley fit the bill perfectly.

Terry proposed on New Year's Eve, and the enchanted couple married four weeks later, on January 28, 1985. It had been a mere four months since Don's high-altitude prayer. God's favor was overtaking this man who had suffered so much. "I feel doubly blessed, like Job," he would tell me a few months later, when the newlyweds were pregnant with Laurie. "I had three children before, but now I'm going to have six!"

I had never seen him happier. "I stayed so busy during my first marriage," he once confided as we drove past Waco to south Texas. "After Jan died I always felt guilty that I hadn't taken more time just to enjoy her and the kids. But this time, Jim, *this* time I'm stopping to smell the roses."

And he did. Instead of scheduling family time around the ministry, Terry and Shirley built each year's ministry calendar around the family. In addition, they began speaking together on Sundays and in weekend marriage workshops. The promises of God were coming true. An extended night of sorrow was surrendering to a future filled with joy.

But that was once upon a time.

Divorce proceedings were initiated in December 1995, and the fairy tale was officially over. Behind the scenes the marriage had been troubled, but Terry still had never contemplated...*this*. It was so wrong, so utterly wrong. And no matter how cordial he and Shirley promised to remain, the whole procedure was inherently ugly.

No bad adjective is too bad—painful, embarrassing, denigrating, tawdry, hypocritical. Divorce is all those dirty words and more. For Terry, especially, it was humiliating.

In fact, like Scot I remember the second time I ever saw him cry. We were both away from home for ministry engagements and had discovered that our schedules would intersect at the Dallas airport. We decided to meet for lunch at the Hyatt Hotel near Terminal C.

I could see that Terry was relieved to be with another old friend and sensed he needed to talk. I knew he was spending day after day in court and figured he had just finished a grueling session. Maybe it was that. We hadn't even ordered water when he began.

"I feel like such a fool," he muttered as we unfolded our napkins. The elegance of the coffee shop enforced a quiet atmosphere.

"What do you mean?" I whispered.

"Fourteen million people read about us, Jim. Our story has gone all over the world. But now..." He grimaced and looked down at his empty plate. "It's all a lie." His voice trailed to a breath, and a tear traced his cheek. The magazine had even done a reprint; millions more would read the tale. And that's all it was, just a tale—without a happy ending. *His marriage was a lie still spreading itself.*[2] For a man who had given his life to delivering Truth to the world, it was almost too much to take.

But things would worsen.

Shirley had retained the services of Warner Jacobs (not his real name), a divorce attorney whose daughter was a classmate of one of the kids. She knew Jacobs was prominent in town, but she did not know how he loathed evangelical ministries. And she certainly could not have expected his services to wipe out her personal inheritance over the next four years.

A stocky man with prematurely white hair, Jacobs was a member of a large Unitarian group whose leader had made a second career of opposing television ministers, especially Oral Roberts. This leader often appeared on network television investigative shows as the token skeptic, although he was billed as a courageous, whistle-blowing Reverend who exposed religious charlatans. Time would reveal that the attorney was a faithful disciple.

The next three-and-a-half years would see Jacobs serve an unending stream of notices and summons, often timed to embarrass Terry—during dinner with the children, or on the golf course with colleagues. Moreover, he made repeated unsuccessful attempts to obtain the ministry's donor records, and bragged to Terry's attorney outside the judge's chambers that he intended to subpoena Oral Roberts and other famous faces.

The attacks were unrelenting, but, of course, they had a purpose. Jacobs wanted a huge cash settlement for the plaintiff and was simply trying to wear down the opposition.

SHAME

Lawsuits against both the ministry and Terry personally meant that the besieged evangelist would have to retain separate firms for his defense. The ministry's long-time attorney, Tom Winters, would surely be called upon as a witness, so his partner, Mike King, himself a committed Christian, agreed to defend World Compassion. For the divorce itself, King recommended another brother in the faith, veteran Tulsa trial lawyer Bob Bartz.

Terry also heeded the advice of his pastor, Bob Yandian, and submitted himself to an accountability panel made up of Yandian, fellow pastor Billy Joe Daugherty, and a third local minister. The three would have unfettered access to Terry's personal records, financial and otherwise, as well as those of the corporation. Ministry donors, pastors, and others who might doubt his integrity could then direct their questions to any of the three. It was a wise move, in keeping with Saint Paul's instruction that an elder must maintain "a good testimony among those who are outside…" (1 Tim. 3:7). It also relieved some of the enormous pressure on a man under fire on all fronts.

"He was concerned for his wife," remembers Pastor Yandian. "It was apparent he genuinely cared for her and wanted her to be taken care of fairly. He was shocked at the attorney she hired and the false accusations leveled at his integrity. He did not want people to believe the lies."

Concerns for his marriage, family, and ministry were taking their toll on a normally robust man. Terry had lost nearly 30 pounds, and his pastor was concerned, yet ultimately optimistic. "His emotions and common sense left him at times," says Yandian, "but his spiritual strength was consistent. He did not know *how* God would deliver him, but he knew He would."

"It was an up and down struggle," Terry admits. "I didn't believe in divorce; I *still* don't. But what could I do? In Oklahoma one party can file, citing irreconcilable differences, and there's nothing the other party can do to stop it.

"I didn't always praise God either," he confides. "There were times when I went into the blackest despair. Isaiah 61 talks about the spirit of heaviness, and I had a running battle with it. To think that people thought I had betrayed them; to think that Shirley and

I had done marriage conferences in major churches across the country—*marriage* conferences—that we had published a tape series on the needs of married couples. All of that brought a shame to me that I cannot describe."

The beleaguered husband was hounded by the unknown as well, with the kinds of thoughts that haunt you when life's most sacred pledge has been rescinded. "Maybe she's already found somebody else. Who is she with right now? What are they doing?"

These were satan's thought-bombs—Terry knew that. He had been utterly faithful to Shirley, and there was no reason to believe that she had been unfaithful to him. The battles in his mind were just like those between the lawyers. Just about the time he would win a small victory, the next attack would begin. The inevitable images conjured up in his mind instantly nauseated him every time.

"I couldn't let my thoughts go there," Terry says. "Images would become pictures, and pictures would turn into scenes that played like movie reels if I let them. I knew that the only way to win that battle was to cast down imaginations and bring every thought into captivity [see 2 Corinthians 10:5]. I *had* to praise the Lord."

CASTAWAY

When death ends a marriage, people rush to your side. They fill your life with flowers and help you face the grave. But when divorce pulls the trigger, the crowd scatters. Instead of admiring your courage, they question your motives. Maybe there's something you've been hiding. Maybe you're just like so-and-so, that other evangelist. And one thing you learn quickly, if some people are not absolutely sure they can trust you, then they won't trust you at all. Worse than going through hell is the prospect of going through it alone.

For a while Terry ramped up his travel schedule, not only to escape the stress of the lawsuits, but also to be some place—*any place*—where people didn't know him and wouldn't stare. But sorrow hung on him like a leaden cloak, even on the road.

"The hardest thing was going to churches," he says. "World Compassion's primary financial support has always come from my weekend meetings, so I had to keep traveling. But it was enormously stressful.

"I would arrive at a church wondering how many people there had heard whispers about the divorce. Had the pastor heard about it? Would he cancel on short notice if someone told him? I kept on believing for reconciliation, so I put off writing a public letter about the whole matter for four years. I just didn't feel like I could talk about it ethically until things were finalized one way or the other in court.

"During the years of legal wrangling, people would walk up and ask me how my wife was, and I didn't know what to say. Should I duck the question and just say, 'she's fine,' or should I tell them what was happening? It was a constant battle. In fact it still is.

"Just this past Easter, I was in England," he continues. "I was sitting with a group at dinner, when the pastor's wife asked me, 'How does your wife handle your constant traveling all over the world?' I've learned over the years that it's best to be frank and accept the consequences, so I looked at her and replied, 'My wife filed for divorce several years ago.'

"You cannot imagine the cold shock that settled down over that table," he says. "Everybody's eyes were looking down. The pastor's wife was mortified. My face was beet red. You never want to lie, but when you tell the truth in that kind of situation everybody gets embarrassed."

Explanations are pointless as well, because if you have to explain, you've already lost. People generally treat divorce like they treat the AIDS virus: It doesn't matter how you got it—you're not welcome here anymore.

Added pressure came from the fact that various churches, even whole denominations, were finding out anyway, and canceling meetings, some of them plainly rejecting any further association with Terry. In one instance, a 5,000-member church called off his Sunday with them just two weeks ahead of time.

"We don't care to get into the issue of whether you are right or wrong in this," the pastor told him. "Our policy is that no divorced minister stands in our pulpit." Integrity and faithfulness to scriptural procedure were irrelevant. Divorce was its own verdict.

"Prominent evangelistic ministries wrote me off as well," he recalls. "Some former good friends wouldn't even take my calls or let me explain." Colleagues with whom he had partnered effectively for years simply dismissed all association with him, as though his stain were contagious.

"The biggest thing was that I believed I had lost my ministry," he says, referring not to his career but to his very calling. "And the biggest lesson to learn was that it wasn't my ministry in the first place. It belonged to God."

SILENT SACRIFICE

Courtroom proceedings finally got under way in July 1999, three years and eight months after the initial petition for divorce. Terry had waged an ongoing battle against depression, but it had not beaten him. He had repeatedly reminded himself that his real conflict was not with flesh and blood, especially not his *own* flesh and blood. This was spiritual warfare, and it called for spiritual weapons. When at long last it was time to go before the bench, he was prepared.

"I took a yellow legal pad into court with me every day," he explains. "There was a verse God had given me, Isaiah 54:17, and I wrote it out in longhand at the top of a new page every morning."

"No weapon formed against you shall prosper, and every tongue which rises against you in judgment you shall condemn. This is the heritage of the servants of the Lord, and their righteousness is from Me," says the Lord.

"Beneath that verse," says Terry, "I wrote, *'Lord I believe you for favor,'* and listed the names of Joseph, Ruth, Esther, and Daniel. During the trial I meditated on their 'trials,' and how God brought them through and gave them favor. And then I added Jesus to the bottom of the list, because He increased in favor with both God and man [Luke 2:52]. Over and over I would thank the Lord under my breath that I too had favor. I did that whenever accusations were being made."

To borrow Terry's terms, he was launching the weapon of God's Word with whisper-quiet rockets of thanksgiving. And there were no temporary cease-fires. Since the entire case against him was based in accusation, the entire trial became a time to pray. Old memory verses like Hebrews 13:15 took on new meaning:

FAVOR

The beautiful thing about any war between truth and fiction is that it's easier to wage the truth. Terry's integrity spoke for him time and again in the eyes of everyone including the judge.

Fiction, on the other hand, is complicated, especially when attempting to spin grasped straws into legal gold. Perhaps Warner Jacobs really believed that no evangelist could be *this* clean, that if he kept procuring papers and deposing Terry and his staff—his *entire* staff—he was sure to find the stain of guilt somewhere. In any case, as time wore on the effectiveness of his charges wore off, and his strategies began to backfire. In one instance he introduced evidence that destroyed his own daylong argument within minutes.

"Jacobs had spent the day trying to disprove the fact that Terry was a prominent evangelist to the communist world," remembers his attorney, Bob Bartz. "Late that afternoon he introduced a book into evidence, because the back cover featured a picture of Terry and Shirley. I objected on grounds of irrelevance, but the judge overruled me and admitted the book into evidence.

"About thirty minutes later the judge interrupted one of Jacobs' questions, and asked him, 'Are you still going on and on and about whether or not Mr. Law has been a minister to Russia?' 'Yes, I am,' Jacobs answered. 'Well,' said the judge, 'I was just looking at this book that *you* introduced as evidence, and that is now part of *your* case...Let me direct your attention to something.'"

The black-robed jurist picked up the evidentiary copy of *Yet Will I Praise Him*, a book the erstwhile couple had written about their respective histories and new life together, and read one of three VIP endorsements *directly adjacent* to the picture on the back cover:

Terry Law was one of the first ones to break through the barrier sur-rounding the Iron Curtain countries and give faith to the rest of us that the Iron Curtain cannot stop the work of the Holy Spirit.

The judge then suggested that the attorney abandon his current line of questioning and move on with his case. "Jacobs turned beet red and sat down," says Bartz. The "evidence" was never mentioned again.

THE PRICE OF VICTORY

The trial had run for three full weeks, the longest divorce case ever in that judge's tenure. Now it was time for summations.

"That day holds the most vivid memories for me," says Terry. "Jacobs paced back and forth in front of the bench. He told the court, 'This man is a wolf in sheep's clothing.' He described me as a religious charlatan with 'the smell of a goat on him.' I sat there with my head down.

"It was so bad that when the judge gaveled to adjourn, I stood up and said to Bob, 'I feel like I need a shower; I've never felt so filthy in my life.' He said, 'I feel exactly the same way.' Warner Jacobs had tried to make me out a liar in every possible way.

"After everyone else left, I was too shocked and mortified even to move. So I just stood there numb. And then this incredible gift from Heaven just fell into my lap. The court reporter, a petite lady, walked over to me and said, 'Reverend Law, we have a prayer and Bible study here at the courthouse. We'd be honored if you would come and share with us.' I blinked at her, and for the first time tears welled up in my eyes."

Hope sparked into faith in Terry's heart. Maybe things would go his way. But a question remained: why had the judge allowed such a browbeating to take place? One onlooker later surmised that his Honor had inwardly decided in Terry's favor at some point during the trial, and that he had given the aggressive prosecutor such enormous leeway in order to let him exhaust his resources. He would have nothing left in his arsenal for a subsequent appeal.

The divorce decree was issued three weeks later while Terry was ministering in Newport, Wales, and Bob Bartz faxed it to his hotel just before midnight in the UK. He had won, hands down, on every count. Moreover, it appeared that the judge had gone out of his way to completely vindicate the besieged minister, awarding the Plaintiff the legal minimum.

"I couldn't believe my eyes," he recalls. "The judge tore apart all four major points, saying that the arguments were completely without merit."

Terry Law was 58 years old and flat broke, but for a couple of priceless assets that no court could take away. For one thing, his name had been completely cleared. His personal finances, as well as those of World Compassion, had been examined stem to stern, and not a hint of impropriety had been found. In fact, he had been brought so low that he was now in a perfect position to see the fulfillment of Psalm 50:23: "Whoever offers [a sacrifice of] praise glorifies Me; and to him who orders *his* conduct *aright* I will show the salvation of God."

Then and there he began to offer up the sacrifice of praise.

"I stood in the hotel courtyard and looked up at the moon and shouted," he remembers. "It was midnight, but I didn't care who heard me. I held up the papers in my hands and shouted, 'Hallelujah! Thank you Jesus!' And then I wept."

FIRST THINGS

His other asset was time, and standing there in the dark Welsh night, an ocean away from home, Terry knew how he had to spend it. "For the first time in years I could look to the future without the present fogging my view. And foremost in my mind was keeping my six children together. I didn't want them split into two groups."

But they already were. Although their wounds varied as much as those of soldiers, the kids shared a common scar. It was one nobody wanted, but it had been carved into them anyway, mainly along maternal lines: Jan's kids versus Shirley's kids.

Terry had brought Misty, Scot, and Rebecca into the marriage. Now they needed healing both from memories lost as well as those all too fresh. Years of conflict had robbed them of remembering their late mother in the meaningful ways they needed, sheer stress having replaced healthy grieving.

Meanwhile Shawna and Jason, Shirley's children from her first marriage, faced utter bewilderment. "To this day I still don't know why a lot of things happened, or how certain people feel about me," says Shawna.

Then there was Laurie, the "ours" in the Laws' yours-mine-and-ours six pack. The dreary contest had lasted a full third of her 13 years, and now she felt lost in the middle. "It was like there was a line drawn in the sand, and I was sitting on it, unable to move. I felt like I was supposed to choose, but I didn't have any siblings who were full-blooded, so I literally believed neither side wanted me."

Their determined father set about to heal the divide, assembling five of the six in Canada for Christmas, and as often as possible after that. In the ensuing years, several have been directly involved in the ministry of World Compassion, including accompanying their dad on overseas missions. The healing continues, a work in progress.

Terry's vision that has since taken him from Afghan villages to the White House, and brought him face to face with terrorists and prime ministers alike. But most important, it also brings him home.

"The thing I marvel at most," says Terry, "is that five of my children have suffered the death of a parent, and all six have experienced the horror of divorce. Yet today every one of them is serving the Lord. They are, without doubt, the greatest pride of my life. Yet I can't take any of the credit; God's grace worked a miracle in them while I was hitting rock bottom."

RESURRECTION

Psalm 103:12 says, "As far as the east is from the west, so far has [God] removed our transgressions from us." That is wonderfully reassuring news to anyone hounded by the past. We are forgiven, and "there is therefore now no condemnation to those who are in Christ Jesus" (Rom. 8:1). Or as one preacher puts it, God casts our sins into a sea of forgetfulness, and then puts up a "no fishing" sign.

Yet when God forgives our sins, He does not rewrite history. We are delivered from condemnation, yes, but not from consequences. That is largely because people are not willing to be as forgetful as God. *God is not forgetful!*

In Terry's case it has been easier to contend with terrorist threats and stone-throwing Muslim mobs than with the friendly fire of Christians who refuse both to forgive and forget.

I brought up the matter in Tulsa recently during our final interview for this chapter. "Terry, after all you've been through, what keeps you going?" I asked. "I know you can handle the death threats and danger overseas, but I'm talking about rejection here at home from fellow Christians. Why keep fighting?" I was baiting him, and my old friend's face brightened as he took the hook.

"Oh, Jim, the greatest ministry opportunities I've ever seen have followed the two big tragedies in my life." He starts reeling off the breakthroughs:

- ❖ The missions training school in China, whose first 19 missionaries, at this writing, are being sent into the Middle East;

- ❖ The widows' houses, work among lepers, and the supporting of a Christian underground numbering several hundred believers, all former Muslims, in Afghanistan;

- ❖ *The Story of Jesus* booklets that have been translated into 72 languages, with more than 270 million copies distributed thus far;

- ❖ The establishment of a network of churches in northern Iraq, composed of and led by former Muslims, and now numbering more than 3,000 members;

- ❖ 5 million Bibles distributed throughout the former Soviet Union;

❖ The burgeoning influence of World Compassion with officials at the highest levels of American government;

❖ Directly influencing the inclusion of a freedom of religion clause in the new Iraqi constitution;

❖ Calls for help from the sheiks of Iraq's Sunni Triangle. These calls subsequently led to their 87,000 troops joining the American war effort to drive Al Qaeda from the country.

The list goes on, but Iraq animates Terry the most, and I know it is because he has seen stunning spiritual victories there in the midst of great danger. He speaks of profound opportunities, including some that he cannot make public for fear of endangering lives. He tells me about frequent trips to the White House, and key believers on the staff who want to facilitate the work in the Middle East.

Then there's the wonderful fact that the number of new opportunities to partner with American churches is fast eclipsing the number of old rejections. Far more doors are opening than ever closed before. Perhaps Terry's proven integrity and sheer tenacity have convinced them to put their hands to the plow with him.

Terry is energized now. He has followed Saint Paul's instruction to Timothy, stirring up the gift within him. I think of what Jesus said in John 4:34: "My food [nourishment] is to do the will of Him who sent Me, and to finish His work." He seems to thrive on serving God, whether bouncing a grandchild on his knee or bouncing across the sands of Afghanistan in a speeding SUV, telling a Muslim warlord about *Isa*, God's Son who died to give him life.

I also think of Saint Peter, and what happened after God restored him from a failure far more spectacular than Terry's or mine or that of anyone who will ever pick up this book.

Even worse than failing a spouse, Peter had failed the Lord of the universe. Worse than abandoning his children, he had abandoned the Son of God. Worse than divorcing a wife, he had forsaken Jesus, cursing—within earshot—the very Savior of his soul. If anyone ever had a reason to throw in the towel, it was Simon Peter.

But even when we give up on God, He does not give up on us. Mark 16:6-7 records that an angel stationed at Jesus' empty tomb gave the two Marys and Salome instructions to "tell His disciples—and Peter" that the Lord wanted to meet with them on a mountain in Galilee. Far from rejecting His dispirited disciple, the Lord then restored and transformed him. A complete flop may have walked up that mountain, but a great apostle and architect of the Church walked back down.

Peter's greatest years in serving God came after his greatest failure, and even among the 11 he was considered a chief apostle. (And you think there's no hope for you!) Moreover, his transformation seems to have taken place during a period of just 50 days, 40 of them spanning several encounters with the resurrected Jesus, and the final ten in a protracted, joy-filled prayer and praise meeting back in Jerusalem.

> *And they worshiped Him, and returned to Jerusalem with great joy, and were continually in the temple praising and blessing God. Amen* (Luke 24:52-53).

Imagine the turnaround that must have taken place in Peter's mind and emotions. The crusty fisherman, a rough-around-the-edges man's man, had shown even more cowardice than the other disciples. They had all fled Jesus' crucifixion in fear, but Peter had sworn and cursed the Lord in spineless terror. Then he sank into indescribable shame.

Any husband who's ever betrayed his wedding vows and destroyed a marriage—any divorcée who's ever tried to "fit in again" at church without her ex—knows the shame Peter felt. And you wonder if you can ever *really* live again, really be happy and know without doubt you're experiencing God's best for your life. Or do divorced folks, especially the ones who were "to blame," have to settle for second-class status in the Kingdom, for spiritual consolation prizes? To put it bluntly, does God consider you "damaged" goods?

Peter had more reason to feel that way than any of us. He could have worn his shame for the rest of his life, and more than likely people would have let him. But instead we see him rejoicing and praising God day after day in the temple, and taking a role of leadership in the formation of Christ's still embryonic Church.

There he is, just a few weeks after blowing his own destiny to smithereens in front of everyone, standing before the other believers, explaining the prophetic significance of Christ's crucifixion, and presiding over the choosing of a new apostle to take Judas' place!

Cut to the Day of Pentecost, and Peter is front and center again, this time speaking in behalf of the whole church, explaining the miracle of the Holy Spirit's coming, and calling the masses to repentance. Three thousand people respond and are added to the Church.

In the ensuing years St. Peter led with effectiveness and excellence, and was even used of God to pen a portion of the Scriptures. Imagine: The same man who had cursed God had a hand in writing the very Word of God!

The thought of Peter's bold preaching at Pentecost brings me back to Tulsa, and to Terry. We're in the car now, and he's taking me back to my hotel, where I will finish this manuscript. Our conversation turns to the subject of grace, his current obsession. Pick any sermon he preaches these days, and no matter what theme he starts with, he'll wind up talking about grace.

We're driving north on Yale Avenue. "When I think about God's blessing on my life, about my children and what the Lord did in them when I couldn't do anything to help—Jim, it just overwhelms me. When I preach, I start to break up every time I talk about the grace of God."

Terry Law has learned the secret of God's grace—only the people who don't deserve it actually qualify for it. It's for the ones who make mistakes, the ones who have blown it so badly they don't deserve another chance.

John Newton, the forgiven slave trader, learned the same secret. That's why his most famous hymn says, "'Twas grace that taught my heart to fear and grace my fears relieved."

Grace puts an exit sign on the grave. The whole world looks different on the other side of death. Your failure wasn't the end after all, but the beginning. Those "greater works" that Jesus talked about—they're still in your future. They're your destiny. And now you realize: Those aren't scars on the Master's hands. *They are the marks of resurrection.*

ENDNOTES

1. H. Page Williams, *Do Yourself a Favor: Love Your Wife* (Plainfield, NJ: Bridge-Logos, 1973).

2. Long after the divorce was final, *Guideposts* magazine republished the original article without checking the facts.

Chapter 10

The Sacrifice of Praise

by Terry Law

Some friends forsook me, and others who stayed took a beating because of me. Even my longtime private secretary resigned after being verbally pistol-whipped on the witness stand. I didn't blame her.

~

An ancient king once said that a "broken spirit, a broken and contrite heart" are a pleasing sacrifice to God (Ps. 51:17). Why? How could the Lord take pleasure in a broken heart? Why does He even require sacrifices in the first place? I thought I had thoroughly learned the answers to those questions after the death of my wife Jan in 1982 (see Chapter 2). But years later I discovered there was more breaking to be done in me, and it happened in the courtroom of divorce.

After Jan's death I was devastated, truly crushed in my spirit. But in the eyes of loyal friends and colleagues my stature grew. Then when I began to minister in the power of a newfound revelation of praise and worship, my reputation grew as well. Healing miracles began to occur in my meetings; spiritual strongholds were broken, and thousands of formerly bound-up believers found new freedom to praise God.

As far as I knew, the second crushing was not a matter of my inner pride precipitating a fall. I had been lifted up—that's true—but not in my own eyes. Instead I had been humbled "under the mighty hand of God," and He had seen fit to lift me up in due time (1 Pet. 5:6).

No, my twice-broken heart was the result of a divorce I did not want and could not prevent, as well as the assault on my ministry and character that accompanied it. The nearly four-year attack decimated my finances, injured my credibility as a minister, and worst of all, wreaked havoc in the lives of those most precious to me, my six children.

Some friends forsook me, and others who stayed took a beating because of me. Even my longtime private secretary resigned after being verbally pistol-whipped on the witness stand. I didn't blame her.

But the first 43 months were merely a prelude to the final three-week trial, a period I can only describe as savagery on parade. Day after day I felt like the prosecutor was describing some notorious mobster, and I was just a listener in the gallery. Yet there I sat in the defendant's chair, and with every smear, a finger pointed at me. My actual innocence or guilt didn't matter inside the courtroom rail. Only the opinion of a black-robed stranger seated behind the massive desk before me mattered. With one bang of the gavel, I would be whatever he said.

Under such circumstances I had only one recourse: I began to offer up a sacrifice of praise in every area of my life. When the prosecutor attacked my ministry I would pray, "Everything is Yours, Lord. It all belongs to You." When he attacked my honor, I'd praise the Lord and say, "It's all in Your hands."

I meant it. I *had* to mean it. In the world's eyes I could lose everything, so I gave everything to God. I was His property, and my ministry was His ministry. That meant that anyone trying to take it would be contending with Him, not me.

The only way I made it through those years—the heartache of losing my marriage; the attack on my honor; the financial loss—was the same way I had survived losing Jan. I offered a constant sacrifice of praise.

Oral Roberts had been right all those years earlier. The sacrifice of praise had saved my life. And now it was saving it again.

In the Beginning

Have you ever wondered why God requires sacrifices in the first place? I can understand praising Him for blessings, but why does He expect me to continue praising Him when everything has gone wrong? I asked those questions many times. Why did He let Jan die? Why was He allowing me to go through the horrors of divorce?

You probably have questions just as puzzling as mine. Maybe you've lost a loved one, or your marriage also has broken up. Maybe you lost your job right after making a big financial commitment on a car or a house. Perhaps you've just been diagnosed with a disease, and it looks like you're going to have to rearrange your whole life. *Why should you praise God?*

The Almighty clearly does not need your sacrifices. "If I were hungry, I would not tell you; for the world is Mine, and all its fullness," He says in Psalm 50:12. Then He explains further in David's song of repentance:

> *Deliver me from the guilt of bloodshed, O God, the God of my salvation, and my tongue shall sing aloud of Your right-eousness. O Lord, open my lips, and my mouth shall show forth Your praise. For You do not desire sacrifice, or else I would give it; You do not delight in burnt offering.* **The sacrifices of God are a broken spirit, a broken and a contrite heart— these, O God, You will not despise** (Psalm 51:14-17).

The principle of sacrifice was first established in Genesis, immediately after the sin of Adam and Eve. In fact God Himself initiated the practice in Genesis 3:21: "Also for Adam and his wife the Lord God made tunics of skin, and clothed them." The fact that God performed an act that symbolically satisfied His own justice offers a big clue: Adam's sin was that he had thrown off God's authority, and through his disobedience had given his earthly dominion to satan. Then he immediately realized that he was "uncovered," and tried to fashion clothing for Eve and himself from fig leaves. The improvised garments did indeed cover their physical nudity, but the couple still tried to go into hiding, because they instinctively realized that they could not cover their spiritual nakedness. They could not reestablish, by their own works, their lost relationship with God.

By killing an animal and covering Adam and his wife, the Lord was showing them that only He could deal with their sin and re-store them to Himself. In other words, Almighty God was already pointing mankind forward in history to His own sacrifice of His Son, Jesus, whose sinless body would be torn, and whose blood would be shed, completely removing man's guilt and restoring him to his place of authority under God.

This is in fact the ultimate purpose of every sacrifice commanded by God—to point to the sacrifice of His Son, Jesus Christ, and the complete satisfaction (propitiation) of God's justice by the shedding of His blood. From Abel's sacrifice in Genesis to the sacrifice of praise in Hebrews, *every sacrifice points to the complete sufficiency of Christ's work on the Cross,* because that work alone makes us acceptable to God. *His flesh* (skin) covers *our* nakedness.

This principle also explains why Cain's offering was rejected while Abel's sacrifice was accepted (see Gen. 4). Cain merely presented the fruits of his own labor as a "tiller of the ground" (Gen. 4:2). His was a religion of works. Abel, on the other hand, believed on Jesus as His Savior thousands of years in advance (see Heb. 11:4), and appealed to God's mercy by sacrificing the blood of a lamb. The act symbolized his faith, while simultaneously exposing Cain's lack of faith. That is why Cain killed him.

Those who would come to God with the fruit of their labors have always opposed those who approach Him on the basis of faith. From that first fratricide to today's Islamic executions of Muslim converts to Christ, the exclusive sufficiency of Jesus' atonement has made Him a "stone of stumbling, and a rock of offense" (1 Pet. 2:8). It is the pattern of history—this confrontation with the one and only Son of God—that no man, no religion can avoid.

Requiring man to reckon with the crucified Jesus is why God has required various sacrifices throughout the ages. They are demonstrations of faith designed (a) to reveal Christ to us, and (b) to reveal Christ in us.

The Old Testament sacrifices of animals were designed to depict the Jews' faith in the coming sacrifice of the "Lamb of God who takes away the sin of the world" (John 1:29). The high priest had to offer a bull for the cleansing of his own sin. The bull represented man's strength, and its slaying showed that the priest knew he could not approach God by his own efforts. A ruler of the people had to offer a ram, whose horn symbolized his power and wealth. The people themselves could bring a lamb or goat, as long as it was their first and best. The poorest believers could bring a dove.

The purpose of each sacrifice was always the same: *to point to God's own provision, the shedding of His innocent Son's blood to cover humanity's sin.* This is an awesome thing. God's holiness could not be violated; an acceptable sacrifice had to be made. Yet because man was incapable of such an offering, God made it for him. If only we truly understood this truth, then *our frequent consternation about a loving God sending someone to hell would turn to utter amazement that He made a way to get anyone into Heaven!*

God's perfect standards have not changed. When Jesus Christ died on the Cross for our sin 2,000 years ago, He propitiated the holiness of God, i.e., He satisfied God's justice. The blood offered at Calvary became the final blood sacrifice for our sin. Yet *the principle of sacrifice remains, because the principle of faith remains.* It is merely the form of the sacrifice that has changed. Today God requires a different sacrifice, one that reveals Christ *in* us.

> *Therefore Jesus also, that He might sanctify the people with His own blood, suffered outside the gate. Therefore let us go forth to*

*Him, outside the camp, bearing His reproach. For here we have
no continuing city, but we seek the one to come. Therefore by
Him let us continually offer the sacrifice of praise to God, that is,
the fruit of our lips, giving thanks to His name* (Hebrews
13:12-15).

Humans are bound by the confines of time. Thus it was appropriate to offer the blood of animals *before* Christ's final sacrifice; such
offerings were statements of faith that redemption was on its way.
But the continued shedding of blood after Jesus died became an
abomination to God, because it demonstrated a rejection of Christ's
sufficiency. The writer of Hebrews understood the timelessness of
true faith, and that is why Abel, Abraham, David, and other Old Testament saints are listed among the just in Hebrews chapter 11.

*God requires your sacrifice of praise, at precisely what seems like
the worst moment, because it reveals Christ Jesus in your life.* In other
words, it's how He shows up! Face it, you need God to show up
right there in the middle of the divorce. You need to know His
presence, to feel Him, in the depths of grief. You need to know
He's walking with you when you're facing a life-threatening surgery. Well, *He shows up in His fullness when you praise Him from
your emptiness, because that is when you truly have room for Him.*

HIGH COST OF PRAISE

Your access to God is an aspect of His grace—it is free, but it is
not cheap. Jesus bankrupted Himself in order to restore your
"free" admittance to the courts of Heaven. As a result you are welcome to approach God's throne boldly to "obtain mercy and find
grace to help in time of need" (Heb. 4:16). But praise is offered
based on God's worthiness, not your needs, and for that reason
alone you should offer something costly, even extravagant.

Every time you go to church you're faced with the lure of getting something for nothing. There might be a liturgy or beautiful choir music. The pastor might preach an excellent message, and everyone present might pronounce the service "blessed." In such an atmosphere it's easy to settle back into the pew and profit from the efforts of others. But God has commanded the sacrifice of praise, and *if it doesn't cost you something, it isn't a sacrifice.*

Moreover, when everything has gone wrong, it is even more crucial that you offer the sacrifice of praise. Whether you're in the midst of great trial or sickness, awash with grief, under attack in relationships or finances, you must not waver; at all times and in all circumstances God is worthy to be praised. And if you offer praise to Him when you're at your lowest, it means all the more to Him. *God is always pleased with the sacrifice of praise and has even attached a promise to it:*

> *Whoever offers praise [towdah, i.e., the sacrifice of praise] glorifies Me; and to him who orders his conduct aright I will show the salvation of God* (Psalm 50:23).

Ordering your "conduct aright" means living an upright life. Note that upright does *not* mean uptight! Right living isn't about keeping a list of rules, but about knowing God. And the sacrifice of praise is what puts us on the path to knowing Him, a path that leads to the life of total well-being inherent in the word, "salvation."

My eldest daughter, Misty, experienced dramatic fulfillment of this promise very recently. For more than a year she had been experiencing mysterious health problems, and they seemed to be getting worse. What she did not tell me was that she had been diagnosed with advanced lupus. Her doctor had told her that she would probably spend the rest of her life in bed. That was like a prison sentence to Misty, because she led such an active life. Besides being a wife, and the mother of two very active little girls, she also worked for a large accounting corporation from her home office. I'm very proud of Misty. She's a loving wife and mom, but she's also tough, and not one to complain. She hadn't told me about the diagnosis, yet I knew from our occasional phone conversations that she was fighting some sort of battle.

Four months passed, and in typical fashion, she remained quiet about her ordeal. Then, in October 2007, she was at church one Sunday morning, singing on the worship team. She had been caught up in praising God, she later told me, when she sensed the power of the Holy Spirit settling on her, and somehow felt a change taking place in her body. Then, after the service, several people—folks who didn't know about the illness—stopped to comment that she suddenly looked healthier, "pinker." A doctor from the congregation asked about her health, and she told him the diagnosis, as well as what had happened during the service. He asked if he might see her and give a second opinion.

Misty saw the doctor right away, and he performed the same regimen of tests the specialists had conducted the previous month. A few days later when the reports came in she called me, crying, and finally told me about the diagnosis of lupus.

I was stunned. "Why didn't you tell me about this before?" I asked in disbelief.

"Dad, let me finish the story," she said in a tone that suddenly didn't sound so sad.

The second doctor had just called her with news that confirmed why she had been feeling so much better of late. Every report, every scan, showed not a single trace of lupus. The disease was gone.

"Dad, it's just like what you wrote about. In the middle of praising God, He healed me. I don't have lupus anymore!"

Misty had been so weak; she could have given up. She could have said, "I'll praise God when He gives me strength," or "when He heals me." But she determined to praise Him when she had no strength, and when everything within her told her it wasn't worth it. Misty knew the high price God had paid for her healing, and she offered a costly sacrifice of praise in return.

The high cost of praise is vividly illustrated in the tabernacle Moses erected in the wilderness. Before the high priest entered into the Holy of Holies to meet with God at the mercy seat, his last stop was at a golden altar immediately outside the veil. There he was required to offer incense to the Lord before crossing through the curtain. If he did not, he would immediately be struck dead.

The incense offered at this altar was symbolic of the prayers and praises of God's people. Extremely costly, and used nowhere else on earth, it was composed of four rare ingredients, ranging from the marrow of a certain tree to mollusk shells from the Red Sea floor. After considerable time and effort in gathering them, the components were brought to the priests, and the whole concoction was ground into a fine powder—a process talcum makers used to call "contriting"—and then blended and salted in a unique fashion for purity's sake.

That's what took place in Misty. She gathered the costliest spices from the far reaches of her soul and laid them before her High Priest for grinding and salting during that time of praise. Then she offered her broken body and contrite spirit to God.

Broken hearts are not only necessary, but inevitable. Jeremiah 23:29 likens God's Word to a "hammer that breaks the rock in pieces." You can either allow the voice of the Lord to break, mold, and conform you to His will, or you can ignore His Word and let the inevitable judgments of life do the job more slowly and painfully. But *you will be broken.*

The good news is that no matter what has broken you, whether you have submitted to the breaking of the Holy Spirit, or been pounded by years of disobedience, God will not despise you when you pour yourself out in praise before Him (see Psalm 51:17). *Your sacrifices and your brokenness are precious to Him.*

DISCIPLINE OF PRAISE

I grew up in Pentecostal circles where we were trained to respond to God on the basis of our feelings rather than faith. But true praise, although it may include emotion, is an act of the will. "I *will* bless the Lord at all times," David said in Psalm 34:1. "His praise *shall* continually be in my mouth." We are to praise God at all times, whether we feel like it or not. Yet it is precisely at this point that our feelings and wills invariably collide.

In one of the many books written about the Azusa Street revival that began in 1906, an author describes the beginnings of what is commonly called "classical" Pentecostalism in America. Pentecostals, he says, do not enter into praise and worship until they are "prompted." I can attest to the fact that, although such practice was not taught as doctrine, it nonetheless became entrenched habit. For the better part of a century we Pentecostals saw praying in the spirit more as a function of emotion than will. And we viewed praise and worship in the same faulty light.

I remember church services in my youth, when the song leader or pastor would encourage everyone to stand up, clap, and raise our hands in public worship. But often I didn't "feel" like rejoicing, and would resent the leader's efforts to get me to enter in. So I stood there in the congregation, arms folded, muttering to myself that I would not be manipulated into praising God. "It's hypocritical of me to raise my hands and say words of praise when I don't feel them," I reasoned. I missed out on the blessings of God because I was imprisoned by a combination of bad thinking and teen angst.

The truth is that the Scriptures command us over and over to "rejoice in the Lord *always*" (see Phil. 3:1; 4:4). Therefore if real hypocrisy lies in knowing the truth and refusing to obey it, then we are being hypocritical when we follow our feelings and refuse to praise God.

Another problem, more prevalent in today's charismatic churches, is that people have been "into" praise and worship for so long that it has become mere liturgical form. They raise their hands, say the right words, and assume all the proper expressions of contemporary praise, yet their minds often are miles away. They are not worshiping anymore than the teenaged Terry Law, arms folded, standing firm in defiance of the poor soul assigned to "lead" him into God's presence.

British pastor Mike Pilavachi, of London's Soul Survivor church, saw something like this happening in his congregation, despite his best efforts to prevent it. "We had become connoisseurs of worship instead of participants in it," he confesses. "We had forgotten that *sacrifice is central to biblical worship* [emphasis mine]. We are called to offer our bodies as living sacrifices...We are called to offer our sacrifice of praise."

"We needed to take drastic action," he continues. "For a while, in order to truly learn this lesson, we banned the band." That meant setting down one of England's most popular worship teams and its leader, renowned singer/songwriter Matt Redman, who later recalled the experience:

> [T]he very next Sunday when we turned up at church, there was no sound system to be seen, and no band to lead us. The new approach was simple—we weren't going to lean so hard on those outward things any more. Mike would say, "When you come through the doors of the church on Sunday, what are you bringing as your offering to God? What are you going to sacrifice today?" …At first the meetings were a bit awkward: there were long periods of silence, and there wasn't too much singing going on. But we soon began to learn how to bring heart offerings to God without any external trappings we'd grown used to. Stripping everything away, we slowly started to rediscover the heart of worship.
>
> After a while, the worship band and the sound system reappeared (sic), but now it was different. The songs of our hearts had caught up with the songs of our lips.[1]

God honored Soul Survivor church's self-discipline, not only revitalizing the congregation's worship life, but also inspiring Redman to compose one of his most popular and effective songs, "The Heart of Worship."

> *I'm coming back to the heart of worship*
> *And it's all about You*
> *All about You, Jesus.*
> *I'm sorry Lord for the thing I've made it*

When it's all about You,
It's all about You, Jesus.[2]

The sacrifice of praise involves a decision to take "drastic action." The will has to grab the mind, focusing our attention upon God and His Word. This must happen not only every time we enter God's house to worship, but it must also become a daily discipline. "Bless the Lord, O my soul," David commanded himself in Psalm 103:1, "and all that is within me, bless His holy name!" That is the essence of the sacrifice of praise.

When a congregation has been trained in the discipline of sacrificial praise, the worship leader's job becomes much easier. He no longer has to be a skilled exhorter or a cheerleader, jumping through a carefully choreographed routine of songs and moods. When the people arrive at church intent upon offering a sacrifice of praise, their songs become God's throne (see Psalm 22:3), and their meeting place His throne room. The inevitable result is the manifestation of His power.

THE CHOICE OF PRAISE

God enjoins us to offer the sacrifice of praise, but it is still a choice, an act of the will that is fundamental to the Christian life. In fact, *you cannot succeed as a Christian without recognizing the importance of choice in offering a sacrifice of thanksgiving and praise.*

Leviticus 22:29 says, "And when you offer a sacrifice of thanksgiving to the Lord, offer it of your own free will." God's Old Covenant laws were many, yet they were never designed to browbeat His people or rob them of willing hearts. It is true that some of His laws were prescribed in precise detail, to be obeyed to the letter. But when it came to offering thanksgiving, the Father said to "offer it of your own free will."

There is something about being willing to praise God that so pleases Him. Remember when your own preschooler decided to "surprise" you with breakfast in bed? Your heart leapt for joy, but not at the sight of the food—it was probably a minor disaster—nor for knowing that a major disaster awaited you in the kitchen. No, you were thrilled because it was an offering not required by you—a gift of pure, unvarnished love! *That* is but a glimpse of the joy our sacrifice of praise brings to the Father.

Tests and trials are as predictable as death and taxes. They *will* come. But they come for a reason. Our moments of insurmountable circumstances are actually invitations from the Lord to *choose* to praise Him. When my friends, Jim and Dolly Gilbert, miscarried their first baby after 21 years of trying to conceive, Jim wrote these words:

> *This letter was to have borne the most joyous tidings of our lives, that after years of praying, we were due to give birth to our first child this December. But on June 4th our gladness was suddenly silenced by a heart monitor that refused to beep the music of a tiny life. Mere seconds into that first exhilarating sonographic glimpse of our baby, the nurse said a gentle, but horrific, "I'm sorry."*
>
> *And then it was all over.*
>
> *Dolly cried hard but quietly. I just stared at the small motionless, black and white image that only a minute ago had been heir to everything of value in our lives. It was too early—only our twelfth week—to call him Jim or her Holly. So we were making*

do with endearments like "precious" and "little treasure," until a future snapshot might let us in on Heaven's little secret.

Dolly's doctor had given us the good news at April's end, thus turning May into an exaggerated Spring ecstasy. Birds no longer flew; they soared. Flowers didn't bloom; they were born. And everything rhythmical, from jackhammers to washing machines, played a merry tune.

On Mother's Day I had been out of town ministering, but coast-to-coast distance couldn't dent our happiness. I sent Dolly two cards and one big, heart-shaped bouquet of roses, with a note that said "I love you both." The flowers had cost a small fortune, but after all, you only have one first Mother's Day. And if you've been waiting for a very long time, why not give something that reflects the overwhelming joy of the occasion!

But then came June 4th.

I have put away the books and videos. Dolly kept two dried roses. And my Father's Day card remains unopened in a drawer upstairs.

So why should you be told such intimate sorrows? And why do I write with uncensored sadness? For two reason dear friends:

1) We want to say, in the face of sorrow, that God is worthy to be praised at all times, even this time. It was easy to praise Him in May. But it is important to praise Him now. You are our witnesses.

2) Our joy was even more profound than it was brief. It is worth enduring the heartache just to relive the wonder. We have been parents, and that can never be undone.

Please pray for us, but do not mourn beyond my signature.

Birds still soared today. There are more flowers to be born and bought and given. And my card will not stay sealed forever.

Jim and Dolly (who now have a beautiful young daughter) didn't allow the devil to make them calloused and bitter. They would not let him erect a stronghold in their hearts. And neither should you, no matter what circumstances you face, because it is precisely at this point that the sacrifice of praise will explode in your spirit and lead to a miracle.

When my wife, Jan, passed away I was filled with grief. Bitterness and self-pity threatened to engulf my heart. I could hear satan saying, "God has been very cruel to you. How could a loving God allow something like this?" I was being bombarded with volley after volley of thought-bombs that were about to sink my spiritual ship. Finally I hit bottom, and when I got there I found myself faced with the most important decision of my life. Then and there, in the very pit of despair, would I praise God?

I knelt down and began to pray, but my words sounded hollow. They were also being drowned out by competing voices. One taunted me: "Why should you praise God when you hurt this badly inside?" Another whispered the words of David in Psalm 34:1: "I will bless the Lord at all times; His praise shall continually be in my mouth." The choice before me was excruciating and seemed so unfair. Why didn't God just overwhelm me with comfort in my misery? Why make me choose to praise Him? If it were so necessary, why not just *force* me to bow down and worship?

I was face to face with what Philip Yancey has called "God's terrible insistence on human freedom."[3] He describes it as "so absolute that he granted us the power to live as though he did not exist, to spit in his face, to crucify him."[4] As I knelt there agonizing,

I began to realize that my choice to praise was the last little bit of power I had in life. I couldn't bring Jan back, couldn't spare my children their grief, couldn't banish loneliness or somehow "fix" our lives to work OK without her. But I could choose to praise God, and the prospect somehow was strangely empowering.

I spoke for a moment to my enemy. "Devil, I *will* bless the Lord, and I command you to shut up! I command you to leave my thoughts alone. I am going to praise the Lord. You can listen if you want, but I'm still going to do it!" And then I did.

Nothing happened right away. In fact, two hours passed before I felt a thing. But I praised God anyway, without emotion, feeling, or tears, without any sense of His presence. But it didn't matter. This was a sacrifice of praise, and I had *chosen* to make it.

And then the moment came. A dam in my spirit broke apart, and torrents of praise began bursting out of what seemed like every part of me, as God made His presence known in my room. That was my initiation into the sacrifice of praise.

Years later when my heart was broken yet again, the ache in my spirit was no less, yet the fountain of praise flowed more readily. And today I know that no matter what the future holds, what once was a pool has become a spring. These waters will not cease.

THE BIG QUESTION

Let's return to the two questions Pastor Mike Pilavachi asked his congregation: What are you bringing as your offering to God? What are you going to sacrifice today? There are so many wonderful sacrifices of praise just waiting to be offered to God, but He's waiting for the unsolicited one, like the imperfect, surprise breakfast in bed.

You can make it quiet or loud, musical or not, practiced or spontaneous, now or later. But *now* is better.

ENDNOTES

1. Matt Redman, *The Unquenchable Worshipper* (Ventura, CA: Regal, 2001), 76-78.

2. Matt Redman, "The Heart of Worship," © 1999 Kingsway's Thankyou Music.

3. Philip Yancey, *The Jesus I Never Knew* (Grand Rapids, MI: Zondervan Publishing House, 1995), 79.

4. Ibid.

Chapter 11

The Lifestyle of Praise

Nothing embarrasses satan worse than seeing someone he has passionately pursued, settled into a lifestyle of praise, happily committed to the Competition.

~

In the wake of divorce I felt like a patient coming out of a coma, someone for whom time seemed to be picking up exactly where it had stopped. For all intents and purposes, I had lost the past four years in ministry, my vision clouded by seemingly endless conflict. But now I was beginning to see clearly again, and although I would have to weather the chill of loneliness, the future looked bright. After the death of my first wife, Jan, praise had been my *lifeline*. But in the aftermath of divorce, I knew it must become my *lifestyle*.

A lifestyle of praise aligns the heart with the purposes of God. And if it is true that our hearts' "abundance" is expressed through speech (see Luke 6:45), then a lifestyle of praise will completely change the way we talk, bringing our words into agreement with the Word of God. Praise is the antithesis of Adam's rebellion, which cost him his dominion and knocked the world off kilter. Praise says, "*You* are the Most High." It puts the world back into orbit around God.

Never underestimate the power of your words. When God says, "Death and life *are* in the power of the tongue" (Prov. 18:21a), He isn't talking about slips of the tongue that bring bad luck, but about the moral and spiritual nature of human speech. Fathers can either ignite or extinguish their children's hopes with a single sentence, simply because to a child, Dad's voice is God's voice (as indeed it should be in the child's early years). Likewise spouses can either build each other up or tear each other down. One Florida pastor understands the power he wields as a husband: "Every time I tell my wife she's beautiful, I'm prophesying to her. When I tell her how much I value her opinion, I can see her rise to levels of wisdom she hasn't known before. The way I talk to her is the most important part of my ministry to her as a husband. I have a sacred duty to speak life to her."

God created the universe by speaking it into existence, and still upholds "all things by the word of His power" (Heb. 1:3). Man, as God's image-bearer, was appointed to govern in like manner. Genesis 2:19,23 says, "whatever Adam called each living creature, that was its name," and quotes him as calling his wife, "Woman, because she was taken out of Man." The next chapter says, "And Adam called his wife's name Eve, because she was the mother of all living" (Gen. 3:20).

Man soon lost his dominion, of course, but Jesus explained that, "the Son of Man has come to seek and to save that which was lost"

(Luke 19:10). As one preacher put it, "Adam turned a garden into a wilderness, but Jesus went into the wilderness and got back the garden." In other words, Jesus regained the title deed to Planet Earth, and then made us joint heirs in His inheritance.

But how do we exercise our restored authority? How do we "proclaim liberty to the captives and recovery of sight to the blind" (Luke 4:18)? A habit of praise is fundamental in restoring the believer's authority *over* creation because it puts him back *under* authority. It tames his tongue, something he cannot do on his own (James 3:8).

The implications of a lifestyle of praise are enormous. *Everything is rearranged.* King David alluded to this in Psalm 50:23 when he said, "Whoever offers [sacrifices of] praise glorifies Me; And to him who orders his conduct [way of life] aright I will show the salvation of God." Praise turns the world right side up.

Let's take a look at how a lifestyle of praise—praise as a *habit*—reorders the Christian's world through several key principles:

❖ Praise silences the devil.

❖ Praise leads us into Christ's triumph.

❖ Praise prepares us for miracles.

❖ Praise brings revelation.

❖ God inhabits our praises.

PRAISE SILENCES THE DEVIL

We have already established the fact that the devil's primary strategy is to use the power of suggestion to erect strongholds, ungodly thought patterns in the mind. He knows that an unrenewed mind is barren ground where he can plant "weeds," cultivate all sorts of ungodliness, and eventually reap a harvest of destruction. But a mentality of praise nips those weeds in the bud; it shuts satan up. In fact, praise on *your* lips can silence the devil's voice in other people.

I learned this in the wee hours of the morning, years ago, when Living Sound was ministering in Katowice, Poland. Nearly 7,000 people had crammed the city's Roman Catholic cathedral that evening to hear the team in concert, while 2,000 more stood out in the night rain, listening and peering through the huge open windows. At the end of the meeting I had given call to Christ, and 2,000 hungry Polish souls had crowded to the front to commit their lives to Him. Now, we were back at the convent, guests of the Franciscan sisters who served the diocese.

I was in my spartan concrete quarters, sound asleep under a warm blanket, when a knock awakened me. I tried to summon my wits as I felt along the cold stone wall for the light switch. It was barely five in the morning. "Who could be knocking at this hour?" I thought as I opened the heavy wooden door.

"This man says he must see you at once," said the sister on duty in her thick Polish accent. "He says he will not leave until he has spoken with you." I looked at the disheveled young man standing beside the diminutive nun. His eyes were red, his hair as mussed as his clothing. He obviously had not slept. Blinking the sleep from my eyes, I invited my unexpected visitor into my room. As we sat on the edge of the bed to talk I sensed that the night, though short for sleeping, had been a long one for his soul.

André was a member of the communist party. "I was assigned to follow you and report on your activities," he explained in halting, but clear, English. "For the past three weeks, every night while you have preached and the group has sung, I have been watching you. At first I thought you were trying to subvert the people with a big American show. But in the past few days I have begun to realize that you are sincere. You believe everything you are saying.

"Last night I saw all of those people responding to your summons to accept Christ, and I...I haven't been able to sleep." He looked straight into my eyes. "I want God. I am not going to leave this room until I have inside of me what you have inside of you." And he didn't! As the sun rose over southern Poland that morning, André knelt by the bed and gave himself to God. He made the Great Exchange: all he had for all Christ has. Today, in a free Poland, he is still actively ministering for the Lord.

What had we done that haunted this man's soul? We hadn't argued against communism or preached on the merits of Western democracy. No, we simply praised the Lord, and the sound of our praises silenced the evil spirits dominating his life and career. King David might as well have been writing about our concert when he composed Psalm 8.

> *O Lord, our Lord, How excellent is Your name in all the earth, who have set Your glory above the heavens! Out of the mouth of babes and nursing infants You have ordained strength, because of Your enemies, that You may silence the enemy and the avenger* (Psalm 8:1-2).

David knew there was a kind of speech so powerful that even a child could speak it and "silence the enemy and the avenger," i.e., make the devil shut up. Jesus quoted the psalmist in Matthew 21:16, when the chief priests expressed their indignation over the fact that the local children were worshiping Him. "Have you never read," He asked the supposed scholars, "'Out of the mouth of babes and nursing infants You have *perfected praise?*'" (Matt. 21:9-16).

But wait a minute! David said "ordained strength," and Jesus said "perfected praise." Was the Son of David misquoting His own Word? To the contrary, He was explaining the very *essence* of what it takes to silence the accuser of your soul. *The simple praises of a child's lips are perfectly capable of shutting satan's accusing mouth.* If you tend to think of spiritual warfare as some exotic discipline, just think about that statement. Children aren't eloquent in their praises, but they are pure. "Dear God, I worship you. Please make Mommy better." That's about it for most little ones. No fancy salutations or introductions—"O, Thou that sittest high above the circle of the earth."

Sure, there's a time to glorify God with poetry and eloquence, but lying on your belly in life's foxhole while the devil lobs grenades of condemnation at you probably isn't that time. Just praise God like a kid: let whatever is in you come out, right there in the heat of your battle. *Praise from your lips is the ordained strength of God to silence the enemy.*

PRAISE FROM THE MOUTH

Jesus said perfected praise comes from the "mouth." It is *the* true launch pad, from which all spiritual weapons, godly or satanic, are fired. Revelation 16:13, for example, speaks of the satan's weapons: "And I saw three unclean spirits like frogs *coming* out of the mouth of the dragon, out of the mouth of the beast, and out of the mouth of the false prophet."

It looks like Mom's warning years ago against "shooting off your mouth" was more literal than figurative. You must guard your mouth, because no matter what you say, you are launching weapons of one sort or another. Your words will land somewhere, whether on satan's head or in the heart of a loved one. They might even boomerang back on you. According to Jesus, "the things which come out of him, those are the things that defile a man" (Mark 7:15). Knowing this, you must consciously choose to launch God's weapons and not the devil's.

Since what comes out of our mouths ultimately determines the winner in spiritual warfare, a lifestyle of praise is paramount. It is the daily strength God has ordained for resisting satan's schemes. And that strength is multiplied when believers unite in praise. I have been in services when we moved into such an atmosphere of high praise that evil spirits oppressing people in the room began to cry out. In fact, Don Moen and I were once in Kuala Lumpur, Malaysia, leading a congregation in praise, when four people with evil spirits began screaming in torment. Thankfully, the church had skilled members who took appropriate action, and the afflicted persons were quickly set free. Afterward the pastors told me that such outbursts were unusual, but that the church usually did not engage in such high praise either.

We both knew this was no coincidence. Praise to God had so upset the demons that it terrorized them, as though a spiritual searchlight had forced them out of hiding. Once exposed, of course, they were easily expelled, and the people they had bound were set free.

GARMENT OF PRAISE

What we wear says a lot about our lifestyles, and the lifestyle of praise is no exception. God has given His Church clothing that is described in Revelation 19:8 as "fine linen...the righteous acts of the saints," and in Isaiah as a "garment of praise" (Isa. 61:3). To put it another way, we are to be outfitted both in deeds and words that glorify Him.

"Therefore by Him let us *continually offer the sacrifice of praise to God, that is, the fruit of our lips, giving thanks to His name.*"

It is one thing to prescribe *regular* praise, but quite another to call for *continual* praise. In fact, it sounds impossible, like praying without ceasing. But what is impossible for mind and body is entirely possible in a man's spirit, where the indwelling Holy Spirit never sleeps, but instead "makes intercession for us with groanings which cannot be uttered" (Rom. 8:26).

By offering a continual sacrifice of praise, Terry found himself "hard-pressed on every side, yet not crushed... perplexed, but not in despair; persecuted, but not forsaken; struck down, but not destroyed" (2 Cor. 4:8-9). Every evening found him worn out from the attacks, but every morning he found new mercies.

The embattled husband wasn't the only one firing spiritual stealth missiles in the courtroom. He had noticed, over a period of days, that his defense attorney's wife and daughter frequently attended the hearing. He knew that Bob Bartz' daughter, Bridgette, was a student, and assumed she must be studying the case. Not so, said Bartz; the two ladies were there to silently pray over the proceedings!

"My wife told me, 'God awakened me last night and showed me I really need to intercede in prayer for your upcoming day in court,'" he explained to his startled client. The weary warrior was not alone after all, a fact that gave him strength.

Immediately after Jesus' temptation in the wilderness He went to His home synagogue in Nazareth, where the rabbi invited Him to select and read a passage from Isaiah. The Lord turned to Isaiah 61, a prophecy everyone knew was about the promised Messiah, and read the beginning:

> *The Spirit of the Lord is upon Me, because He has anointed Me to preach the gospel to the poor; He has sent Me to heal the brokenhearted, to proclaim liberty to the captives and recovery of sight to the blind, to set at liberty those who are oppressed; to proclaim the acceptable year of the Lord"* (Luke 4:18-19; see also Isaiah 61:1-2).

After reading through the opening statement of the prophecy, Jesus closed the sacred scroll and added one fateful sentence that marked the first steps of His three-year walk to Calvary: "Today this Scripture is fulfilled in your hearing" (Luke 4:21). He had announced the "year of the Lord," the beginning of His reign as the promised King of Israel.

But the famous passage in Isaiah 61 does not end with verse 2. The Lord had restricted Himself to the opening statement because it suited His announcement. The prophecy actually continues through verse 3, where the Savior says God has anointed Him to give His people "beauty for ashes, the oil of joy for mourning, the garment of praise for the spirit of heaviness."

This is a wonderful three-fold exchange. When we preach the good tidings of Christ to someone, we give them beauty for their ashes, the ruins of a burned life. We soothe and revitalize their scarred spirits with the healing oil of joy, the Holy Spirit. And we release them from the heaviness they have borne, clothing them with a beautiful, much lighter, garment of praise.

So many people in today's world wrestle against the spirit of heaviness, what we would call *a spirit of depression*. In fact several studies on chronic depression place the number of adult Americans in its relentless grip at nearly ten percent of the population.[1] I believe that depression, while most of the time induced by circumstances, can also be an actual principality, a stronghold of satan. Behind it is an evil personality that binds, discourages, and frustrates, a spirit that robs the heart and mind of all hope. In any case, depression is the doorway to the pit of despair.

David undoubtedly was facing depression when, hiding in a cave, he wrote Psalm 142. In verse 3 he said, "my spirit was overwhelmed within me," and in verse 6 confessed to being "brought very low." But the sweet psalmist had an exit strategy! "Bring my soul out of prison, that I may praise Your name," he sang in the final verse.

King David knew that the way out of depression was to exchange the spirit of heaviness for a garment of praise, because he was a covenant child of God. "You shall deal bountifully with me," he exulted (Ps. 142:7). He was a hunted man, running for His life, yet there in the cave He chose to rejoice, to dress his mind in the fabric of praise.

More than just a covering, clothing is part of a person's identity and personality. It functions psychologically very much like a second skin. When you tumble out of bed each morning and get dressed, you decide exactly whom your friends and colleagues at work will see. That is precisely why Scripture calls praise a "garment." It is something you *choose* to wear, a frame of mind you decide to put on before the devil and the world. And although it's beautiful, the garment of praise is also tough. You could even think of it as armor for your attitude.

Of course, you can also choose *not* to wear the garment of praise, and the Lord certainly won't force you to wear it. The Bible says He has been anointed to give it to you, and assumes you will want to put it on. If you choose, you can wear a bruised ego on your sleeve and a chip on your shoulder. You can let discouragement come from your mouth and paint the whole world gray, if you choose. But that's just it: *the choice is yours.* The garment of praise is God's gift to empower you, to let you share in the thrill of His victory over satan, whom He has disarmed and humiliated (see Col. 2:15).

Your praise to God only adds to the devil's humiliation, because his desire for your worship is what drives him most. Seeing you clothed in praises frustrates him, like the rejected suitor who sees his coveted date all dressed up for someone else. Nothing embarrasses him worse than seeing someone he has passionately pursued, settled into a lifestyle of praise, happily committed to the Competition.

PRAISE LEADS US INTO CHRIST'S TRIUMPH

We did not participate in Christ's victory over satan; that was His alone. We do, however, fully share in the Lord's *triumph* over His enemies, as Paul makes clear in Second Corinthians 2:14: "Now thanks be to God who always leads us in triumph in Christ, and through us diffuses the fragrance of His knowledge in every place."

Most people think the verb "to triumph" means to win a victory, but in reality it means *to exult in a victory already won.* That's huge, because winning and celebrating are as different as bullets and confetti. One happens on the field of battle and the other on the streets of home. Furthermore the New King

James Version of the Bible's rendering of "triumph" as a noun is a purposeful reference to a specific event, rather than jubilation in the general sense. The apostle was citing a particular kind of Roman celebration that was well known to his readers. It was an allusion not to the winning of a battle, but to the special festivities that followed a definitive victory over a foreign power.

A triumph was the highest honor a Roman general could receive; a magnificent ceremony was awarded him by the state for completely vanquishing a foreign foe (which required a minimum of 5,000 enemy casualties). Dressed in purple and white robes, the hero rode a special circular chariot led by four horses in a grand procession through the streets of Rome.

The day of triumph was a legal holiday, so the people of the city would line the streets to cheer the general and the spectacle that accompanied him. Leading the parade, bound in chains, were the chiefs of the conquered peoples. For the general this was a victory procession; for them it was a death march, ending at a prison where they would be executed.

Next came numerous celebrants bearing the spoils of victory, featuring slaves, wagons of gold, valuable artifacts, and even exotic animals. The grand display often included enormous placards, depicting the battles and detailing the winning strategy.

Behind him a detachment of troops, and sometimes his entire army, marched in splendor all their own.

Colossians 2:15 explains how Jesus celebrated in similar fashion when He conquered satan: "Having disarmed principalities and powers, He made a public spectacle of them, triumphing over them in it." Like a feted Roman general, Jesus totally vanquished His enemy, the devil. He stripped satan of all his powers, inflicted mass casualties amongst hell's principalities, and then "made a public spectacle" of them before all creation.

But there is one part of the procession that we have not described: What about the victor's family? Where are they? In fact, where are *you*? Are you watching from a grandstand, or merely cheering from the sidelines? Or are you running along with the procession, trying your feeble best to keep up?

St. Paul reveals exactly where you are in Second Corinthians 2:14: "Now thanks be to God who always leads us *in* triumph *in* Christ." Where are you? *You are in the chariot with Christ.* The general's family always rode with him in the chariot. And *you* are family!

Notice the adverb: God *always* leads us in triumph in Christ. There is no time or place that God does not lead us in triumph. It is a never-ending celebration, or as one modern translation puts it, "a constant pageant of triumph in Christ" (Moffatt). Furthermore our defeated—no, *utterly* defeated foe is ever on parade before us, a spectacle of perpetual humiliation.

Just picture the scene. There is the shame that clung to you after your divorce, bound in chains, along with the other spirits that have hounded you: fear of cancer, sexual compulsions, substance abuse, career disappointment—they're all there, and they're all chained! So are the hurts from your childhood, even the long-submerged anger at your dad. All the things that bound you have been bound by the Man beside you in the chariot, the One who wears a crown and commands the army that forms your rear guard in this procession. Ephesians 4:8 says, "He led captivity captive." *This is Jesus, your elder Brother. He has bound your past, and you can celebrate now!*

The old idea of preachers admonishing the saints to win the victory is neither biblical nor logical. You cannot win a victory that has already been won. However, you have been invited to join in Christ's triumph. The government of Heaven has declared a perennial, legal holiday, and angels line the boulevards of history, jeering the devil, and cheering the conquering Lord with whom you ride in magnificent procession.

Praise is the way you share in Christ's triumph; it is your place on the program, your contribution to the pageant. King David lived a thousand years before the Romans devised their first triumph, but his words in Psalm 106 are nonetheless prophetic and perfectly appropriate: "Save us, O Lord our God, and gather us from among the Gentiles, to give thanks to Your holy name, *to triumph in Your praise*" (Ps. 106:47).

The lifestyle of praise is one of perpetual celebration, not because you've learned to "fake it" on your off days, but because you are right there with Christ in the Victor's chariot. He has already defeated disease, financial worries, "chronic" depression, and all other snares. *You are set free from your bonds as you release your faith in celebration!*

I'm not speaking figuratively when I say that a lifestyle of praise means continuously celebrating God's goodness. Some people are down all the time, and for some reason, society has come to accept that condition as normal, even naming it "chronic depression." Yet when we speak of a lifestyle of praise, many Christians would call it abnormal or fake. Why? Why not be so practiced in celebrating God's goodness that praise becomes your natural frame of mind? If Romans 12:2 says to "be transformed by the renewing of your mind," doesn't logic dictate that it's possible to actually *be* transformed?

Of course, being transformed doesn't mean undergoing some personality change like the victims in the old B-movie, *Invasion of the Body Snatchers*. It means becoming the *real* you, the person God created you to be. Only that person can offer "perfected praise." If you're a truck driver with oil-stained fingernails, you shouldn't be expected to dance a cute little two-step at church on Sunday morning. But you certainly can lift holy hands to God, as First Timothy 2:8 specifically commands *men* to do. And in any case, whether you're a man's man or a wisp of a woman, as long as you're still breathing, Psalm 150 says you should praise the Lord in one way or another.

PRAISE PREPARES US FOR MIRACLES

You've read about King David's "exit strategy" when he was under attack: "Whoever offers praise glorifies Me; and to him who orders his conduct [way of life] aright I will show the salvation of God" (Ps. 50:23). Praise *as a way of life* puts you in the path of blessing.

But why does the Lord say He *will* show you salvation when you've already been saved? The word for *salvation*, throughout both Testaments, refers to more than the salvation of the soul. It refers to restored health, redeemed relationships, plenty of provision, deliverance from satanic attack—in short, total well-being.

When you develop the habit of praising God, you should expect to see a demonstration of His salvation and deliverance, like Jonah in the Old Testament and Paul and Silas in the Book of Acts.

You already know Jonah, the disobedient prophet whose stubbornness landed him in the belly of a big fish. It took a gut-churning combination of stench and stomach acid to convince the reluctant preacher to repent, and indeed his prayer was desperately eloquent. But then the dying castaway made a startling commitment: "But I will sacrifice to You with the voice of thanksgiving; I will pay what I have vowed. Salvation is of the Lord." *Jonah's vow was the hot button!* The very next verse records God's response: "So the Lord spoke to the fish, and it vomited Jonah onto dry land" (Jonah 2:9-10). The prophet had discovered a literal exit strategy from his acrid prison. When he began to prophesy and to offer thanksgiving to God, he became distasteful to his enemy.

Your enemy, the devil, is in the same predicament. When you offer thanksgiving and praise to God in the midst of suffering, satan finds it utterly nauseating. And not only will the Lord deliver you—your captor will be glad to see you go.

In Acts 16 Paul and Silas were beaten and thrown into the "belly" of a Philippian jail for preaching the Gospel and healing the sick. Badly injured and bound in leg irons, they had no way of escape.

"But at midnight Paul and Silas were praying and singing hymns to God, and the prisoners were listening to them," says Acts 16:25. Their response to suffering was as preposterous as Jonah's, and, of course, so were the consequences. First, there was an earthquake, and their chains fell off. Then, after stopping their panicked jailer from killing himself, they led him to Christ. Before the sun rose they had (a) led his entire family to Jesus, (b) done the same for their fellow inmates, (c) baptized the lot of them, and (d) were released from prison.

Did Paul and Silas start praying and praising God because they thought it might "work" for them, and get them out of jail? No! Praise and thanksgiving was their *lifestyle*. These men knew they were free even behind bars, so they voluntarily stayed put when the dungeon doors had fallen off their hinges. And in a twist that only praise makes possible, the captives set their captor free!

You might not be in a jam like Jonah, and your "midnight" may not be as drastic as that of Paul and Silas, but I have no doubt you're facing problems just as real. In fact, I know it, because I know the enemy of your soul wants to destroy you just as badly as he wanted to destroy them. He fears you, because your praises are just as dangerous to him, and just as damaging to his plans. *When you praise God you destroy the obstacles satan puts in your way.* Praise sets you up for a miracle!

PRAISE BRINGS REVELATION

Revelation comes readily to the Christian for whom praise is a mindset. David said in Psalm 49:4, "I will incline my ear to a proverb; I will disclose my dark saying on the harp." When the spirit of prophecy came upon David, he often uttered "dark sayings," mysteries that he himself did not easily understand. He sang and praised God, as was his habit, and the Holy Spirit frequently would "disclose" just the right lyrics to him. Psalm 22 is a perfect example. The young shepherd who became a king was such a man after God's own heart (see 1 Samuel 13:14) that he actually foresaw the agonies Jesus would experience hundreds of years hence, as He hung dying on the Cross. "My God, My God, why have You forsaken Me?" the song began, before going on to describe Jesus' crucifixion with uncanny accuracy. Praise brought David revelation.

The biblical connection between prophecy and musical expression is important. Old Testament prophets were often also musicians, and the written forms they employed suggest that the *normal* way of expressing prophecy was lyrical, either in poetic odes or songs.

There certainly was something about praise that opened David, as a composer, to the mind of God. His music became a doorway into what Saint Paul would later describe as "a mystery, the hidden wisdom which God ordained before the ages for our glory" (1 Cor. 2:7). For *our* glory—did you see that? *I can promise you, if you submit your heart, mind, and voice to God in a lifestyle of praise and worship, the wisdom of the Scriptures will open to you in ways that will enhance, if not surpass, your intellectual study.*

That kind of flash hit me after the terrorist attacks of September 2001. For the first few days I was in the same state of shock that you probably experienced. I was stunned and almost paralyzed by the sheer enormity of the destruction, especially at Ground Zero in New York City. One evening, I was watching news coverage of the Afghan refugee crisis that had been brought on by the Western coalition's assault on Taliban extremists. Although these savage Muslim radicals were at last being flushed out into the open, the attacks were leaving thousands of widows and orphans in their wake. The sight of those sad, terrified little faces stayed with me day and night.

But amid the gloom, a light was starting to shine in my spirit. Radical Islamists like the Taliban had been wreaking havoc in nation after nation for years, yet staying under the West's radar all the while…until now. Now there would be no more hiding: The demonic mindset of Islam that had grown like a cancer for centuries and now held a billion souls captive, was being exposed at last.

I began to see opportunity rising from the ashes of the attack. *Satan had overplayed his hand, and God must be at work,* I thought. And although I didn't understand the how and when, I knew in my heart that from that one awful day of destruction would come a massive harvest for Christ in the Middle East.

I looked at the television again. Surely those widows and orphans fleeing into the cold, unforgiving Afghan desert, would be open to the Good News. Suddenly I felt my spirit rising, and a voice spoke very distinctly in my heart: "Terry, do you want to sit here like the pundits and curse the darkness, or would you rather light a candle?"

The question came so clearly to my mind that I actually answered it: "Lord, of course I'd rather light a candle." I had no idea in practical terms what lighting a candle would entail, but a few days later my assistant Joel and I were in Afghanistan, ready to find out.

The relief effort that ensued was the beginning of what has become the most productive time of ministry I've ever known. As I write, there is now an underground network of several hundred "Christ-followers" in Afghanistan's principal city of Kabul. Our work subsequently took us into Iraq, where in 2003 we were able to help a handful of local believers plant a church in the city of Irbil. At this writing that congregation numbers more than 3,000 former Muslims, and is by far the largest Christian congregation in the history of the Islamic Middle East. We have also have been privileged to print and distribute millions of pieces of Christian literature, including Arabic Bibles, all over Iraq. And the Lord has allowed us to befriend presidents and prime ministers, and even to influence the writing of the new Iraqi constitution, so that it mandates freedom of religious choice without reprisal.

How did such wonders begin? They started when I sat in front of the evening news, heavy in my spirit, and decided to put on the garment of praise. Then I caught a glimpse of "the hidden wisdom which God ordained before the ages for our glory," and the adventure began. But I would not have seen it, and Heaven's dazzling plan would have gone undone, had I not begun to praise God there at my own Ground Zero.

You may have given up reading the Bible because you feel like you just don't "get it." Well, it's true that the mind of God is inscrutable, and in fact, First Corinthians 13:12 compares trying to understand His will with squinting into a dim mirror. But while you will never see with perfect clarity until you behold the Lord face to face, praise will at least take some fog off the mirror! Let a spirit of praise illumine your contemplation of God and His Word, and you *will* start to get it. And don't be surprised when some strange little seed of a thought blossoms into a grand accomplishment of God's will in your life.

A mindset of praise, like a good pair of bifocals, will sharpen your ability to distinguish the subtle shadings of God's Word. That's important, because revelation is not optional. "Man shall not live by bread alone," Jesus told the tempter in Matthew 4:4, "but by every word [*rhema*] that proceeds [is now proceeding] from the mouth of God."

There is a *now* Word of God for you, a *now* revelation from the Holy Spirit, that has direct bearing on your circumstances. Praise prepares you to receive this Word, by which God will reveal "the mystery of His will, according to His good pleasure which He purposed in Himself" (Eph. 1:9).

PROTOCOL OF PRAISE

Everyone has a fundamental hunger for God's presence; you and I were *created* for His fellowship. Yet many Christians feel far from the Lord when they pray, as though there is a gulf between them that they cannot cross. Maybe you know the Scriptures and you've memorized your church's key doctrines, yet you're still like the pastor that once lamented to a friend of mine, "I feel like I know everything about Christianity except Christ." So what's wrong?

The Scriptures are quite clear that praise is man's only avenue of access to God. King David was both eloquent and straightforward about this fact in Psalm 100:4: "Enter into His gates with thanksgiving, and into His courts with praise. Be thankful to Him, and bless His name." This is not a formula; it is a protocol. If you want to enter into God's presence, there is no other way. **Praise is the palace protocol.**

I learned about protocols when the Lord took my missionary team, Living Sound, to Vatican City. In 1974, during a concert in a Roman Catholic church in Tampa, Florida, the Holy Spirit had impressed me that He was going to give us a season of worldwide ministry to Catholics. Three months later we found ourselves in St. Anne's Cathedral in downtown Warsaw, Poland, where at the close of our very first concert, hundreds of people jammed the sacristy, responding to Christ's claims on their lives.

Within days the nation's primate, Stephan Cardinal Wyszynski, had invited us to sing and preach in all of Poland's cathedrals. He told me that the ruling communists thoroughly controlled his country's school system, and they were telling the students that God was dead. "But," he said, "they will listen to your music and your praise to God."

The next year Cardinal Wyszynski opened his homeland's dioceses to us, and we blanketed the nation, singing and preaching in packed Catholic basilicas, cathedrals, and churches. We were also his Eminence's guests of honor at the Festival of the Black Madonna in the city of Czestochowa, where 150,000 celebrants gathered on the grounds of a Paulite monastery called Jasnagora.

In 1976 we returned to the festival, this time leading nearly 300,000 spiritually hungry Poles before God's throne in praise and worship. Also attending that year was Poland's junior cardinal from Krakow, Karol Cardinal Wojtyla, a smiling, vigorous man in his mid-50s. He listened to us sing and preach, and later invited us to his home in southern Poland for fellowship. It quickly became apparent that he loved young people, and also loved our music.

When Joel Vesanen, our team manager, asked Cardinal Wojtyla for a letter of recommendation, he hesitated, saying that he was just an obscure cleric from the south of Poland, with a name no one in the West would know. Nevertheless, he wrote the letter of blessing. Two years later Karol Wojtyla took a new name, Pope John Paul II, as the College of Cardinals stunned the world by electing him the first non-Italian pontiff in four centuries!

In 1980 Pope John Paul II invited us to give a special concert at the Vatican in Rome. I will never forget August 13, 1980, when we stood on the steps of St. Peter's Basilica, testifying and singing the praises of God before 60,000 people. I will also never forget the protocol laid out for us by Monsignor Monduzzi, the Pope's personal secretary. The monsignor took me aside and instructed me in the ways that a Protestant addresses the Pope. It quickly became clear that our visit would be quite different from the one in his living room back in Poland. The regulations were simple, but precise, and very strict. Yet knowing them somehow set me at ease.

Protocols are necessary, and they vary greatly, depending upon the dignitary and his domain. There is one protocol for meeting the Queen of England, and quite another for meeting the President of the United States. There are even special protocols for these two heads of state when they meet, procedures that vary depending upon where the meeting takes place.

There is also a protocol for obtaining an audience with the King of kings, a requirement that must be met by prince and pauper alike: approach His royal presence with a song of praise. This certainly doesn't mean you can't bring your petitions—and even complaints—to God. Quite a few of the psalms were composed by songwriters getting things off their chests. But according to Heaven's protocol, petition and supplication do not grant you access to the King. That's why the psalmists invariably couched their complaints in praise. It was their *admission ticket*.

"You shall call your walls Salvation, and your gates Praise," Isaiah rhapsodized about the City of God (Isa. 60:18b). Old Jerusalem is ringed with several gates, among them the Sheep's Gate, the Lion Gate, even a Dung Gate. Likewise the heavenly Jerusalem, the place of total provision, is also gated on all sides. Yet unlike those of any man-made city, every gate leading into God's presence—into the fullness of salvation—bears a single name: Praise.

GOD INHABITS OUR PRAISES

You've read about entering into God's presence through praise, but in another sense praise also invites the Lord into *your* presence. Psalm 22:3 says, "But You are holy, enthroned in the praises of Israel." That is why it is so necessary for you to praise God; *it brings the power of His presence into your life.*

God is always King of kings, always worthy of praise whether you bow or not. He is completely sufficient in Himself, the all-knowing, all-powerful, omnipresent Possessor of all things. Yet He waits for you to build Him a throne with your praises, your *tehillim* (see Chapter 8). When you offer up spiritual songs, you are building a throne, and Psalm 22 is your guarantee that He will come and seat Himself upon it.

When we, as the Church, join together to praise the Lord, aside from the myriad benefits cited throughout these pages, we literally offer a throne to our King, one He finds most attractive. The Hebrew word for enthroned is *yashab*, meaning "to sit down," but in a permanent sense. In ancient times it meant more popularly "to move in," and was even used in some instances to refer to the commencement of a marriage. In other words, the Psalmist is saying that *God wants to "move in," to take up permanent residence in the spiritual songs His people sing to Him.*

The opposite is also true, of course. When we do not praise the Lord, we are withholding His chair, blocking the throne of our hearts. That is why any church service without praise is truly pointless. If we go to church to enter God's presence, but do not enthrone Him with our praises, then the service is null and void. Our time and effort have been wasted.

Of course, we know that Jesus promised in Matthew 18:20 that, "where two or three are gathered together in My name, I am there in the midst of them." But notice that He specifies "in My name," i.e., in the *unity* of His name. The Lord spoke these words about the exercise of governmental authority in His Church, but let's not fool ourselves. Such unity is not achieved because of membership cards or denominational status. Indeed, there have been many gatherings where Christians were technically "one," but the Lord was in no way present.

To the contrary, our unity in Christ is a *living*, dynamic oneness. We are His Body, filled with His Holy Spirit, empowered by His love (see Gal. 5:6). And it is praise that stills the cacophony of a thousand cultures and gives us a single voice. *Our unity is in praise*, and that is what forms His throne. *Our praise, as one people joyfully gathered in His name, is God's favorite place to rest and relax.*

WORLDVIEW

Lifestyle is an all-encompassing word. It speaks of one's life choices and habits. We use the term to describe people whose lives we find attractive, as well as those who repulse us. In this chapter I have spoken of praise as a lifestyle because I want you to understand that it is not merely one Christian activity among others. Praise is not an optional or "alternative" lifestyle. It should permeate your *worldview*, the way tinted sunglasses color their wearer's world. *Life should be seen through the lens of praise.*

Your worldview is the set of assumptions you make concerning the way the world works. It's something you generally don't think about, yet depend upon all the time. Berkeley Professor Phillip Johnson describes it perfectly:

> Understanding worldview is a bit like trying to see the lens of one's own eye. We do not ordinarily see our own worldview, but we see everything else by looking through it. Put simply, our worldview is the window

by which we view the world, and decide, often sub-consciously, what is real and important, or unreal and unimportant.[2]

It should be no surprise, then, that God also finds some lifestyles attractive, but is repulsed by others. Thus, really knowing Him, really knowing "the love of Christ which passes knowledge" (Eph. 3:19), means adopting a lifestyle that enthrones the Lord and humiliates the devil.

THE LIFESTYLE OF PRAISE

Did I feel like a fake at first, always praising God when every-thing in my life seemed to be going wrong? Sure I did. But the beauty of adopting praise as a lifestyle is that it eventually be-comes a habit, if not a reflex. Praising God became my natural response to adversity, because I had been "transformed by the re-newing of [my] mind" (Rom. 12:2).

I believe the same thing can happen to you. *I believe praise can become your regular frame of mind.* Now, let's take another look at the ways in which such a transformation takes place.

❖ First, I told you that praise on your lips silences the devil's accusations against you.

❖ Second, I have encouraged you to "put on" the gar-ment of praise that Christ Jesus has given you, be-cause a mindset of praise is like a coat of armor on your attitude.

❖ Third, I have painted the picture of your place in Christ, which is right beside Him in the Victor's chariot, and pointed out that praising Him is your official assignment in the grand pageant of His triumph.

(handwritten margin note: how about holiness?)

❖ Fourth, praising God sets you up for God's power to be displayed in your life, and His wisdom to be unfolded to you.

❖ Fifth, I have shown you that praise is the official protocol for entering into God's presence, and that no other way is acceptable or even possible.

❖ Sixth, I've shown you how your songs of praise enthrone God, not just temporarily, but for permanent residence in your life.

❖ Finally, I have emphasized the importance of adopting a mentality of praise, that you "wear" it like a pair of glasses, so you can look at the world through it.

Allowing praise to become a mentality—a permanent frame of mind—will enable you to prove the will of God, regardless of the difficulties you face. Sure it will make the devil angry. But I can tell you from years of experience that it also wears him out!

ENDNOTES

1. http://www.nimh.nih.gov/health/publications/ the-numbers-count-mental-disorders-in-america. shtml#MajorDepressive; accessed 4/24/08.

2. Phillip Johnson, in Nancy Pearcey, *Total Truth* (Wheaton, IL: Crossway Books, 2005), Foreword.

Chapter 12

The Confession of Praise

So the mouth: more important than the heart.[7]

Satan's strategy is to capture our hearts in order ultimately to gain control of our mouths, because whoever controls the mouth takes dominion.

~

On October 29, 1941, British Prime Minister Sir Winston Churchill, visited his childhood alma mater Harrow School, and during the course of speaking to the students, made a statement that became one of his most famous:

Never give in. Never give in, never, never, never, never—in nothing, great or small, large or petty—never give in, except to convictions of honour and good sense! Never yield to force; never yield to the apparently overwhelming might of the enemy.[1]

Churchill was speaking about England's war against Adolph Hitler, of course, but his words also could easily have been spoken about his frequent bouts with depression, what he called "my Black Dog." Many psychologists and historians believe, in fact, that the great statesman suffered what is sometimes called "bi-polar disorder," or "manic depression." In any case, most of them agree that his gift for oratory not only rallied the soul of the British people, but his own as well.

Fewer people know, however, that Sir Winston's speaking gift was no gift at all, but a hard-earned skill. Author and Churchill expert Stephen Mansfield explains:

> Among Churchill's chief obstacles in becoming an effective speaker was his maddening lisp...[He] also wrestled with his inner self in becoming a great speaker. He was very emotional and during his speeches he was often so overcome that tears streamed down his cheeks and he could not continue. It embarrassed him and made some of his speeches uncomfortably sentimental, but he never found the key to containing his emotions. It is probably good that he did not, since the genius of his words were their passion, tempered only by vision and learning, not by stifling self-control.[2]

According to Mansfield, Churchill wrote his speeches word for word in longhand, writing detailed cues in the margins—including when to stutter—in order to create the "illusion of spontaneity."

> To master these, he practiced sometimes up to eight hours for one speech-in front of a mirror, often doing his best work in the bathtub...[He] knew his limitations: "I am not an orator. An orator is spontaneous." Instead, he worked on the "carefully pre-

pared impromptu" until it became second nature, and it paid off. "His speeches set the whole kingdom on fire," Lord Ismay said. "He gave you a kind of exaltation. He made you feel that you were taking part in something great and memorable."[3]

The world—and England in particular—is fortunate that the Old Bulldog never gave up on himself, but instead "mobilized the English language and sent it into battle."[4] Winston Churchill knew better than most the critical importance of a good confession.

CONFESSION OF PRAISE

Hebrews 13:15 is the classic New Testament verse on the sacrifice of praise: "Therefore by Him let us continually offer the sacrifice of praise to God, that is, the fruit of our lips, giving thanks to His name." The Amplified Bible broadens it: "Through Him therefore let us constantly and at all times offer up to God a sacrifice of praise, which is the fruit of lips that thankfully acknowledge and *confess* and glorify His Name."

Acknowledge, confess, and glorify. When I first saw that I was intrigued. I could understand how acknowledging and glorifying God were connected to praising Him, but why was the word *confess* included? Most people invariably associate that word with an admission of guilt or the recounting of their sins before a priest. But those are negative connotations. On the positive side confession is similar to *profession*; it is a declaration of one's faith in God's Word.

This is what the writer of Hebrews means by "the fruit of our lips, giving thanks to His name." The phrase "giving thanks" is a liberal interpretation of the Greek word *homologeo*, which in most other New Testament passages is translated as "confessing to." The latter part of the verse, then, is more literally translated as "the fruit of lips confessing to His name." The American Standard Version, in fact, renders it "the fruit of lips which make confession to his name,"[5] and the Berkley Version of the New Testament translates it as "confession in His name."[6] This distinction is crucial if we are truly to comprehend the sacrifice of praise.

W.E. Vine's *Expository Dictionary of New Testament Words* reveals the full weight of the word *homologeo*: "*to speak the same thing,* to assent, agree with; to confess, declare, to confess by way of admitting oneself guilty; to confess or declare openly by way of speaking out freely, such confession being the effect of deep conviction of facts; *to confess by way of celebrating with praise.*"[7] In other words, confession is either a frank admission of sin or a strong declaration of praise.

There is the key! *Your sacrifice of praise, more than anything else, means that you constantly glorify God by continually saying the same thing with your mouth that He says in His Word.* It means bringing your day-to-day speech into agreement with the written Word of God.

Very few Christians realize the doctrinal importance of confession in both the Old and New Testaments. Paul, in fact, quoted Psalm 116:10 in his second letter to the Corinthian church: "And since we have the same spirit of faith, according to what is written, *'I believed, therefore I spoke,'* we also believe and therefore speak, knowing that He who raised up the Lord Jesus will also raise us up with Jesus, and will present us with you" (2 Cor. 4:13-14).

That's a good description of the process of confession. If you're going to enjoy a living faith, it must have a means of expression. *Faith that does not speak is stillborn.*

No one understands that truth better than General Georges Sada, Iraq's deputy national security advisor, who also works extensively with my ministry, World Compassion.[8] The only Christian ever to serve in Saddam Hussein's cabinet, Georges now travels with me, telling his story and proclaiming the Gospel throughout the Western world. Together we are spearheading a mission to Iraq that has taken us from the villages of Kurdistan to the streets of Baghdad, and on numerous recent occasions, to the White House.

When I met him after the war of liberation in 2003, Georges was Iraq's newly appointed defense minister. It was a dangerous job to be sure, but not nearly as perilous as the ethical tightrope he had walked for years before—a modern Daniel, he had served God and Saddam at the same time, and lived to tell about it.

In 1990 when Saddam wanted to invade Israel with 98 jet fighters laden with chemical weapons, "the Christian"—as the dictator called him—single-handedly talked him out of it. When the Iraqi strong man's demonized son, Qusay, wanted to execute 45 downed coalition pilots, including 21 American POWs, during the first Gulf war a few months later, General Sada—at peril of instant execution—invoked the prisoners' Geneva rights. Their lives were spared. When Brazilian officials offered him a $4 million bribe during negotiations for military aircraft, Georges refused. A few days later Saddam executed a fellow negotiator, who had succumbed to an identical bribe.

How did Georges Sada manage to survive in such treacherous surroundings? Like King David and Saint Paul, this servant of the

Almighty *believed*, and therefore he *spoke*. His firm commitment to confessing the truth is the reason he is alive today.

REEDUCATING THE HEART

The Scriptures consistently demonstrate a connection between the mouth and the heart. Jesus said in Matthew 12:34, "...For out of the abundance of the heart the mouth speaks." It is inevitable. Whatever fills the heart eventually will be spoken, because *the mouth is the faucet of the heart.*

Does that statement strike you in a good way or a fearful one? If your heart already abounds with God's Word, it probably gladdens you to read it. But if your heart is filled with fear, and your mind is gripped with worry, it probably just adds to the pressure. Truth cuts both ways.

Satan wants to build strongholds in your mind that crowd out everything else, so that there is no room for God's Word to enter and prosper there. He wants his lies to so pervade your thoughts that they become things you meditate upon and accept as truth. His strategy is to capture your heart in order to ultimately gain control of your mouth, because *whoever controls the mouth takes dominion.*

God created the world with His Word (see John 1), and still rules His creation accordingly (see Hebrews 1:3). He also created man in His image, to rule the earth under Him by obeying and enforcing that Word. Therefore if satan can turn man's heart and capture his tongue, he usurps man's dominion over the earth.

That is why your mouth is ground zero in the war for the universe. Once your heart is captured, the devil knows your mouth will speak from its abundance. *Whoever controls the mouth controls the man.* Then satan can spread his war on God to other hearts, as he uses you to fire his rockets of gossip, backbiting, division, hatred, fear, and every other conceivable evil.

Like Peter's Galilean accent, a person's speech betrays him. I have found that I usually only need to spend about half an hour with a person before I know what's in his heart, because he reveals it with his mouth. The more our words line up with the enemy's thought system, the deeper it takes root in our souls, controlling us from the inside out. Disease often captures people in exactly this way. That is why physicians and medical researchers alike note that a good attitude helps the body in fighting diseases like cancer, while those who "give up" in their minds succumb much sooner in their bodies.

In fact Dr. Jim Winslow, long-time physician and former director of a well-known Midwest hospital, once told me that 60 to 70 percent of all disease begins with a thought. Fear of disease, for example, initiates chemical reactions in the body that create an opportune environment in which disease can flourish.

LEARNING BY MOUTH

Jesus declared in Matthew 10:32, "Therefore whoever confesses Me before men, him I will also confess before My Father who is in heaven." And in Romans Paul expounds on what the Savior meant. Notice the connection he makes between heart and mouth.

But what does it say? "The word is near you, in your mouth and in your heart" (that is, the word of faith which we preach): that if you confess with your mouth the Lord Jesus and believe in your heart that God has raised Him from the dead, you will be saved. For with the heart one believes unto righteousness, and with the mouth confession is made unto salvation (Romans 10:8-10).

In verses 8 and 9 the apostle mentions the mouth first and then the heart, but in verse 10 he reverses the order, emphasizing the heart first and then the mouth. This pattern is both deliberate and sensible. For example, suppose you are ill. You must begin by putting God's Word in your mouth, acting on will rather than feeling, bringing that Word against the sickness. By confessing with your mouth the same thing God says in His Word, you receive it into your heart. And the more often you confess it, the more firmly you establish it there.

At some point your heart will become fully persuaded by the Word in your mouth. This is the moment of *rhema* revelation. Until now your mouth has been in the lead, but from now on your confession will *follow* your heart. You have reeducated your heart, and your mind has been renewed and transformed with regard to the sickness (see Romans 12:2). In other words, agreeing with God's Word has become your natural response. This is the faith that brings healing.

When my coauthor, Jim Gilbert, first proposed to his future wife, Dolly, she told him she would marry him only if her father could walk her down the aisle. "I took it as a 'no,'" he says. "Dolly's dad had multiple sclerosis and hadn't taken a step in seven years. It's an incurable disease, so I just about gave up hope we would ever marry."

But the situation wasn't such a dead end after all. "I got everybody at our little church in Baltimore praying regularly for her dad," he grins, admitting that his motives were partly selfish. "But one Sunday morning, as I started to lead the congregation in prayer, an inner voice stopped me with my mouth open. 'Don't ask me again,' the Holy Spirit said. I know some people hold the opinion that we should never ask God for anything more than once, because it means we didn't asked in faith the first time. But I really sensed that God was directing me."

Jim told the congregation what he was hearing. "We all think in pictures. If I say 'pink elephant,' you can't help but see one in your mind. Well, from now on when we think of Mr. Holste, let's not picture a sick man lying in a bed. Let's think of him as well and strong, up and walking around, and let's praise God for healing him!"

From that day forward the congregation did just that. They praised God with every mention of Dolly's father. Then, a couple of months later, Jim had to make a trip overseas.

"I had been gone for about two weeks when a letter arrived from my own father, who pastored a church nearby. He had gone to visit Mr. Holste and was completely shocked when the man, himself, answered the door!

"I quickly called home and Dolly told me what had happened. Her dad's back had been hurting lately, so he had gone to the renowned Johns Hopkins Hospital for tests. The doctors were baffled, and told him that his back was hurting because he just needed exercise, that he didn't have a trace of MS in his body. I still remember the quote: 'We know you had it, and now you don't. But MS is incurable, so we can't explain what has happened.'

"The following February, Dad Holste walked his daughter down the aisle at our wedding," says Jim. "In fact he nearly upstaged the bride, because so many people were crying at the sight of him walking. He lived another 28 years, and the doctors at

Johns Hopkins never did give him a release, because they didn't know what to write."

Jim's entire church renewed their minds and reeducated their hearts with the Word of God, and when they heard the Lord's direction they devoted themselves to a continuous sacrifice of praise. I have no doubt that Dolly's dad was healed as a direct result.

In English we refer to *memorization* as "learning by heart," but Jim's church in Baltimore did what in Hebrew is called "learning by mouth." It's really a more accurate description of the way we learn. I still remember poems I memorized in grade school, because I repeated them over and over by mouth until I knew them in my heart.

Spiritual warfare demands that you develop the same self-discipline. Every time the devil attacks you, whether in mind or body, you must counter him by confessing God's Word. Obviously this involves a struggle, since the Word of God is saying something contrary to what you are experiencing. And if a predisposition already exists in this area, the struggle will be more pronounced, because your feelings will tell you that God's Word cannot be true.

The sacrifice of praise is in essence a good confession focused upon the Person of Jesus. It is an act of the will rather than a reaction to emotion. It quite literally is confessing to the name of Jesus, not because we feel fit to make such an offering, but because He is always worthy to receive it.

Some people take the sensible practice of scriptural confession and abuse it. When approached mechanistically or legalistically, confession degenerates into nothing more than a mind-over-matter technique. Emile Coue, the "prophet of autosuggestion," told his followers to repeat daily, "Every day and in every way I'm getting better and better."[9] But God is not a cosmic puppet who dances when we pull His strings. He is a Father who delights in answering the requests of His children, as we attempt—however imperfectly—to imitate His ways.

A legalistic confession is as damaging to one's faith as a bad one. Remember when you learned your multiplication tables? You recited them over and over, the twos, the threes, and so on. You dwelt on them so much that you might even have dreamed of numbers stacked on numbers. Why were you so slavishly devoted to learning them? The answer is that *you were a slave to them in order to become their master.*

This is key to understanding a proper confession. The sacrifice of praise keeps you close to Father's heart. It colors your approach to Scripture, and keeps you from lapsing into "vain repetition" (see Matt. 6:7). A good confession is motivated by love for God and His Word. King David said, "Oh, how I love Your law! It is my meditation all the day" (Ps. 119:97). That's what makes His Word become a living *rhema* in you, and allows the Holy Spirit to open your eyes to His will. Remember, you can only confess those things in Scripture that are His expressed will for you. You don't simply pick and choose Bible promises to suit your tastes, as though you were customizing a gourmet hamburger. Instead, you must ask God to give you His taste!

I have referred to confession as a "process." God has made it a matter of cause and effect, i.e., when *this* happens, then *that* happens. In Romans 10:10 Paul said, "For with the heart one believes *unto* righteousness, and with the mouth confession is made *unto* salvation." The word *unto* indicates a progression. In other words, as you continue to make the right confession with your mouth, you advance into the various provisions of your salvation. But what exactly are those provisions?

In the New Testament the Greek verb *sozo* is usually translated "to save." But the meaning of this word goes far beyond the forgiveness of sins. Salvation involves redemption and healing in every aspect of life, including deliverance from evil spirits, healing of the body, even resurrection from the dead. It is a word that sums up all the benefits provided in the death and resurrection of Jesus.

DOORWAY OF FAITH

A good confession is the doorway of faith. You can lay hold of the myriad benefits of salvation by walking through that doorway into the realm of unswerving faith. And because it focuses upon confession to the name of Jesus, I believe *the sacrifice of praise will lead you into a total manifestation of the salvation Jesus purchased for you on the Cross* Think of it as a room containing healing for your child, freedom from the depression that has hounded you since high school, liberation from the shame of divorce, and guilt for that abortion. And the key that unlocks that room is the song of praise on your lips.

The sacrifice of praise essentially is a profession of heartfelt agreement with the Word of God. It is the deliberate, joyful repetition of Father's Word back to Him. You can take the words of the Psalms and other truths of Scripture, and sing them as a triumphant anthem in the presence of God. This will move your emotions, and even your physical state, into line with the declared Word of Almighty God, who delights in displaying His healing power in response to praise.

This is why people are consistently healed in my meetings. As they enter the presence of God through a sacrifice of praise, their spirits are released to believe for miracles. And when an entire congregation offers a sacrifice of praise with one voice, their collective confession becomes an awesome force, toppling strongholds that have bound individual minds and bodies. I saw this happen at Mt. Paran Church near Atlanta. Thousands of us gathered for a Sunday evening healing service. The people, I'm happy to say, were enthusiastic, praising God with all their might. In the middle of the service I sensed that someone was being healed of multiple sclerosis, but no one responded when I asked who it was. After the service I was walking to my car with Dr. Paul Walker, the pastor, when a lady approached us on the parking lot. She had been diagnosed with MS eight years earlier and lately had begun rapidly losing control over her motor functions. She knew something had happened during the service, but since the change wasn't visible she hadn't come forward when I called. Seven years later, however, when I returned to Mt. Paran Church, the same lady greeted me. She had been perfectly healthy ever since.

I also saw a different kind of "congregation" praise God for a different kind of "healing" several years ago in communist Cuba. My daughter Shawna and I had been caught with Bibles stuffed in our suitcases and clothing, and were relieved when the customs officials decided to let us go. We hurried outside, a blast of tropical air hitting us in the face, and found our "ride," a vintage flat-bed truck from the World War II era. Our hosts were nervous and just as eager to leave as we were, so they hustled us into the slat-sided bed and quickly took off.

Being seen with foreigners would mean big trouble for the men up front, so they asked Shawna and me to lie down. We rode for hours in the heat and noise, shifting from our backs to our stomachs and back again as we made our way into the mountains east of Havana. The battered old machine had no muffler, and blue smoke constantly billowed up the sides and into our faces. Out in the countryside we'd occasionally stand up to get a breath of fresh air, quickly ducking for cover every time we saw headlights.

I had been trying to sleep, counting potholes instead of sheep, when a curious odor stirred me at about 2 A.M. I remembered these fumes from my farm days in Canada and rolled over close to Shawna. "We're in trouble," I whispered. "The transmission is burning up." No sooner had the words left my lips than the clutch began to slip. In seconds the truck ground to a halt, and the air filled with the acrid odor of burning oil and hot metal.

Now we were in bigger trouble: we faced a long nighttime hike through mountainous tropical terrain and stood a very good chance of getting caught by the police to boot. But our Cuban brothers thought differently.

They cheerfully invited us to get out of the truck and join hands with them in prayer. Within moments they were chattering enthusiastically in Spanish, and I could tell they must be praising God. After a few moments, one of them broke ranks and crawled under the truck, while the other two kept praying. Then he gingerly touched the hot transmission casing and spoke loudly in Spanish. I couldn't believe it—this man was laying hands on the truck and commanding it to be repaired!

This is ridiculous, I thought, as they finished praying and motioned us back toward the truck. Since they hadn't tried cranking the engine yet, I just stood there. "There's no use," I told my daughter. "It's pointless." But the brothers insisted that we climb back aboard, so I helped Shawna to her spot and then followed suit.

The next thing to backfire was Terry Law's pride. The driver fired the engine and let out the clutch, and off we hurtled at full speed. In a little while we had reached our destination, and the next morning, while Shawna and I slept, the driver headed for the mechanic's shop in Camaguey. There was nothing wrong with the truck, the repairman said, topping off the fluid. And the old Cuban miracle truck was indeed "healed," and served us well for the rest of our mission.

Those Cuban brothers might not have known the theology of a triumph (see Chapter 11), but they sure knew how to celebrate one! Exulting in the liberating greatness of God ultimately means that disease will have to go. You may waver at first, as I did, when you're caught in the tension between your all-too-real symptoms and the immutable truths of the Word, but a true sacrifice of praise will get you up the mountain!

THE HIGH PRIESTHOOD OF JESUS

The main theme of the Book of Hebrews is the high priesthood of Jesus Christ. It is a profound revelation of His ministry as your Advocate before the Father. Christ is enthroned at the Father's right hand, where He "always lives to make intercession for [you]" (Heb. 7:25). The upshot is this: Jesus prays for you, and has become your personal Guarantor of God's promises. He is your full-time, personal Attorney.

But there is a potential limitation upon His priestly ministry in your behalf. *The high priesthood of Jesus Christ is directly linked to the confession of your mouth.* Hebrews 3:1 calls Him "the Apostle and High Priest of *our confession.*" Lest this sound like heresy—that we can manipulate God—let me point out a key aspect of the ministry of a priest: *he can only offer to God what the worshiper brings to Him.* So what should you bring to Him: grumbling, pessimism, worry, or complaints about someone who wronged you? No, you should offer His own promises back to Him, like Jehoshaphat in Second Chronicles 20 and Nehemiah in Nehemiah 1, who stood there before God, quoting His own covenant to Him. God is delighted when you remind Him of His Word, because it gives your High Priest something to work with.

In my meetings, when an entire congregation is caught up in singing God's Word back to Him, their combined faith rises like incense before His throne. Then healings begin to take place naturally, a sure sign that our High Priest has taken our confession directly to the Father in our behalf.

HOLD FAST

Hebrews 4:14 stresses the importance of holding fast to your confession: "Seeing then that we have a great High Priest who has passed through the heavens, Jesus the Son of God, *let us hold fast our confession.*" Once you have brought your own words into alignment with God's Word, resolve to keep them that way. The writer—in fact, the Holy Spirit who *inspired* the writer—knew that his readers would encounter resistance, changing circumstances, and stress. So he emphasized the importance of perseverance, of doggedly clinging to God's Word, which does not change.

Hebrews 10:21-23 makes the same point again, with added emphasis:

> *[A]nd having a High Priest over the house of God, let us draw near with a true heart in full assurance of faith, having*

our hearts sprinkled from an evil conscience and our bodies washed with pure water. **Let us hold fast the confession of our hope without wavering, for He who promised is faith-ful** (Hebrews 10:21-23).

This passage actually completes a progression. It begins at Hebrews 3:1, where Jesus is called "the Apostle and High Priest of our confession." Then Hebrews 4:14 adds that you must hold fast to your confession, an allusion to the fact that winds of opposition are inevitable. Finally, Hebrews 10 emphasizes holding fast *without wavering*, because "He who promised is faithful." **You can hold fast with confidence to a confession that does not change because it is linked to a High Priest who cannot change!**

Jesus is *continually* before the Father on your behalf. His blood *continually* cleanses you from sin, making you *continually* presentable before the Father. Therefore, a *continual* confession of praise on your part keeps the blessings of salvation flowing. What great force praise unleashes on the earth!

Satan tries to make your sacrifice of praise and worship dependent on how you feel. He attacks your mind in every way possible to tear you away from praising God. He knows as soon as you enter into praise you will begin to confess the name of Jesus. You will use the Word, the Name, and the Blood as the weapons God designed them to be, smashing the strongholds of disease and bondage the devil intended to permanently wreck your life.

"You're not worthy to praise God." That is probably the most common thought-bomb launched against Christians, no doubt because it has proven the most effective. *But you must never praise God based upon your worthiness to offer praise.* After all, if you were worthy, you wouldn't need a High Priest.

When the Queen of England rides in royal procession along the avenues of London, everyone waves—noblemen, commoners, even the pickpockets, if only with one hand! They are not concerned about their worthiness to honor Her Majesty. Instead they deem her worthy to *receive* honor. How much more should you praise the King of Heaven who, at all times, in every circumstance, is worthy to receive all praise!

Holding fast to your confession of praise means yielding "in nothing, great or small, large or petty." The Word of God is always true, and your High Priest is always interceding for you. Surrendering, even wavering a little, must be unthinkable.

My mandate from God to take the Gospel into closed countries has, over the years, brought me into increasingly precarious situations. After all, today's world is much more dangerous than it was in 1970. Ministering in places like China, Afghanistan, Cuba, Iraq, and North Korea has tested the limits of my confession. But like Paul, I am determined that I will "not lose heart. Even though [my] outward man is perishing, yet [my] inward *man* is being renewed day by day" (2 Cor. 4:16).

Like Sir Winston himself, I will "never give in. Never give in. Never. Never. Never. Never."

ENDNOTES

1. Winston S. Churchill, *Never Give In! The Best of Winston Churchill's Speeches* (New York: Pimlico, Random House UK Limited, 2003).

2. Stephen Mansfield, *Never Give In: The Extraordinary Character of Winston Churchill* (Nashville, TN: Cumberland House Publishing, Inc., 1995), 175.

3. Ibid., 176–177.

4. Ibid., 174.

5. The American Standard Version. Copyright 1901 by Thomas Nelson & Sons and 1929 by International Council of Religious Education. Published by Thomas Nelson, Inc., Nashville, TN.

6. The Modern Language Bible: The Berkeley Version in Modern English. Copyright © 1945, 1959, 1969 by Zondervan Publishing House, Grand Rapids, MI.

7. W.E. Vine, *An Expository Dictionary of New Testament Words,* vol. 1 (Old Tappan, NJ: Revell, 1966), 224.

8. General Sada's book, *Saddam's Secrets,* was published in 2006 by Integrity Publishers and is available at www.worldcompassion.tv, and in bookstores.

9. http://www.durbinhypnosis.com/coue.htm; accessed 3/30/08.

Chapter 13

Praise and Angels

---

by Jim Gilbert

Twenty-seven years later those words proved accurate. As they say, the proof of the pudding is in the eating. If I doubted before, I do not now.

~

When Iraq's fugitive ex-dictator Saddam Hussein was captured on December 13, 2003, multitudes of jubilant Iraqis quickly filled the streets of Baghdad. Women cried, grown men danced, and celebrating soldiers fired AK-47s into the air. I know because they woke me from a hard-earned mid-afternoon sleep.

I had checked into my hotel in the wee hours that morning. The Baghdad airport had been bombed out of commission, so my team and I had traveled the dangerous 600-mile trip from Amman, Jordan, on the ground. Even Nebuchadnezzar's wildest dreams had not included the specter of a white Chevy Suburban streaking across the sands of Babylon at a dozen times camel speed. But that's what you do when your route takes you past terrorist hotbeds like Ramadi and Fallujah.

Four days later we had finished our ministry business and were ready to retrace the perilous route back to Amman. News of the fallen strong man's capture meant it would be even more perilous. Pro-Saddam insurgents would surely attempt to show themselves still strong.

We left under the cover of early morning darkness, made even darker by a blanket of heavy fog. The thick mist might slow us down, but it would also make us less visible to would-be attackers.

I sat up front next to our Arab driver, my knees propped against the dashboard. The hum of the tires had me nodding off before we'd left the city limits. Fallujah and Ramadi were within the first hundred miles—if I were fortunate, I'd sleep right through that part of the trip.

Suddenly I awakened to the sound of cursing, and then a crash that coincided with an instantaneous, excruciating pain in my knees. There was blood on my left leg as I tried to climb out of the mangled mess that moments ago had been our SUV. *We've been ambushed*, I thought. We were now on the outskirts of Fallujah, and Al Qaeda was known for staging roadblocks like this one.

We had been speeding through the fog at more than 80 miles an hour when we hit the front quarter panel of the other car. We would learn a little later that the other motorist had simply run out of gas. But that relatively reassuring fact was still unknown to me, as I paced back and forth beside the wreck, trying to walk off the pain while I waited for Al Qaeda machine guns to appear.

At that very moment—as suddenly as the crash—the peace of God settled on me, as I remembered something a man had told me nearly 25 years earlier.

> *You have been chosen and prepared by God for a very special work, that of being in the forefront of His work in penetrating darkened countries with His life-giving light...God has opened to you long-closed doors and has accompanied you by His Spirit. You are a chosen messenger. The Father has given you guidance and protection. He has provided for you in ways you have not known by His Spirit, by men, and by angels of the Lord.*

Darkened countries...guidance and protection...angels. At once I knew my friends and I would be all right, and that the pain in my legs was only temporary. I smiled inwardly and thought of Psalm 23:6, that says, "surely goodness and mercy shall follow me all the days of my life." "Goodness and mercy—those must be the names of my guardian angels," I joked to myself. "They sure are getting a workout this week."

The words spoken to me a quarter century earlier had proven truly prophetic. As they say, the proof of the pudding is in the eating. If I doubted before, I do not now.

A KEY MINISTRY OF ANGELS

Angels are "ministering spirits" from God. They are protectors, warriors, and celestial errand runners, delivering everything from messages to miracles (1 Kings 19:6). In Jesus' parable about a dying beggar, it was angels who carried the spirit of Lazarus to Heaven (see Luke 16:19-22). In Acts 5 an angel freed the apostles from prison. In Acts 8 an angel directed Philip to his preaching appointment with an Ethiopian man. Two chapters later an angel told an Italian officer named Cornelius to send for the apostle Peter, who would explain the Gospel to him. In Acts 12 it was an angel who again freed Peter from jail, and yet another who struck Herod with a fatal disease.

More than anything else, however, the Bible depicts angels as praising and worshiping God around His throne. Saint John described the staggering scene in Heaven:

> *Then I looked, and I heard the voice of many angels around the throne, the living creatures, and the elders; and the number of them was ten thousand times ten thousand, and thousands of thousands, saying with a loud voice: "Worthy is the Lamb who was slain to receive power and riches and wisdom, and strength and honor and glory and blessing!"* (Revelation 5:11-12).

Ten thousand times ten thousand is 100 million, and although Saint John is being figurative in his description, it is safe to say that no other angelic assignment in the Scriptures involves anything close to such a number. Of course it's understandable that angels or anyone else standing before God's throne in Heaven would worship Him; the only alternative ever mentioned is falling down dead!

Angels have always been involved in praising the Lord. Job 38:7 says that at the beginning of creation, "the morning stars sang together, and all the sons of God [angels] shouted for joy." Then when Jesus was born, Luke 2:13-14 says, "...suddenly there was with the angel a multitude of the heavenly host praising God and saying: 'Glory to God in the highest, and on earth peace, goodwill toward men!'"

Isaiah chapter 6 reveals a setting similar to what John saw in Revelation, as the mighty seraphim hovered over the throne of God, crying out, "Holy, holy, holy is the Lord of hosts; the whole earth is full of His glory!"

All of these scenes taken together raise a question: **if angels are so involved in praise and worship to God, how is their praise related to ours?** Hebrews 12:22-24 gives us our first clue: "But you have come to Mount Zion and to the city of the living God, the heavenly Jerusalem, to *an innumerable company of angels, to the general assembly and church* of the firstborn who are registered in heaven, to God the Judge of all, to the spirits of just men made perfect, to Jesus the Mediator of the new covenant, and to the blood of sprinkling that speaks better things than that of Abel."

We worship in the company of angels because, as the Church of Jesus Christ, we are already seated in "the heavenly places" (Eph. 2:6). In other words all of us, saints and angels alike, are assembled before God's throne in Heaven, our praises intermingled in a never-ending symphony.[1]

WAR AND PRAISE

But Heaven is not the only place where you and I interact with angels, as, for example, the story of Elisha's attempted abduction in Second Kings chapter 6 shows. The king of Syria was making war on Israel, yet time after time his most private strategy sessions were being "leaked" to his enemies. Informed that Elisha, the Israelite prophet, was able to know his thoughts, the Syrian king determined to kidnap, and presumably kill, the man of God.

Elisha's servant was the first to spot the approaching band of Syrian raiders, and he panicked. "Alas, my master! What shall we do?" he asked the prophet in verse 15. "Do not fear, for those who are with us are more than those who are with them," answered the man of God. And then he prayed that the Lord would "open his eyes that he may see." With that the young man's spiritual vision was opened and he saw that the surrounding mountains were full of horses and chariots of fire (see 2 Kings 6:8-17).

This should encourage you if you've been led to believe that the devil is in charge in the world around you. Most Bible scholars assume—based on an obscure passage in Revelation—that one-third of the angels were cast out of heaven with satan. I agree with their interpretation, and would hasten to add that two-thirds of the angels did not fall! No doubt Elisha's servant got a glimpse of the *real* balance of power.

Clearly, angels are involved both in war and praise. But as we noted in Chapter 3, these two ventures are one and the same. In fact, when you have praised God and seen spiritual success, it is because God has sent angels to war on your behalf. They are the enforcers of Christ's victory. You sing; they fight; you win! Such is life for the heirs of God!

JOINT WARFARE

Revelation chapter 12 describes a war in Heaven wherein God's angels cooperate with believers in the casting down and ultimate defeat of satan and his angels:

> *And war broke out in heaven: Michael and his angels fought with the dragon; and the dragon and his angels fought, but they did not prevail, nor was a place found for them in heaven any longer. So the great dragon was cast out, that serpent of old, called the Devil and Satan, who deceives the whole world;*

he was cast to the earth, and his angels were cast out with him. Then I heard a loud voice saying in heaven, "Now salvation, and strength, and the kingdom of our God, and the power of His Christ have come, for the accuser of our brethren, who accused them before our God day and night, has been cast down. And they overcame him by the blood of the Lamb and by the word of their testimony, and they did not love their lives to the death" (Revelation 12:7-11).

This passage makes it clear that *God's angels and God's children are involved in a joint operation to defeat satan and his forces.* In verse 7, Michael and his angels cast satan down, but in verse 11 it is believers that overcome him "by the blood…and the word of their testimony." How can both statements be true?

The saints simply made use of the weapon of the blood of Jesus, launching it against the devil with the rocket of their spoken testimony. The Lord subsequently deployed the archangel Michael and his angelic troops to enforce the power of that Blood, in response to His people's confession.

It is logical to assume that Michael and his angels could have fought and prevailed against the dragon and his angels at any time, under any circumstance. If God had told Michael to cast them out of Heaven, he would have cast them out. Yet the heavenly voice in this passage attributes satan's defeat to believers and angels, as though the angels were actually waiting for believers to become active in spiritual warfare before they would enforce what the believers had requested in prayer. *One can only conclude, then, that believers and angels cooperate in casting down the devil.*

Am I implying that you can control angels? Absolutely not. I believe that angels can only act on orders from God the Father.

He alone commands them. I do believe, however, that when you act according to scriptural principles of spiritual warfare, then angels are released by God to enforce His will accordingly. Angels will not act in your behalf against the powers of darkness until you recognize your authority and responsibility in this regard.

GOD'S BATTLE PLAN

Second Chronicles chapter 20 tells the story of someone who not only used the Word with prayer, but also launched the weapon of the name of the Lord with the rocket of praise.

Jehoshaphat was the king of Judah during Israel's period as a divided kingdom, and in Second Chronicles chapter 20 his tiny nation was invaded simultaneously by an alliance of three others. The king immediately "set himself to seek the Lord, and proclaimed a fast throughout all Judah" (v. 3). After assembling the entire populace in Jerusalem, Jehoshaphat stood before them and prayed an eloquent, but honest, prayer. "[W]e have no power against this great multitude that is coming against us; nor do we know what to do," he admitted in verse 12, "but our eyes are upon You."

Then the spirit of prophecy came upon Jahaziel, a Levite from Asaph's lineage, a designation that identifies him as a musician. Jahaziel's prophetic word outlined an innovative, but highly unusual battle plan for the next day.

The professional temple musicians, all Levites, were to lead the army into battle, singing a song of praise. They would encounter the enemy at a place called the Ascent of Ziz. "You will not need to fight in this battle," the Lord assured them in verse

17, instructing them instead to take their positions, stand still, and watch Him bring victory in their behalf.

If any situation ever illustrated the fact that "we do not wrestle against flesh and blood, but against principalities," this one does (Eph. 6:12). God wasn't interested in the might of the oncoming army, what kind of armor they were wearing, or how much firepower they possessed. Spiritual warfare called for spiritual weaponry.

Judah marched into battle singing a perennial national favorite: "Praise the Lord, for His mercy endures forever" (2 Chron. 20:21). In doing so they used the rocket of praise to launch two spiritual weapons at once, singing both the Name and the Word of God from Psalm 106:1. As a result the battle was over before it had begun. The Lord set ambushes against the enemy, and they fell into disarray, turning on one another until they were dead to the last man.

GOD'S AMBUSHES

How did God "ambush" Judah's enemies? I believe He used angels. Here's why. *First*, He did the same thing in dealing with a single man, Balaam. Of course, the disobedient prophet's spiritual perception was so dull that he failed to see the ambushing angel that was blocking his path with a sword, so God used his donkey to point him out. Then Balaam fell on his face and repented (see Numbers 22). *Second*, an army of angels assisted Elisha in Second Kings chapter 6, assembling a massive ambush against the unsuspecting Syrian invaders, striking them with temporary blindness. *Third*, in Second Kings 19:35, a single angel ambushed and killed 185,000 Assyrians invaders in one night.

Based upon these precedents, I believe God consistently uses angels to ambush His enemies, and that He did exactly that to Judah's allied enemies in Second Chronicles chapter 20. *Furthermore, the ambush coincided exactly with the time that the army of Judah began singing and praising God. Like a bugler signaling "Charge!" their sounds of praise summoned heaven's troops.* The mighty host already possessed the power to destroy the spiritual stronghold that motivated Judah's enemies, but they did not move an inch against them until God's children engaged in spiritual warfare according to God's Word. Only then did the angels confound their enemies so uniquely that they self-destructed.

How did they confuse them? Let's turn some tables. If the devil's angels can sow thoughts of bondage, fear, and disobedience in the minds of Christians, then logic suggests that God's angels could easily have whispered in the ears of Judah's enemies, sowing seeds of doubt and distrust among them so effectively that they turned on one another. In any case, the angels appear to have been standing at the ready on God's orders, responding directly to His children when they exercised the correct principles of spiritual warfare.

Tell me, who is whispering in your ear? When you face life's battles, whose marching orders do you follow? It ought to be clear to you by now that Almighty God loves you as fiercely as satan hates you, and that He has angels standing at the ready to defend your cause. No doubt He has deployed them for your good many times in the past, but like Balaam you failed to recognize His hand. You may have even thought the devil was attacking you, when in reality God was frustrating your plans in order to protect you!

It's tempting to downgrade reality to mere visibility, to disregard the work of angels, or file them under "fantasy" right beside Santa Claus and Superman. But they are real, and they're on assignment where you live and work and play, ready to perform God's Word in your behalf. If you're wondering what's keeping them, I suggest that they may be waiting for the sound of the bugle from your lips, celebrating the mercies of God.

ANGELS IN ACTION

Angels are still in the same business today that they were in Second Chronicles and the Book of Acts, assisting the saints and ambushing the enemy. In fact, they're also involved in the ministry of healing. John 5:1-15 tells the story of how Jesus healed a man at a pool near Jerusalem's Sheep Gate. Of note, however, is the fact that at least one angel frequently also brought healing to people at that location. The spirit apparently operated invisibly, showing his presence by stirring the waters. Then, whoever jumped in first was healed. But every once in a while God gives somebody a peek at His celestial servants in action.

Several years ago Don Moen and I were ministering at a large church in Baker, Louisiana. As usual, after Don led the people in praise to God, I led them in a general prayer for healing. The crowd numbered about 5,000 that morning, and the music was loud, the way I like it! But to one woman, just to my right on the second row, it suddenly seemed too much. She caught my eye as she began to jump, and I saw her wince as her hands flew to cover her ears. She soon took them down, however, and began weeping profusely. At that point I called her to the microphone.

"Did you see them?" she asked as soon as she could talk. "You were looking right at me, so you must have seen them."

I had no idea who she was talking about, but I was intrigued.

"Eight years ago I lost my eardrums to a degenerative disease, and I've been deaf ever since. Tonight two large angels stood on either side of me and touched my ears, and they both came on at once! The loud sound in here startled me, and I had to put my hands over my ears. When you stopped the music, I asked my friend there beside me to whisper in my ear. Now I can hear a pin drop!"

Six weeks later Don and I were in Dallas, Texas, and the scene from Louisiana almost repeated itself. In the middle of the praise service I saw a little boy step into the center aisle, and pause for a moment. Then he dashed up the aisle and out the back door, into the parking lot. About 15 minutes later he came back in, and I invited him down to the front. He was sweaty and breathing hard, and I asked if he had been ill.

He had been born with asthma, he said, and had never been able to walk far without his lungs hurting. The neighborhood boys had called him a sissy because he couldn't play sports with them. In the middle of the interview he looked at me.

"Did you see them?" he asked.

"See who?" I asked in return. He obviously thought the rest of us could see whatever he had seen.

"The angels!" he said. "There were a whole bunch of them up there by the loudspeakers." He pointed to the sound equipment hanging from the ceiling. "The big one in the middle came down and put his hand on my chest, and then I knew the asthma was gone, so I started running. I don't have asthma anymore! I'm healed!"

Angels Watching Over Me

According to Hebrews 1:14 millions of angels are sent "to minister for those who will inherit salvation." That's a staggering statement. Thus, during my 600 hours of preparation for writing *The Truth About Angels*, one question loomed as primary in my mind: What action can I take, or what principles can I obey, that will cause angels to work in my behalf? I discovered five:

- ❖ Submission to Authority: God dispatches angels to minister to those who submit themselves to the authorities He has established in the family, church, and state;

- ❖ Sacrifice: When you sacrifice your time to serve the Church, offer hospitality, or participate in missions, God sends angels to serve you as you serve Him;

- ❖ Prayer: God sent angels to protect Daniel in the lions' den when he refused to stop praying. An angel set Peter free from prison because the church was praying for him;

- ❖ Praise and Worship: We have already seen this principle at work in the story of Jehoshaphat, king of Judah;

- ❖ Giving: In Acts 10 God was pleased with Cornelius' aid to the poor, so He sent angels to make sure the Roman officer received the message of the Gospel from Peter.

The last principle, giving, played a huge part in the ministry of angels in my life. When I was nineteen, and starting my third year of Bible School in Canada, I was required to attend church on Sunday mornings, so I chose Central Tabernacle in downtown Edmonton. One Sunday Pastor Bob Tatinger invited a missionary to Kenya to join him on the platform. Then he told the congregation that he wanted to raise the airfare to get the man back to Africa. "How many of you will give $100?" he asked.

I looked down from my perch in the balcony at the people I thought had money. Nobody was responding. Suddenly a strange feeling swept over me, and I thought, "Oh no, not me!" I was a poor student who lived six miles from campus and had to take the bus to school every day. Today it was twenty degrees below zero outside. If I gave $100 it would leave me with six bucks to my name, and I'd have to start walking. But somehow I mustered the courage to give it anyway.

The next Thursday I ran out of money and went to the chapel to pray a while before my long walk home. I heard someone walk up beside me, put something on the bench, and walk away. But I didn't look up and just kept praying. The something turned out to be an envelope with $50 in it. I was floored, and not a little relieved. Two weekends later my father called and asked me to come home and speak at church, so I spent the $50 to make the trip. After the Sunday evening service a local rancher named Ed Stahl knocked on our front door and asked for me. When I walked over to him, he held up three crisp $100 bills and smiled. I was overwhelmed! But, of course, I haven't yet mentioned any angels, have I?

The next summer Ed invited me to work on his ranch, where he was crossbreeding thoroughbred Hereford cows with a prize Simmental bull from Switzerland. Soon Ed would have larger, friendlier, leaner cattle. He was a smart businessman, and I jumped at the chance to work for him.

Oral Roberts came to preach at the Edmonton hockey arena that summer, so I begged a day off. It was my first time to see him, and I was impressed. So as I left for home I picked up a brochure that advertised the university he had built in Tulsa, Oklahoma. Oral Roberts University looked spectacular, and I immediately felt compelled to submit an application. But it would cost $8,000 a year, and I only earned $50 a week, so I dismissed the idea as hopeless. In fact I dismissed it over and over for the next two months, but it wouldn't leave me. I prayed and praised God every night anyway, but I felt like my praises were hitting a brick wall. Somehow I *knew* I was supposed to go to ORU.

I finally gave in and told Ed about it out in the field the next morning. He abruptly put down his tools and headed for his pickup truck. "Come with me," he said, and I thought I saw a tear in his eye. We drove two miles across the prairie and parked on a hill.

"Do you see that spot?" he asked, pointing his finger. "Two months ago an angel appeared to me right there and told me you were going to go to ORU. He said that when you decided to go, I should pay for everything."

Now it was my turn to tear up. For the first time in my 19 years, God had asked me to make a huge sacrifice in giving. I gave to the point of being embarrassed, beyond my ability, like the Macedonians in Second Corinthians 8. But the Holy Spirit had been watching, keeping track like He did with Cornelius. And then He dispatched angels to make the impossible happen: they turned a meager $100 into a university degree, and then a worldwide ministry and life of adventure beyond my wildest dreams.

THE PLEASURE OF YOUR COMPANY

Angels are not chubby babies, nor are they the spirits of devoted loved ones who have "earned their wings." They are powerful messengers and mighty warriors from God, ready to work in your behalf as much as mine. In fact, here are two theological points that might just revolutionize your point of view forever:

First, *you don't live in the company of angels so much as they live in yours.* Powerful and perfect though they are, there is not an angel in the universe that God calls His son or daughter. That high privilege is yours; it puts the Good in the Good News.

Second, *angels are as intrigued by your salvation as you are by their powers.* First Peter chapter 1 explains that the prophets of old studied hard to discern when their visions and decrees would eventually come to pass, and that the Lord showed them they were speaking to a future generation. The apostle described it as a marvelous plan, full of glorious twists and turns and "things which angels desire to look into" (v. 12).

Angels know their place in that plan as it relates to you, and now you know yours as it relates to them. You are a child of the Most High God, created to "reign in life" through Christ Jesus (Romans 5:17). But in order to reign you first have to take some territory currently in the hands of rebel holdouts. This involves warfare, which Second Corinthians 10:5 describes as "casting down arguments and every high thing that exalts itself against the knowledge of God, bringing every thought into captivity to the obedience of Christ." But you're not fighting empty-handed! God has given you His Word, Jesus' name, and Jesus' blood, powerful warheads with which to establish His Lordship, as well as the means to fire them: prayer, preaching, praise, and your own testimony.

Now, take your place!

ENDNOTE

1. To learn more about angels see my book, *The Truth About Angels*, available at www.worldcompassion.tv and in bookstores.

Chapter 14

Praise and Music

---

by Jim Gilbert

What will happen when some performer decides to combine the power of music with the power of the occult? I can tell you the answer: Millions of young people will follow such a person, like rats running after the Pied Piper, into an abyss of spiritual oppression and destruction.

~

More than 20 years ago a ministry colleague of mine met the manager of one of the most successful rock bands of all time. Although he would not name the group, he did say that in his eyes they were just "another brick in the wall," which happens to be the name of a 1979 Pink Floyd song from their rock opera, *The Wall*. A darkly spiritual recording, it is the fifth largest-selling album in history, with an estimated 40 million sold as of this writing.[1]

The evangelist was shocked at the intelligence of the manager, and quickly perceived him to be a musical and marketing genius. So he decided to ask him a question. "What's next on the rock-and-roll agenda? We're emerging from the era of punk rock and new wave. Where do we go from here?"

The manager didn't hesitate. "We're just like any other business. How do you sell cosmetics, clothes, or cars? You find motivational triggers. And we have discovered that the strongest motivation in the world is religious commitment. No human being ever makes a deeper commitment than a religious one. We've decided that in the '80s we're going to turn our concerts into religious services. We will proclaim ourselves as messiahs, and we will be worshiped."

Interestingly, Pink Floyd—if indeed they were the band in question—broke up shortly thereafter, even though *Dark Side of the Moon* remains a sales phenomenon. Other rock bands, however, did indeed go on to add a religious, in fact overtly satanic, flair to their images and live concerts. Rocker Marilyn Manson picked up the theme, and even went so far as to name one of his albums *Antichrist Superstar*, which rose to #3 on U.S. Billboard chart in 1996.[2]

No matter how you view the music, one fact is beyond dispute. The moguls of the rock industry know that *(a) nothing stimulates sales better than controversy and (b) religion and sex are the two most sensational subjects in that regard.* Moviemakers and television networks have to exercise care in crossing such boundaries, but violating taboos is pure gold in the hard rock music industry. In fact, with hindsight, adding a religious element to the marketing and performance of stars like Manson and Madonna was inevitable.

But the question arises: what will happen when some performer discovers that the arena of the supernatural is real, and decides to combine the power of music with the power of the occult?

I can tell you the answer: Millions of young people will follow such a person, like rats running after the Pied Piper, into an abyss of spiritual oppression and destruction. And critics will hail that "artist" as a bold innovator and trendsetter, with awards to follow.

What will the Church have to say to such a generation? *If we do not combine the power of musical praise and worship with the supernatural power of God, then we will have no answer for "the next big thing."* But I believe God has already equipped us to counter any bill of goods the devil's minions try to sell.

Innovation is not invention. God is the Father of all true invention, the Creator of *everything*. I believe that rather than trying to sound like, or be just as good as, secular hit makers, the Church can accomplish an "end run" around them and take young people to a place today's rock charlatans could never go—into the very throne room of God. But since, as we have established elsewhere, spiritual warfare and praise are one and the same, then we must take Christ's triumph into this arena. The spirits that motivate and control so much of today's creative community must learn that we're not going to let them go unchallenged any longer. *We must trumpet Christ's victory and announce His rightful dominion over the arts.*

It's imperative that we understand why the devil operates the way he does. That means gaining a biblical perspective on the source of his authority and power with regard to music. Any search will lead us straightway to two classic Old Testament passages that Bible scholars generally agree are about satan: Ezekiel chapter 28 and Isaiah chapter 14.

PERVERSION OF MUSIC

Ezekiel 28:13 gives us a description of the devil and his devices:

You were in Eden, the garden of God; every precious stone was your covering: the sardius, topaz, and diamond, beryl, onyx, and jasper, sapphire, turquoise, and emerald with gold. The workmanship of your timbrels and pipes was prepared for you on the day you were created.

The New American Standard Bible (NASB) has changed "timbrels and pipes" to "settings and sockets," and the more recent English Standard Version renders it "settings and engravings." **But an examination of the original Hebrew text verifies the accuracy of "timbrels and pipes,"** and even the NASB offers "tambourines and flutes" as an alternative translation.

This verse admittedly is poetic rather than literal in its description of satan's "workmanship." Spiritual beings cannot have physical parts. Nonetheless, he undoubtedly possesses certain qualities and abilities that are best described in human terms as tambourines and pipes—rhythm and wind instruments. We could even think of them as his hands and lungs, two of the three physical organs human beings use to make music.

Isaiah 14:11 gives further confirmation of satan's musical prowess, when it refers to "the sound of your stringed instruments." This would add vocal chords, or the voice, to the description. Thus we have percussion, wind, and strings, the three major types of instrument in a symphony orchestra, described as somehow built into satan's being. I believe these passages describe him as a master musician, Heaven's former "worship leader."

The subsequent verse in Isaiah calls him lucifer, the "light-bearer" or "day star" (see Isa. 14:12). As a virtuoso, with music emanating from his very being, this anointed cherub would have been involved with covering the glory of God with the musical praises of Heaven. I am certain satan was present at the creation when, according to Job 38:7, "the morning stars sang together, and all the sons of God shouted for joy."

The fact that Scripture singles him out, and that—as is generally accepted—he led one third of the angels in rebellion, leads me to believe that satan, in fact, was the chief worship leader and guardian at the throne of God. Of course, as broader readings of both Isaiah chapter 14 and Ezekiel chapter 28 reveal, lucifer was cast out of Heaven when iniquity was "found" in him. He turned his eyes from the glory of God and began gazing at his own beauty and brilliance. "I will ascend into heaven," he said in Isaiah 14:13. "I will exalt my throne above the stars of God." He began to desire worship for himself, and that sin brought him down "like lightning" (Luke 10:18).

Satan lost all his privileges when he fell from Heaven, but there is no indication that he lost his musical abilities. They were perverted yes, but not lost. His creativity and originality, being cut off from God, degenerated into a spirit of rebellion and theft. In a sense then, when satan fell, music fell with him, insofar as it was no longer exclusive to the worship of God. It is no wonder the devil still uses it to incite rebellion in the human heart, and to appeal to the lower nature of humans.

There is nothing in Scripture to indicate that lucifer does not still have musical ability, and the power to use it for his own nefarious purposes. To the contrary, Romans 11:29 says, "the gifts and the calling of God are irrevocable." So satan's anointing remains, and by it he seduces the spiritually blind to worship him instead of God.

Satan craves the worship of humankind, if for no other reason than simply to divert us from worshiping God, for whose pleasure we were created. That is why he vowed to be like the Most High, and to exalt his own throne above the stars. He is not omniscient, omnipresent, nor omnipotent, so the only remaining way for him to be like God is to receive humanity's worship.

Could not repent

The devil actually tried that gambit against Jesus in the wilderness and lost. Still he did not repent, and even though Jesus has legally wrested creation from his evil grasp, this father of lies still offers the same seductive arrangement to humankind today, especially to the young, because the future is theirs. He offers talented artists the same proposition he gave to Jesus: the kingdoms of this world. He offers them popularity, fame, and enough money to choke themselves on excess. He wants the music of our generation to glorify him instead of God, and he inspires the music-makers themselves to divert large groups of people into various religions, because *any false religion will do*. From recent popular sensations like Kabbalah and Scientology to ancient Buddhism, this former light-bearer will shine false beams on *any* path other than the true one.

IMPORTANCE OF MUSIC

We need to take a fresh look at the subject of music and learn how to use it in praise and worship to launch our spiritual weapons, in order to dethrone the current rulers of darkness over the arts. This was my strategy with our teams, and today my heart is warmed to see worship leaders like Living Sound alumnus Don Moen featured in national television commercials that advertise the power of God in praise and worship. But a gifted few are not enough. Filth and perversion have become the currency of the arts in America. As humorist P.J. O'Rourke has noted, "What used to be called shame and humiliation is now called publicity."[3]

The day for sacred-secular arguments is past. Now it's time to take effective action, to use praise and worship the way Jehoshaphat's army used it in Second Chronicles 20, where the "sons of Asaph" were theologically educated, adequately funded, and under proper authority. Such qualities made them fit to lead God's people onto a battlefield that appeared physical but was truly spiritual, and to plunder the wealth of their defeated foes.

The Bible mentions music more than 800 times. That is no minor emphasis. And for that reason it will serve us well to compare how Scripture accentuates the ways we are to respond to God with how it stresses some of our fundamental doctrines. My purpose is not to downplay the importance of doctrine; it gives indispensable structure to our faith. But we need to see that the Bible dedicates more space to our response to God than it does to doctrinal belief.

The virgin birth, for example, is mentioned twice in the Bible, while dancing is mentioned five times. Missions is mentioned 12 times, but shouting is commanded 65 times. Justification rates 75 mentions and sanctification 72, but thanksgiving is emphasized 135 times, and singing 287 times. Baptism is mentioned 80 times, while rejoicing is commanded 288 times. Repentance is mentioned 110 times, while playing musical instruments is mentioned 317 times. Praise is mentioned or commanded 332 times.

It is only logical to conclude, then, that God places great importance on how we respond to Him, and that music is one of the primary vehicles He has given us for doing so. Psalm 100:2 commands us to "come before His presence with singing." That is *His* protocol, not merely one option among others. If we are going to come before the King of kings and Lord of lords, we must come in the prescribed way, with singing. That's how important—how *cherished*—music is in our Father's heart.

Lucifer no longer hovers by the throne, covering the glory of God with praise and worship. But God still requires the praise that is due Him from all creation, and He will have that praise from His Church. He will receive it from a race of beings who praise Him not simply because it is His command, but because they want to worship Him, and have made the decision to do so.

This redounds to the honor and glory of God in a much greater way than the praise of angels, greater, in fact, than lucifer's praise before he fell. *There simply is no comparison between the commanded praise of angels and the freely lavished love of sons and daughters.*

CREATION WAITS…AND WAITS

The Church for several centuries merely reacted to "worldly music" instead of blazing new trails for the world to follow. In the Middle Ages, for example, the Roman Catholic Church frowned on certain musical intervals, even banning one they called "the devil's interval" (a diminished 5th in today's terms). The Reformation introduced a better theology of music, giving us Bach, Beethoven, and other masters, but within a couple of centuries Christian creativity seemed to crawl back into its restrictive little box.

In my parents' era musicians like Glenn Miller and Cab Calloway used orchestras, so of course we stuck with pianos and organs (and accordions if we traveled). When the 1950s came rockin' along, bands used drums, so churches banned them. Elvis "the

Pelvis" Presley gyrated, so we Christians had to stand still. The Beatles had long hair, so we wore "whitewalls" around our ears.

When the Church finally OK'd contemporary methods, for the most part we spawned "sound-alike" artists in an effort to give Christian young people wholesome alternatives to glittery secular filth. But we had merely torn down a fort and built a ghetto. By the time we actually began turning out true originals like Larry Norman and Andrae Crouch, the world had largely quit paying attention.

King David, however, was both innovative and inventive. He considered the musical instruments of his day inadequate to give God the glory He deserved. By the Spirit's inspiration, he invented new musical devices, exclusively for worship (see 2 Chron. 7:6), while redeeming others that had originated in pagan cultures (see Ps. 150). Until now Israel's worship had never been particularly musical, save for the occasional use of the *shofar* and tambourine. From the time of David forward, however, every revival in the nation's history was marked by the reinstatement of Davidic praise.[4]

Some people still dismiss certain musical instruments and styles as intrinsically evil, but physical objects and sounds are neither good nor evil in themselves. They cannot convey evil anymore than they can impute righteousness. Rather, their effectiveness, for good or bad, depends upon the character and skill of the musician. And although there is musical ability within all of humanity, some instrumentalists and singers are set apart by God and specially equipped to communicate His message through their music. George Frideric Handel, Fanny Crosby, the late Larry Norman, and today's talented British songwriter Martin Smith and his group "Delirous?" are four sterling examples. Some, like Handel of "Messiah" and "Hallelujah Chorus" fame, have been justly celebrated, while others, such as Larry Norman, were too little appreciated. But all have brought the spirit and skills of King David to their generations.

ON EARTH AS IN HEAVEN

Music was created to glorify God, not only in heavenly worship but also in earthly evangelism. In fact, if Jesus taught us to pray for God's will to "be done on earth as it is in heaven," then clearly *God's will is for His praises to bathe the earth just as completely as they permeate Heaven.*

Yet sometimes we live in a dry and thirsty land of our own making. A case in point was the Russian church under communist rule. When I first began traveling into the USSR and associating with believers there, I noticed a complete absence of praise to God. They revered Him, yes, but they didn't praise Him. Songs in major keys were dismissed as frivolous; only minor keys honored the suffering Savior. They sang every verse of every hymn like a dirge, and a song with four verses could take 15 minutes. In a way it was understandable; most of their leaders had been in prison.

In 1983 a young musician from Estonia joined my coauthor to attend a famous church in Moscow. As they sat on the front row of the balcony during the service, Taavo made the mistake of smiling. In a flash he was face to face with a little *babushka* (a "granny") who had been watching the two strangers. "You should repent of your sins," she scolded him, pinning him to the pew with a wagging finger. "The church is no place to smile."

That little woman had unintentionally summed up the Soviet-era church. It was no place to smile, and really had no reason to. Yes, there was love, and yes, there were times of sweet

who is done in Heaven?

fellowship. We often held secret meetings where the people wept for joy at our stories of God's work in the West. But for the most part "worship" meant sorrow and weeping.

Back in America something wonderful was happening. A "worship movement" that had begun in the late 1970s was now in high gear. Churches were abandoning 15-minute "song services" in favor of extended times of praise and worship. Conferences like the International Worship Symposium were drawing thousands of pastors and music ministers. There was even a new "praise and worship" record label called Hosanna! Music. Don Moen had left my employ (with my full blessing) to join Integrity Communications' new company after "Give Thanks," his first CD with them, had put the company on the map.

I thought of Don and the burgeoning worship movement during one of my visits with some leaders from the "underground" church in Russia. These men had suffered greatly for their faith in Jesus, and even though they were downcast, they continued to persevere. "I wish they could hear the kind of music Don is making," I thought. And then another thought hit me: "Why not?"

As soon as I got back to the States, I flew to St. Louis where Don and Mike Coleman, the company's founder, were recording. I took them to lunch and challenged them to do a Russian-language praise and worship CD. It would change the church in that nation, I assured them. Besides, we already had a means of distribution. Some years earlier Living Sound had smuggled cassette tapes and commercial duplicators into the USSR in order to disseminate the Bible on tape. We already had 75 duplicators in place around the country, and half a million blank cassettes ready to use. What did they think?

It didn't take long for Mike to give the go-ahead, and soon Don was headed to San Francisco to record a group of Russian emigrés who were translating and learning the songs. Within weeks the master tapes were ready for us to smuggle into the Soviet Union. But first I needed to try them out on the Russian leaders of the underground. They would be the hardest sell of all.

My assistant, Joel, and I flew to the northwestern city of Riga, Latvia, to rendezvous with the bishops. Someone found a boom box, and we took it to an old farmhouse out in the country, where leaders from virtually every region of the USSR had secretly assembled. I stood and welcomed them, and told them we had something in their own language that we wanted them to hear. I was nervous, because I knew that, for better or worse, the music on that little boom box was about to shake them to the core.

Joel pushed the plastic button on top of the player, and soon a strange, sweet sound in Russian diffused the room. *Kvahlah teebyah nash Gospod*—"Give thanks with a grateful heart." For at least thirty seconds not a man there moved, as the music wafted across the drafty room. Then the bishop from Moscow gasped, and it was as if a valve had opened. Tears were stealing down cheeks, and all over the room hands began to rise. When the first song ended, I motioned for Joel to stop the tape. A holy hush filled the air. The leaders of the persecuted church were lost in worship.

"We must have this music in our nation," said the Bishop of Moscow, brimming with emotion. "How can we get it here?"

"We have 75 duplicators and 500,000 blank tapes," I responded. "We want to give them all to you."

That album, *Heal Our Land*, became the signature of the Russian church. Its distribution took place during the crumbling of both the Berlin Wall and the Soviet Union, and in fact probably hastened the collapse of the latter. In any case, no publicity team could have positioned it more perfectly for the flood of evangelists and missions teams that began arriving in 1991. Along with the five million Bibles we distributed later, it changed the face of the church in Russia and several other former Soviet republics.

Nearly 20 years later it still is. Don Moen called me from Omsk, Siberia, in 2006. "Terry, you're not going to believe this!" he laughed. "There's a four-thousand-member church here, and the pastor became a Christian because of that little tape."

Heaven invaded earth on that first day with the bishops, and once unleashed, there was no way to keep the lid on the demonstrations of God's power that followed. Such victory had never been known until the Holy Spirit turned their mourning into dancing (Psalm 30:11). Yes, they had to deal with sorrow from time to time in life, just as you and I do. But praise and worship are never about licking our wounds. There is no place for mourning in Heaven, and *there is no place for mourning during worship*.

Of course, you *should* freely pour out your complaints to God. Psalm 142:2 says, "I pour out my complaint before Him; I declare before Him my trouble." You have the *right* to spell out every last detail of all your troubles to your heavenly Father. He wants to hear them. But when it comes to praising Him, there is only one acceptable protocol: "Enter into His gates with thanksgiving, and into His courts with praise. Be thankful to Him, and bless His name" (Ps. 100:4).

PSALMS, HYMNS, AND SPIRITUAL SONGS

Much ado has been made about the "degrees" that exist as we move from thanksgiving to praise to worship. I agree that these three, to a certain extent, are distinct from one another, but I also agree with worship leader, Barry Griffing, who says that if there is an actual identifiable progression in worship, it most likely is found in Ephesians 5.

> *Therefore do not be unwise, but understand what the will of the Lord is. And do not be drunk with wine, in which is dissipation; but be filled with the Spirit, speaking to one another in* **psalms** *and* **hymns** *and* **spiritual songs***, singing and making melody in your heart to the Lord, giving thanks always for all things to God the Father in the name of our Lord Jesus Christ, submitting to one another in the fear of God* (Ephesians 5:17-21).

Note the three types of music mentioned here: psalms, hymns, and spiritual songs. The Psalms were the songbook of ancient Israel. Unlike any other collection of songs on earth, they are the very Word of God, and as such, are incredibly effective in spiritual warfare. *When we sing the Psalms, we are launching the weapon of the Word with the rocket of praise and worship.* There is a great release of spiritual energy when we sing them. Even those that express distress and discouragement always resolve into a message of faith and hope. That is why the Holy Spirit is reintroducing them to the Church today.

Hymns are religious odes, whose modern form is traceable all the way back to Greek theater, where the audience was part of the cast, chanting scripted responses to the actions of the actors onstage. God inspired Moses to write a hymn intended not only for his current listeners, but to be transcribed and taught from one generation to the next. That is the purpose of hymns. They carry the "faith of our fathers" from generation to generation in the Church.

Whereas the Psalms celebrate God, hymns tend to deal with enduring themes and doctrines. Classics like "Amazing Grace" and "How Great Thou Art," declare the Lord's goodness, grace, and even His judgments. And their timeless character gives them timeless authority.

Spiritual songs, the third category Paul mentions in Ephesians 5, relate more to the subjective, often spontaneous, songs we all sing. Psalm 42:8 says, "in the night His song shall be with me—a prayer to the God of my life," and Psalm 32:7 rejoices that "You shall surround me with songs of deliverance." Spiritual songs are true prophetic songs in that they come from the Holy Spirit. The spiritual song may well be what Paul is referring to in First Corinthians 14:15, when he says, "I will sing with the spirit, and I will also sing with the understanding."

When you sing spiritual songs you needn't worry about rhyme, syntax, or even vocabulary; the Holy Spirit will help you to express the depths of your spirit in ways that go beyond language. And when those moments come, the Spirit—if you ask Him—will also give you understanding, so that your mind can be fruitful as well. These are spiritual songs, and singing the Psalms and hymns can certainly help to jump-start them in your heart.

This, perhaps, is the true progression in worship. Singing the Psalms is the healthy repetition of God's Word, the sowing of it into our minds and hearts. Likewise hymns, with their emphasis on truth, essential doctrine, and the story of redemption, renew our minds and encourage our hearts in the Lord. And spiritual songs are the Spirit-inspired outflow of all the goodness back to God. This is not an attempt to establish a new doctrine, but a logical case for such a natural progression can certainly be made.

ONE LORD, ONE CHURCH

I have learned a valuable truth about the Church from Roman Catholic theology: They see the Church in two parts. One part is the Church Militant, and the other is the Church Triumphant. The Church Militant is alive on earth and is made up of all believers in every nation. The Church Triumphant is that part of the Body of Christ already gone from earth to Heaven. Roman Catholic ecclesiology emphasizes the fact that we are *one* Body in two places. Thus while part of the Body worships God here on the earth, our other half is before His throne in Heaven, worshiping him there. When we gather at the table of the Lord in holy communion, we break the bonds of time, and celebrate with everyone who ever gathered there and everyone who ever will. We worship Him *together*.

I have come to appreciate this concept so much since my wife, Jan, died. I know she's in eternity, before Heaven's throne, covering God's glory with her praise and worship. I know that the two of us, while we do not communicate with each other, nonetheless worship Him together in the true communion of saints.

The Church *up there* is encouraging the Church *down here*—you and me—to join with them in praise and worship. They no longer see Jesus through the dim mirror that Paul lamented in First Corinthians chapter 13. They see Him face to beautiful Face. And they cheer us on, because they fully understand the glory that is set before us. They have seen it. They see it now!

If God's will is going to be done "on earth as it is in heaven," then the Church Militant must do what the Church Triumphant does. *Your song of praise is your connection.*

THE FRONT LINES

I cannot overemphasize the importance of being sensitive to the Holy Spirit in the area of music. As the spiritual war for the souls of nations intensifies, we need inspired singing and instrumental music in the Church more than ever before. God uses music to powerfully express His will to the Church, and in turn the Church should use music not only to praise the Lord, but also to proclaim God's will to the world.

As history progresses toward its climax, praise and worship will continue building, ascending to God with great power from the congregation of the redeemed. We must abandon ourselves to Him as musicians and singers so that He can use us to display His might and glory to a world in darkness.

I have listened to a pianist being led by the Spirit in a spontaneous anthem of worship, sometimes with lyrics, sometimes not. As the song progressed other instruments would join in, following the moment rather than a written score. The result invariably was a prophetic song of great power; effective warfare the way God would have it. If congregations on the whole will begin moving in the Spirit like this, miracles will become the signature of the Church.

The armies of the world historically have marched into battle to the beat of a song. Why should God's army do any less? Whether it was Joshua's troops marching on the walls of Jericho with trumpets, or Jehoshaphat's army putting the singers on the front lines, music was employed in battle after battle in the Old Testament. The lesson: *Worship should be both the beginning and end of missions.* If you and I will wholeheartedly commit ourselves to biblical praise and worship we will prevail in the spiritual war for the American soul. Then, if we are willing, we can lead the Church to win the hearts of other nations as well.

TAKING NEW TERRITORY

You might occasionally hear about Kurdistan in the news, but you will not find such a place on the map. That is because the Kurds have no homeland of their own, their "nation" straddling the corners of four others: Syria, Turkey, Iran, and Iraq. World Compassion, as mentioned several times in these pages, has been working in northern Iraq's Kurdish province since 2003, distributing humanitarian aid, conducting conferences, and helping to plant a church that at this writing has grown to more than 3,000 members, the largest congregation of ex-Muslims in history.

I have noticed a growing desire among these "Christ-followers," as they call themselves, to sing their praises to God. We have been able to import a few CDs from Integrity and other companies, and these prized items are passed from person to person. Groups of believers will play them and sing along in broken English, but they are hungry for versions in their own language. Hence, we are working with Don Moen's new company, Worship2Action, to produce Kurdish praise and worship CDs.

This is a significant project, because 39 million Kurds live in the Middle East, with 4 million of them in Syria, 7 million each in Iraq and Iran, and more than 20 million in Turkey. The fact that they cross their common borders quite freely presents great opportunities for spreading the Gospel. I believe if we produce an album combining Kurdish national songs with praise songs, it will shake the whole region.

Furthermore, Iraq's Kurds are not only friendly to America, but are also far and away the most forward-thinking people in the Middle East. Their own provincial constitution guarantees freedom of religious choice, full women's rights, and defines marriage as between one man and one woman. I believe the Kurds are the key to penetrating the entire Middle East with the Good News of Jesus Christ.

MUSIC TO THEIR EARS

Music and the other arts are unique to man. That fact ought to bother Charles Darwin's disciples, because it sets us so far above our "ancestors." Look *down* the evolutionary ladder, and there's simply no reason for the words we sing or the melodies we make. In fact *evolutionists can give no reason why we humans sing for no reason!* Look *up* the ladder of creation; however, and it makes perfect sense: *Music is a unifier.* It is God's gift to enable us to sing His words and express His heart at the same time with the same intensity. We can be one voice or a sea of voices, virtuosos or team players. We can fill the heavens with harmony or terrorize hell with a single note.

Before you turn to the next chapter, I suggest you put down this book, lift up your voice, and do what Darwin's smartest monkey could never do: sing for joy to the Lord!

ENDNOTES

1. *Billboard* magazine's online edition cited this figure as early as May 2006. See: http://www billboard.com/bbcom/news/article_display.jsp?vnu_content_id=10 02463719; accessed 4/25/08. More recent but less reliable usage of this figure is available at http://en

.wikipedia.org/wiki/List_of_best-selling_albums_
worldwide; accessed 4/25/08.

2. http://en.wikipedia.org/wiki/Antichrist_Superstar;
accessed 3/31/08.

3. P.J. O'Rourke, *Give War a Chance* (New York: Atlantic
Monthly Press, 1992), 125.

4. These revivals occurred under Solomon (see 2 Chron.
8:14), Jehoshaphat (2 Chron. 20), Joash (2 Chron.
23:18), Hezekiah (2 Chron. 29:25), Josiah (2 Chron.
35), and Nehemiah (Ezra 3:10; Neh. 12:36). Furthermore, I believe James' conclusion that the Church is the
restoration of the "tabernacle of David" (Acts 15) mandates an indefinite continuation of musical excellence
and innovation in praise and worship.

Chapter 15

The Vow of Praise

by Jim Gilbert

"We cannot force the Iraqis to put something into their constitution," said President Bush's assistant. "But you as an American citizen have a moral authority, and if you raise your voice, perhaps they will listen."

～

I was in Irbil, Iraq, in April 2005, when I received a phone call one afternoon from the Mother Superior of the Sisters of the Sacred Heart.

"There are many Muslims in Iraq who want to convert to Christianity," she said, "but they dare not because of the Qur'an and Sharia law, both of which declare that if any Muslim ever converts to another religion, he must be given three opportunities to repent. If he fails to do so, he is an infidel, and his family is encouraged to kill him.

"Dr. Law," she continued, "Iraq is in the process of creating a new constitution. Never before has there been an opportunity like this to introduce freedom of religion to our nation."

She cited Article 18 of the Universal Declaration of Human Rights, which declares that people have the right to change religions without fear of reprisal. Yet only one Muslim nation, Afghanistan, had incorporated the declaration into its constitution. She asked me if I could help in getting such a clause written into the new Iraqi constitution.

I vowed that I would try, realizing that I was making a sacred promise that would be taken as seriously in Heaven as I meant it on earth.

When I returned home to Oklahoma, our staff at World Compassion put together a petition directed to then Iraqi Prime Minister Ibrahim al-Jaafari, and posted it on our Internet site.[1] In the petition we requested that the Universal Declaration of Human Rights—specifically Article 18—be included in the new Iraqi constitution. Thousands of Christians throughout the United States, Canada, the United Kingdom, and other Western nations responded by joining the petition.

Soon the White House learned about our efforts, and I found myself in the West Wing, meeting with Meghan O'Sullivan, Special Assistant to the President, Deputy National Security Advisor in charge of Iraq and Afghanistan. She was very encouraging.

"Our government has asked for this," she said, "but we cannot force the Iraqis to put something into their constitution. However, you as an American citizen have a moral authority, and if you raise your voice, perhaps they will listen."

I looked at Ms. O'Sullivan and made the same commitment I had made to the Iraqi nun: *I made a vow.*

By early August, when my assistant Joel and I flew to Baghdad, thousands more concerned citizens had signed onto the petition. Time was critical—the new constitution would be ratified and published within two weeks.

The ride into Baghdad was harrowing. General Sada was behind the wheel, zigzagging along the airport road at breakneck speed. I glanced over at the gauges. The speedometer sat on 100 miles per hour. "Why are you swerving back and forth?" I asked, half-holding my breath.

"There are lots of RPG's [rocket propelled grenades] launched in this area," he explained, "and I'm making us harder to hit."

Our guards in the car behind us sped around us as we neared the first stoplight into town. It was red, but they kept going, swerving straight into the lanes for oncoming traffic. The general sensed our fear and calmly explained.

"The suicide bombers wait at intersections," he said. "They look for VIPs and foreigners, so they can maximize their kills." I suddenly felt very foreign. Going fast and running red lights suddenly didn't seem so bad after all.

Over the next five days we met with most of Iraq's major leaders: President Jalal Talabani; National Security Advisor Mowaffak al-Rubaie; Minister of Planning Barham Saleh; the Ayatollah of Baghdad, Hussein al-Sadr; and finally with Prime Minister al-Jaafari himself.

We presented our thousands of petitions to the Prime Minister, and then I posed a question: "Sir, when Muslims come to America, we allow them freedom of their religion. We let them build mosques and share their message with anyone who wants to listen. Are you willing to guarantee Christians the same rights in Iraq?"

It was the first time in my life that I had confronted a head of state. He looked at me, and before he could answer I added a second question. "We sent our young men and women over here to die for the freedom of the Iraqi people. We believe that one of the most basic freedoms is freedom of religion. If an Iraqi citizen should decide to change to another religion and is persecuted or killed for it, is that not the most basic abuse of human rights possible?"

I moved straight to the point. "The Universal Declaration of Human Rights[2] has been signed by most of the nations of the earth, including Iraq in 1948. Would you be willing to include it in your new constitution?"

For more than an hour the prime minister avoided answering me, switching from one subject to another. By the time we left I thought that perhaps our visit had been futile. But two months later, when the new Iraqi constitution was published, all of our requests had been honored in Articles 39-41 and 43.

Today 27 million Iraqi citizens have the right to choose their religion. Already thousands are deciding to follow Jesus. God honored the faith of a soft-spoken Iraqi nun, a brave government official, and *the vow of an Oklahoma preacher* to change a nation.

DAVID'S VOW OF PRAISE

The Psalmist David's station in life was even lower than mine. He was a shepherd boy, the insignificant runt of his father's litter.

Yet this teenager made history by facing down big bad Goliath on the battlefield. *Where did he get such faith and courage?* Out in his father's fields!

David had practiced more than his harp out there with the flocks. He had, in the words of Brother Lawrence, practiced the presence of God. He had learned how to flow in praise to the Lord, and had discovered the power therein. I believe that's why he was able to kill both a lion and a bear (see First Samuel 17:36) long before he ever faced an armed giant. When you are consumed by the presence and power of the Lord, your perspective changes and every foe fades by comparison. *David's passion for God gave him the power and faith to face Goliath.*

First Samuel 17:45 says that the young Hebrew went against the Philistine giant with the "name of the Lord of hosts," the Name he had spent countless hours praising in the plains, with only his flock for an audience. He had discovered its awesome power, and had learned to unleash its force with the rocket—or in this case a small stone—of praise. First Samuel 17:48 says he "hurried and ran" toward his foe, drew the stone from his bag, and slung it straight into the flesh of Goliath's forehead. The giant fell with a mighty thud. Then David stood on top of his body and severed Goliath's head with his own sword. The Israelite army, now emboldened, went on to defeat and plunder their Philistine enemies. And no doubt, from that moment on the heart of Israel belonged to David more than to Saul.

The future king had discovered a spiritual perpetual motion machine: The stronger the faith, the more praise reverberates in the soul; the stronger praise reverberates in the soul, the stronger the faith. Praise is more than occasional contact, more than a pragmatic spiritual cure-all or the latest "formula" for spiritual victory. *Praise is the generator of powerful faith.*

If praise is a rocket for the weapon of God's Word, then faith fuels the rocket. Your praises go nowhere without faith coursing through them, lifting them off the launch pad of your lips. Praise is what triggers the combustion of faith, and faith is what elevates the song of praise. Together they wield the awesome power of the living Word against the evil spirits that, given the opportunity, would literally harass you to death.

Praise turns your walk of faith into a dance of triumph. You might have prayed for years in dogged determination for a wayward son, but praise will turn your battle into a song of salvation. Praise and faith together rejuvenate the soul, transforming sedate patience into genuine, joyful anticipation.

I'm speaking of true praise, of course, not the posturing that tries to manipulate God. Praise is not a coin in a cosmic vending machine. Yet according to Scripture, it is perfectly proper to praise the Lord when faith gives present substance to future fulfillment.

The alternative is to sit back and passively accept whatever life throws at you, but I warn you, such an attitude will disarm you and render you as helpless as a toddler in traffic. To the contrary, you grow into maturity by exercising the authority and dominion Jesus has bequeathed you.

Someone has said, prayer asks, but praise receives. Prayer presents the problem, but praise embraces the answer. This is not to denigrate prayer, but to distinguish praise. The time to praise God is when the valley is darkest and the pressure greatest. *That* is when praise releases faith.

A VOW IS A CHOICE

Psalm 61:8 is a short verse, but it provides an excellent model for our own vows of praise: "So I will sing praise to Your name forever, that I may daily perform my vows."

This is where praise must always begin, with the will. "I *will* sing." There's no "when I feel like it," or "when I really mean it." Before the world began you and I were appointed to praise God. And as for me, I *will* sing, even when I don't want to. I *will* sing even when—*especially* when—things go from bad to worse. I *will* sing even when the accuser whispers that I'm a hypocrite for singing! *Praise is God's command, yes, but it is also my choice, and I will do it. I will daily perform my vow.*

At one point David was in exile, running from the wrath of King Saul, while simultaneously trying to dodge a Philistine ruler also out to kill him. Yet in the midst of such horror, such sheer dread, he wrote Psalm 34, which begins with a vow: "I will bless the Lord at all times." I *will* bless Him when I'm forced to act like a madman. I will bless Him when my enemies are about to destroy me. His praise shall continually be in my mouth.

It was a vow made by the boy, but kept by the man. It had not been abandoned due to disappointment, nor was it even tempered by experience. David knew that no matter what had befallen him in life, he was still responsible for his own will. You may claim that you can't overcome your past, that you can't forgive an abusive father or unfaithful spouse, but that's not true. What you mean is that you *won't* forgive, that you *choose* not to overcome, because forgiving and overcoming bring responsibility.

The good news is that they also bring *freedom*. Remember that. Exercising your will to praise God "at all times" means walking into freedom. It means staying free even after you're thrown into prison like Peter in Acts chapter 12, or Paul and Silas in Acts chapter 16. Bad things may have happened to you, and you might feel like you can never again forgive or function normally. But God has given you the ability to respond—responsibility is *response ability*—and exercising it is your first step to freedom.

This is why Paul said we should, "rejoice always, pray without ceasing, in everything give thanks; for this is the will of God in Christ Jesus for you" (1 Thess. 5:16-18). It is also why David made his vow of praise. He accomplished God's will by exercising his own.

Furthermore, David almost always fulfilled his vows by singing them. There is a faith—a determination—that is uniquely expressed in singing. Even the saddest songs, the laments, can take flight on wings of praise. What might otherwise be a spiritual tantrum, when it is sung *to* God rather than yelled *at* Him, becomes instead the first step on the path to healing.

The vow of praise was David's key to spiritual power. He understood the principles of spiritual warfare. He knew that God had given him the powerful weapon of His name, and that he could launch that weapon in praise. In Psalm 61:8 he promised to sing praises to God's name forever, in order to perform his *daily* vows. In other words, *David made a permanent commitment in order to achieve a daily discipline.*

A friend of mine needed to lose weight, but had never achieved success in dieting. In fact, he had steadily gained weight for years. But then he heard his pastor refer to having made a permanent change in his own lifestyle. "Something clicked," he told me. "I realized I had never been able to commit to a diet because it was something temporary. I always looked forward to a reward or to the end of the regimen. But that day it dawned on me that I could make a permanent commitment more easily than a temporary one." My friend went on to lose nearly 30 pounds, and more importantly, made permanent dietary changes and lasting improvements to his health.

Some people praise God *as long as* things go well, or *until* something bad happens, but that's exercising an option, not keeping a commitment. Praise is unconditional. It is crucial and should be constant, no matter where you are or who is looking. "I will praise You with my whole heart," David said in Psalm 138:1. "Before the gods [authorities of all kinds] I will sing praises to You." In Psalm 22:25, a song which actually prophesies the very words of Jesus Himself, the psalmist promised that "My praise shall be of You in the great assembly; I will pay My vows before those who fear Him."

A VOW IS SACRED

We are concerned primarily with the vow of praise, but it is important to understand the nature of vows in general. They are sacred promises, and the Scriptures show that God views them with great seriousness. Hannah, for example, made a vow that her son, Samuel, would be the servant of the Lord, and God rewarded her commitment by establishing Samuel as one of the greatest prophets of all time. The Nazirites were an order of Jewish ascetics whose vows established their very identity. These vows showed them to be extraordinarily devoted to God, and in turn God used several of them, including Samson and John the Baptist, in extraordinary ways.

King Solomon wrote of the importance of vows in Ecclesiastes 5:4, where he said, "When you make a vow to God, do not delay to pay it; for He has no pleasure in fools. Pay what you have vowed." Then he adds, in verse 5, the wisdom for which He is so well known: "Better not to vow than to vow and not pay."

God's promises to us are ironclad, and since we represent Him on earth, He expects a similar commitment from us. For example, the Lord ordained marriage as a life-long covenant, so entering it entails making vows. Yet in today's America marriage has become a mere contract easily broken. In fact, matrimonial vows have become so meaningless in Western society in general that many people have dispensed with them altogether. That is why we are in cultural collapse.

I have written about my own excruciating experience with divorce (see Chapter 9). Much of the pain was due to the fact that I had made a lifetime vow to my wife and was determined to keep it. Sure, divorce would have been easier after hope seemed lost, but it also would have brought reproach upon the name of Christ, because I had also taken a vow to represent Him before the world. In my mind, to break one was to break them both.

Although I have made—and done my best to keep—many promises over my 40 years of ministry, I have made a few specific ministry vows as well. I have described two earlier in this chapter, one made to an Iraqi nun and another to a presidential aide. But there were two others, and they seemed just as impossible to fulfill.

BACK TO JERUSALEM

In the late 1990s my assistant Joel and I flew to Beijing, China, to meet one of the five primary "uncles" who lead somewhere around 50 million believers in that nation's burgeoning house-church movement of more than a 100 million. Although China appears to have adopted many Western customs and liberties, it remains a communist nation, a fact made very evident by the government's relentless persecution of Christians. So it came as no surprise that our driver had to take us all over town, on a very circuitous route, before we eventually made it to our back-room rendezvous in a local restaurant.

We were profoundly honored to meet these apostolic leaders and to hear them describe their service to God and His wonders among them. Eventually one of them, "Uncle Z," began to unfold an incredible vision that is shared by millions of Chinese believers.

"When the Gospel went out of Jerusalem in the first century," he began, "it traveled primarily northward to Europe and Asia Minor. Over the succeeding centuries it has continued moving west, and also spread southward into Africa and South America. Eventually the message of Christ crossed the Pacific Ocean and came to the Asian nations, and has spread across China."

I was impressed by this humble man's grasp of church history as well as his apparent wisdom. *Where is he headed?* I wondered as Z continued.

"We believe that Jesus' Great Commission to the Church will be fulfilled only when the circle is complete. We believe that God has called us to take His Gospel across Asia, through the Muslim world, all the way back to Jerusalem. But we do not know anything about Islam, and we know that we need formal training in order to prepare for such a mission. Will you help us to fulfill our vision?"

Equally stunned and inspired, I vowed that we would help in every way possible. My son, Scot, and daughter-in-law, Kathy, subsequently developed our China Mission School that now trains Chinese believers to evangelize in Muslim lands. We soon relocated the school to a neighboring country for security purposes, and in 2006 graduated our first 19 missionaries. We are currently helping to place them in Muslim countries.

As I write, Uncle Z is in prison for his faith in Jesus, but his vision cannot be stopped. I believe in years to come there will be a flood of Chinese evangelists taking the message of Jesus to every corner of the Middle East.

MY VOW OF PRAISE

I made my first vow in missions ministry during a time of praise, even though I had not yet connected the two subjects. I made it directly to God in a whisper.

During my first trip behind the Iron Curtain in 1968, I was stirred by the commitment of the Christians I met. They had risked life and limb just to take me to a secret prayer meeting, and I still recall the moment, sitting there in a crowded, dark room in Tallinn, Estonia, when I made a vow that I would readily return to minister in the Soviet Bloc if God called me. Two years later, as I've described elsewhere, He did call me. I was required to fulfill my vow to God.

Doing so has taken me and my partners in the Gospel around some blind curves and down a few dangerous paths. Several times I faced questioning and threats from the KGB, the Soviet secret police. I have watched as the young men and women of our Living Sound team stood against a wall with soldiers' rifles pointed at them, and more than once crossed a border, knowing that if the guards looked in a particular bag or compartment I would go to prison. I have rejoiced at successfully smuggling a man out of communist Romania, and cried over the murder of a beloved

Chinese brother. But I have kept my vow.

The importance of not breaking vows points to their potential, not their fragility. The vow I made in 1968 became foundational to my ministry. Within a few years Living Sound and I had ministered all over the nation of Poland at the invitation of the Roman Catholic Church. We became a spiritual influence in the lives of men like Lech Walesa, leader of the Solidarity movement, and Karol Cardinal Wojtyla, the Bishop of Krakow who later became Pope John Paul II. Roman Catholic platforms all over the world opened up to us, including Vatican Square.

Our fame in Poland was instrumental in getting us into the Soviet Union, where underground believers actually prayed us into their nation. We were eventually able to establish a ministry beachhead in Soviet Estonia in 1978, and the revival that took place there was reported on wire services around the world.

I am still reaping the benefits of that very first vow today, more than four decades later, because of one very important principle: *God not only takes vows very seriously, but He also richly rewards those who keep them.*

The vow of praise is far more than a promise to wash behind our spiritual ears. It is a commitment that turns shepherd boys into giant killers, and groups of singing kids into world changers. It is a choice *you* can make with enthusiasm, not resignation, knowing that *your promises to God will be met in flight by promises from God.* And take it from me, the echo is far more beautiful than the song.

ENDNOTES

1. http://www.worldcompassion.tv.

2. Article 18 of the Universal Declaration of Human Rights says, "Everyone has the right to freedom of thought, conscience and religion; this right includes freedom to change his religion or belief, and freedom, either alone or in community with others and in public or private, to manifest his religion or belief in teaching, practice, worship and observance." The complete document is available online at: http://www.un.org/Overview/rights.html.

Chapter 16

The Pattern of Praise

by Jim Gilbert

We can choose to praise God, but we must await His divine invitation to actually enter into worship. It is His and His alone to initiate.

~

Twenty years ago when I wrote the first edition of this book, there was no "praise and worship" section in Christian bookstores. Some places carried it in "Christian living," while others put it on the "theology" or "music" shelf. I was just glad it wasn't put on clearance.

The ensuing two decades have seen a worldwide transformation in the way Christians worship. Congregations that once followed song leaders are now led by worship teams, and it is more unusual to see a platform without drums than with them. Thousands of wonderful praise songs have been composed and distributed by the millions via CDs, DVDs and computer downloads. In fact, Christian music has been transformed to such a degree that music industry awards in the religious field now often go to artists whose repertoires focus on praise and worship.

Width does not equal depth, however, and even though Christians today are fervent in praising God, enthusiasm is not enough. Joyful feelings are not the goal of praise, but the byproduct. *If a "praise experience" becomes our goal, we will miss our destination altogether.* In First Chronicles 15, King David assembled a huge throng to celebrate the Lord, but failed to consult God's Word about the "proper order" (see 1 Chron. 15:13). The Scriptures specified exactly how the priests were to lead the people into the Lord's presence. These rituals were symbolic of the way you and I, as a "royal priesthood," are to seek God's presence today.

The biblical pattern for praise is vital because it touches on something ultimate—God's presence. *The presence of the Lord is your destination; don't ever let it change.* You dare not—cannot— "move on" to another subject, to some new experience or more advanced material. *Worship is the reason you exist.*

THE PATTERN

I believe the Bible contains a divine design for entering God's presence. Psalm 100 gives us a general pattern, of course. Verse one exhorts us to "make a joyful shout to the Lord," and verse two insists that we "come before His presence with singing." As stated in chapter 11, this is not a formula, but it is Heaven's protocol. And it is one that the Old Testament Hebrews were careful to observe.

Whereas Psalm 100 provides an overview, the Book of Hebrews harks further back to a more detailed pattern for entering His presence. It is found in the Tabernacle of Meeting, a tent built by Moses as an earthly "copy and shadow of the heavenly things" (Heb. 8:5). In other words, the tabernacle was an earthly representation of God's heavenly throne room, so it had to be built to God's exact specifications.

We should not confuse Moses' Tabernacle with David's Tabernacle, which has received a fair amount of attention in recent years from prominent Bible teachers such as Dr. Graham Truscott and Kevin Connor, and from ministries like the International Worship Symposium and Portland Bible College. King David erected a tabernacle at Mount Zion, and it typifies the earthly Church (see Acts 15) in the same way that Moses' Tabernacle typifies Heaven's throne room.

Moses' Tabernacle, on the other hand, has been largely ignored by the modern church. Perhaps people think David's Tabernacle rendered it obsolete, in the same mistaken way that some have thought the New Testament somehow replaced the Old Testament. But nothing could be further from the truth. More than 50 Old Testament chapters directly reference Moses' Tabernacle, and the New Testament Book of Hebrews devotes 131 of its 303 verses—43 percent of the entire book—to explaining it. Yet I asked you, "What do you know about the Tabernacle of Moses?" I wouldn't be surprised if you drew a complete blank. Frankly, so would most pastors.

Let's rectify that and take a walk through gates of thanksgiving and courts of praise. Let me help you discover the pathway into God's presence.

ENTERING IN

Hebrews 9 describes the tabernacle that Moses built, and the ministry the priests performed at each station.[1]

Then indeed, even the first covenant had ordinances of divine service and the earthly sanctuary. For a tabernacle was prepared: the first part, in which was the lampstand, the table, and the showbread, which is called the sanctuary; and behind the second veil, the part of the tabernacle which is called the Holiest of All, which had the golden censer and the ark of the covenant overlaid on all sides with gold, in which were the golden pot that had the manna, Aaron's rod that budded, and the tablets of the covenant; and above it were the cherubim of glory overshadowing the mercy seat. Of these things we cannot now speak in detail.

Now when these things had been thus prepared, the priests always went into the first part of the tabernacle, performing the services. But into the second part the high priest went alone once a year, not without blood, which he offered for himself and for the people's sins committed in ignorance; **the Holy Spirit indicating this, that the way into the Holiest of All was not yet made manifest while the first tabernacle was still standing** (Hebrews 9:1-8).

Verse 8 makes it clear that the Holy Spirit has a pattern for entering God's presence that the original tabernacle only symbolized. Jesus made the symbol a reality, of course, and paved the way for you and me to follow Him into the throne room. *I want you to know that you are welcome to approach God's throne boldly* (see Heb. 4:16), by following the pathway Jesus opened. It was always there, but like Jerusalem's Eastern Gate, no one was fit to open it until He came.

The birth of Jesus meant that God had set up His tent among men in the body of a little baby. That's why John 1:14 says "the Word became flesh and dwelt [tabernacled] among us." In Jesus,

God was taking up residence in the community of man, in the same way that the tabernacle sat in the center of Israel's camp. The Son was His Father's dwelling, which is why Paul's letters talk so much about living *in* Christ instead of for Him. And of course He did this to become your bridge to God.

The tabernacle structure consisted of three rooms, rich in symbolism. They mirror, among other things, the redemptive work of Christ, as well as the pathway to God that Jesus opened for us. The latter is our concern.

Generally speaking, the Outer Court represents your body; the Holy Place represents your soul, your mind, will, and emotions; and the Holy of Holies depicts your spirit. Since God is a spirit, and must be worshiped in spirit and in truth, the tabernacle reveals a path from the realm of the natural to that of the spiritual. It shows you presenting your body a living sacrifice, also submitting your mind, will, and emotions in praise to the Lord, and finally entering—by divine invitation—into the place of worship, of intimate fellowship with the Spirit of God.

We can also say—although I do not want to draw these lines too sharply—that the three areas of the tabernacle represent the threefold process for entering God's presence: thanksgiving, praise, and worship. Let me emphasize again that there are overlaps among the three, transitional phases from one to the next. Just as red becomes yellow becomes green in a rainbow, so thanksgiving becomes praise becomes worship. Don't try too hard to separate the "colors" along the way. If they seem sharply drawn, that's a good indication that you're standing too far off. But if you'll move in close, then just as with a rainbow, the lines will become indistinguishable and *unimportant*. (I have heard people criticized for "backing out" of God's presence simply because they momentarily gave thanks during a time of intense praise.)

It is probably more accurate to picture three concentric circles, and to think of praise as greater than, yet inclusive of, thanksgiving, and worship as greater than, yet inclusive of, both thanksgiving and praise. But even here I'm measuring the immeasurable. The truth is, *when you truly encounter the shekinah glory and respond to God's invitation to worship, you will experience a mystery that any attempt to explain only profanes.*

Still, even if you can only "see in a mirror dimly" (1 Cor. 13:12), that's better than having no mirror at all, so don't be ashamed to use it. Illustrations are helpful. As the old Jewish saying goes, "to study is to worship."

THE OUTER COURT—THE BODY

The Outer Court was where the priests dealt with sin and forgiveness by sacrificing animals, symbols of man's fleshly desires and the coming offering of Jesus' body for our sins. Today's Outer Court is the place where you are called to present your body as a living sacrifice (Romans 12:1). How? By offering the *towdah*, the sacrifice of thanksgiving.

Psalm 100:4 says to "enter into His gates with thanksgiving." Remember, thanksgiving relates to what God has done for you. As you begin to recount the great deeds of God in your past—when He saved you, filled you with His Holy Spirit, healed your body, rescued you from financial foolishness, gave you babies, and then healed them when you prayed—you prepare yourself. An attitude of gratefulness will overpower the worries you bring home from work, or the hunger pangs you feel halfway through church.

Songs that express gratitude for your salvation are wonderful for stirring up a spirit of thanksgiving. Feed your mind with songs that remind you of your righteousness in Christ, that you stand before God with no condemnation, that you are a member of a holy priesthood, with a right to approach God!

Lift up your hands once in a while as well, even if you're a conservative sort. Raising hands is an act of humility that from time immemorial has symbolized surrender. It gets your body involved with your heart and mouth. Such physical gestures are appropriate—even necessary—because in celebrating God your body must be brought into submission *from the start*. Otherwise your flesh will have you heading for the lunch buffet by the third verse.

Thanksgiving should involve physical expression like clapping your hands and dancing before the Lord. Sure, not everybody dances, but *somebody* should! Some of God's children should come before Him with singing, and with instruments making a joyful (but skillful) noise. Others should come with shouting, with the voice of triumph. Someone somewhere should celebrate Him with drums, and someone else should honor Him with a violin. And somewhere in all this variety, you should do something!

You know, you're the only "you" God made, so you have something to bring to God that no one else on earth can offer. Sing out loud in the car; dance with your kids in the living room; give Him something! Psalm 150:6 says that "everything that has breath" should join the party. That's the only qualification. If you're breathing, you're in!

The sacrifice of thanksgiving will gradually become a song of praise as you are drawn from what God has done to who He is. But with all the distractions of life, especially modern, electronic, fast-paced life, you should start by presenting your body to God in that Outer Court before moving into praise. This is not a hard and fast rule, but it is in keeping with something Paul recognized in Romans 12:

> *I beseech you therefore, brethren, by the mercies of God, that you present your bodies a living sacrifice, holy, acceptable to God, which is your reasonable service. And do not be conformed to this world, but be transformed by the renewing of your mind, that you may prove what is that good and acceptable and perfect will of God* (Romans 12:1-2).

The apostle mentions presenting the body and renewing the mind, not as a strict sequence, but in their natural order. You should do the same things for the same reasons. It is a matter of grace, not law.

CLIMBING ONTO THE ALTAR

The Outer Court featured two large items of furniture. First there was a huge brass altar, 7 1/2 feet square. It was situated front and center at the entrance to the court, just as the Cross of Christ Jesus confronted you when you gave your life to God. Upon this altar the priests shed the blood of innocent sacrifices. This was also the blood that the High Priest carried into the Holy of Holies once a year on the Day of Atonement.

Admission to the Outer Court requires a sacrifice from the very start, and this is what Paul was alluding to in Romans 12. The sacrifice of thanksgiving involves placing yourself, your flesh, upon the altar of God. It is the "reasonable," sensible first step on your way to the Holy of Holies.

The big brass altar was the site of daily blood sacrifices for the cleansing of people's sins. It's fulfillment is found in the types of declarations I suggested in Chapter 6, declarations concerning what the Blood of Jesus constantly accomplishes in your life. These declarations— that you are forgiven, redeemed, cleansed, made righteous, and sanctified—are your sacrifices of thanksgiving that prepare you to enter into God's presence.

CLEANSING YOUR BODY

Just as the Blood cleanses us our hearts, there is also something that cleanses our minds, that deals with the dust of life that clings to us in the form of bad memories, dirty jokes, and the like. It is pictured in the tabernacle as a second item in the Outer Court, a brazen laver. A large bowl filled with water, the laver had been fashioned from the mirrors of the women of Israel. Whenever the priest looked into the water, he could see his reflection in the brass *through* the water. This refers to the Word of God, and is why the Scriptures refer to the washing of water by the Word in Ephesians and Hebrews 10:22.

It is important that you "wash" your flesh with the Word of God. That's why it's a good idea to sing songs of thanksgiving that relate to the power of God's Word and the great deeds He has done for you. Popular choruses certainly have their place, but *the power of the Scriptures is unparalleled.* When you sing the Word of God, you launch powerful spiritual rockets against the strongholds that otherwise would keep you earthbound.

THE HOLY PLACE—THE SOUL

Having made your declarations concerning the Blood, and having reflected upon your salvation through the mirror of God's promises in songs of thanksgiving, you are prepared to move to a second place patterned by the tabernacle. Psalm 100:4 calls you to "enter...His courts with praise." The word for praise here is *tehillah*, meaning to sing *halals*. The word *halal*, in turn, means to make a show, to boast, to be clamorously foolish, to rave, to celebrate. In more contemporary language, it means *to party*—to celebrate Christ's triumph—in the spirit! *Tehillah*, therefore, means to sing praises extravagantly, and according to Psalm 22:3, it is in the *tehillim* of His people that God makes Himself at home. *Your praises are God's comfort zone!*

The way into the Holy Place—the tabernacle's second chamber—is with extravagant singing and boastful praise. Such praise may or may not be physically loud, but there certainly is an *intensity of intent*. For this reason, **once you move to songs of praise, you ought to stay with praise, and not revert to songs of thanksgiving.** This is not to contradict what we said earlier; there is a degree of overlap among thanksgiving, praise, and worship. But reverting to songs of thanksgiving during a time of focused praise usually indicates aimlessness. Remember, your destination is the Holy of Holies, where God dwells.

Of course, this ultimately depends upon God's invitation, not your performance. In fact, when you're at church, never judge a service on whether the praise time is or isn't "good" that day. To the contrary, since worship is for God, only He can judge how good it is. *You are not after the thrills and chills. You are after God.*

Your songs of praise will eventually focus on the character of God more than what He's done for you. You will extol Him for His goodness. Praising God, in a sense, means *appraising* Him. Every homebuyer or seller knows what an appraiser does. He examines the various individual features of a house and assigns *value* to them.

Yet he always keeps in mind the whole. So also in praise, you should *appraise* the Lord in all His wonderful aspects, all the while remembering that He, not His characteristics, is the Object of your affection. In other words you are "into" Jesus, not into praise.

Praise, then, takes you beyond what God has done for you to who He is. His steadfast character and utter majesty now captivate you, and your heart is convinced that He can do now what He has done in the past. You have made the subtle transition from thanksgiving to praise.

SACRIFICING YOUR WILL

The second chamber of the tabernacle, the Holy Place, contained three pieces of furniture Unlike the brass altar and laver in the outer court, these furnishings were made of gold. Brass is an alloy of copper and zinc, but gold is *unalloyed*. It is pure. The same thing is true of you. You came to God full of impurities and climbed up on the altar of Christ's sacrifice, where you died with Him. Then God washed you with the water of His Word, and welcomed you into a purer level of fellowship and understanding.

Now, when you celebrate Him, you commemorate your salvation with the sacrifice of thanksgiving, as the water of His Word continues cleansing and renewing your mind. *God has made you fit to enter in!*

The first item of furniture in the Holy Place was the table of showbread, with 12 loaves of freshly baked bread aligned in two rows of six atop its blue cloth. The bread and table represent your will, the arena of your soul.

Praise issues from the soul, and begins as an act of your will. It is not the product of emotion, although your emotions are bound to be involved. *Praise is your deliberate choice.* You decide to put on the garment of praise for the spirit of heaviness (see Isa. 61:3). No doubt Paul and Silas had such an exchange in mind when they sat in the Philippian jail, praying and singing hymns at midnight (see Acts 16:25). Did they *feel* like singing? No, but they *chose* to sing anyway.

Hot, fresh bread is a wonderful thing, but it doesn't make itself. First, the wheat must be ground into flour. Likewise when you are on your way into God's presence, you must grind up your own will and *choose* to praise the Lord. This is why Jesus said, "My food is to do the will of Him who sent Me, and to finish His work" (John 4:34).

Bread also has to bake, and that means putting it in a fire. (You know what's coming, don't you?) The same is true of the human will. You aren't submitted completely to God's will—the bread isn't "done"—until your will has been through the fire of difficulty and testing. Jesus was going through the fire when He said to His Father in the Garden of Gethsemane, "not My will, but Yours, be done" (Luke 22:42). Without submitting His will, He could not have entered into the Holy of Holies. *Such a sacrifice of praise is essential, and it is the reason God allows the furnace of your life to get so hot.*

ILLUMINATING YOUR MIND

The second item in the Holy Place was the seven-branched golden candlestick, the *menorah*. Crowning each branch was a bowl of burning oil. This lamp stand was the inner court's only means of light.

The candlestick represents your mind, illuminated by the fire of the Holy Spirit. This is in line with the progression cited by Paul in Romans 12:2. After you have presented your body to God as a living sacrifice, then you wave goodbye to the ways of the world in order to be transformed by the renewing of your mind. This happens not only through studying God's Word, but also through singing His Word in your time of praise.

It is precisely at this point that spiritual warfare happens. Remember the primary Scripture of this book: "For the weapons of our warfare are not carnal but mighty in God for pulling down strongholds" (2 Cor. 10:4). Strongholds exist primarily in the mind; they are thought systems. All arguments must be cast down, including "every high thing that exalts itself against the knowledge of God, bringing every thought into captivity to the obedience of Christ" (2 Cor. 10:5). When you sing God's Word back to Him, your mind is renewed.

RELEASING YOUR EMOTIONS

The third piece of furniture in the Holy Place was the golden altar of incense. Every time the High Priest entered the Holy Place, he was required to take a handful of this priceless, exclusive incense and to sprinkle it upon the altar's smoldering coals —coals originally lit with fire from the brazen altar and kept perpetually aglow. The resultant cloud of perfumed smoke permeated the linen veil that separated God's *shekinah* glory—His manifest Presence in the Holy of Holies—from the priests. The smoky fragrance also saturated the linen clothing of the priest.

The altar of incense represents your emotions being released to God. When you have surrendered your will in a sacrifice of praise, and submitted your mind to the Holy Spirit through spiritual song, you can expect a powerful, healthful outflow of emotion. This is not simply an indiscriminate release of feeling; emotion should *never* dictate praise. In fact, that wouldn't be praise at all. But true praise does involve the emotions. You may or may not cry on any given occasion, but if you truly praise God there will be a complete surrender of your emotions, and you will be able to express them as much as you need to at the moment. *The important thing is to enjoy the Lord.*

In fact, the Holy Spirit expresses Himself *through* human emotion, just as surely as the Son of God was born through a human womb. And He does it in such a way that you also should feel completely expressed. Don't ever distrust or feel ashamed of emotion in this context, as long as you control it rather than letting it control you. *It is emotional surrender, not emotional intensity, that makes the incense.* This is an essential, costly, and sacred aspect of praise. It is at the golden altar where the Holy Spirit sets your heart on fire, and a pleasing sacrificial fragrance wafts up to the nostrils of God. And it is this thrust that finally brings you through the veil into an act of worship.

THE MOST HOLY PLACE—YOUR SPIRIT

Your praises will not always take you into the Holy of Holies, but this third and most sacred chamber of the tabernacle should always remain your destination. Entering therein is the ideal, and should be your constant desire. Nevertheless, sometimes you'll stop at thanksgiving and walk into the grocery store. Sometimes you will move into the golden court of praise, even into the high praise that takes place at the altar of incense, and the baby will cry, or you'll have a flat tire.

Worship, however, is a matter of God's sovereign choice. You can decide to praise God, but then *you must await His divine invitation to actually enter into worship.* It is His and His alone to initiate.

In my meetings around the world I have occasionally seen this priceless moment happen. Without a sign from anyone, I have watched an entire congregation bow the collective knee. I have seen them prostrate themselves on the floor, overwhelmed by the presence and power of Almighty God. Sometimes the people have gone into a hushed silence. At other times someone played music that seemed to be more *from* God than to Him. There is no way of programming that moment of worship, of turning the spiritual volume up or down.

I appreciate Don Moen's sensitivity to the Lord in this regard. He knows that sometimes you just need to stop playing and be quiet. Such a moment came one time in Boise, Idaho. Don had been leading the people in a time of praise that seemed to grow in intensity by the moment. Eventually he just stopped the music and let the wonderful hush of God's presence fill the room. The people had been standing, some with hands in the air, but now everyone across the room began to kneel.

Then the power of the Holy Spirit came upon a teenaged girl who had been born deaf, and her ears opened. She ran to the front, fell to her knees, and began to praise God. More amazing, she could perfectly understand my speech without having to read my lips.

I had not called that girl to the front for prayer, and no one had laid hands on her. We weren't even singing the high praises of God anymore. But the invitation to worship had been extended to everyone there, and her flesh responded the way all flesh must in God's presence—what was dead began to live again!

Someone has said true worship should move beyond physical expression, that there should be "no dancing in the inner chamber." But the spiritual does not exclude the physical; it merely transcends it, as that young lady's healing proves. Indeed, as one South African pastor told a Living Sound member years ago, "Brother, when we get to Heaven, perhaps we will sing your American songs, but the dancers will be Zulu!"

It is God's privilege to extend the invitation to worship. It is your privilege to respond.

Someone has called worship "extravagant love and extreme submission." You must extravagantly pour yourself out at the Lord's feet, just like the woman who broke the alabaster bottle and splashed priceless perfume on the feet of Jesus. This is the purpose of praise and worship, to *waste* our greatest gifts at His feet. The wondrous fact that He should grace us with His presence is the greatest miracle of all.

ENDNOTE

1. This particular passage deals only with the Inner Court and Holy of Holies, and does not mention the Outer Court, which contained the brazen altar and laver.

Epilogue

One afternoon in 2004 my daughter, Rebecca, came home from her classes at Oral Roberts University and told me that a tragedy had occurred just two doors down. Rick Wolfer, a history professor from ORU, had just passed away from esophageal cancer. His wife, Barbara, also a professor, was at home, and Becca suggested that I walk over to the house and offer her counsel from my own experience in having lost a spouse.

I followed the advice and spent two hours with Barbara. She and her husband had been married quite happily for 23 years, and now she was stricken with grief and needed time to mourn. My time of ministry finished, I said goodbye and walked home, giving her a copy of the previous edition of this book as I left. After that evening we spoke occasionally by the mailbox, or when I was out in the cul-de-sac, playing football with my grandson, Taylor.

Then, three years later on February 6, 2007, I decided to invite Barbara to join me for dinner. That evening will always live in my heart, because God sparked something special in both of us. Having being widowed in 1982 and then divorced in late 1995, I had spent 12 years as a single father, endeavoring to raise my children, as Ephesians 6:4 instructs, "in the training and admonition of the Lord." In addition, I had been wracked by shame after my divorce, and for the sake of my children still living at home, had banished the thought of ever marrying again. They were—and are—still recovering from the trauma of a battle they did not choose. But to be truthful, I was pretty gun shy myself.

Now, at dinner, I sat face to face with a woman of great quality, an English professor at ORU, with an intense love for the Lord, and whose life had known the same refining fires as my own. I prolonged the meal as long as I could that night, the smile on my face broadening as the conversation deepened. We both were, in the words of C.S. Lewis, "surprised by joy."

We spoke freely to one another after that, and discovered to our delight that our two broken hearts made one whole one. Finally, on November 16, 2007, in a little restaurant on the corner of 81st Street and Yale Avenue in Tulsa, she agreed to become my wife.

Our engagement was a wonderful fulfillment of a word in Isaiah that the Lord had placed in Barbara's heart some time earlier.

Do not fear, for you will not be ashamed; neither be disgraced, for you will not be put to shame; for you will forget the shame of your youth, and will not remember the reproach of your widowhood anymore (Isaiah 54:4).

Barbara and I were married on May 31, 2008. We have a new home, and her son, David, also an ORU student, will live with us until he graduates. Meanwhile my youngest daughter, Laurie, completed her degree just weeks before the wedding and makes her home nearby.

In these pages I have confessed much grief, pain, and shame. Now, it is a delight to end the book with this wonderful news of God's grace and mercy. I love my wife deeply, and look forward to the rest of our life together.

It is only fitting that I say thank You, Father. I praise You with my whole heart!

> *I am like a green olive tree in the house of God; I trust in the mercy of God forever and ever. I will praise You forever, because You have done it; and in the presence of Your saints I will wait on Your name, for it is good* (Psalm 52:8-9).

About the Author

Dr. Terry Law, founder and president of World Compassion Terry Law Ministries, is known internationally for his powerful evangelistic and teaching ministry. He digs deeply into Scripture, bringing up a treasure trove of instruction and encouragement to the Body of Christ, while also reaching those who need to respond to the call of salvation.

Terry was born and raised in western Canada. As a young man he journeyed to Tulsa, Oklahoma, where he attended and graduated from Oral Roberts University. In 1969, he founded Living Sound International, which later became known as World Compassion Terry Law Ministries.

Terry has become one of America's foremost speakers on praise and worship and is in demand as a missionary statesman throughout the world. For nearly 40 years, he has been fulfilling the call of God to open doors for the Gospel in closed nations, ministering to the physical and spiritual needs of hurting people in places such as the former Soviet Union, North Korea, Albania, and more recently Afghanistan, China, Iraq, and Myanmar (Burma).

Terry has met with many government and religious leaders around the world as an ambassador for Christ and is frequently called upon for his observations and insights on the Middle East. His Christian ministry, World Compassion, has made a concerted effort in recent years to bring the message of Jesus to the Muslim world, including Afghanistan and Iraq. In addition to his international travels, Dr. Law frequently speaks at churches across the United States, Canada, and the United Kingdom.

He is the author of several books including *The Power of Praise and Worship, The Fight of Every Believer, The Truth About Angels,* and *Come Before Winter.* Many of his teaching messages are available on CD as well (visit www.worldcompassion.tv. for more information). Terry and his wife Barbara make their home in Tulsa, Oklahoma.

CONTACT INFORMATION:

Terry Law Ministries

PO Box 92
Tulsa, OK 74101

Website: http://worldcompassion.tv
Phone: 888-492-2858

About the Author

Jim Gilbert was a charter member of Living Sound in 1969, and has ministered in nearly 60 nations since then. He founded Jim Gilbert Ministries in 1983. A missionary statesman in his own right, he is a speaker, author, singer, and songwriter. Jim was featured soloist on Hosanna! Music's "Lamb of God" worship CD. His first book, *How a Man Stands Up for Christ*, was published in 1996.

Jim and his wife and daughter, live in Gainesville, Florida. His ministry abroad is devoted especially to pastors and to men, and concerns the necessity of developing a biblical worldview, and then imparting it to the next generation.

CONTACT INFORMATION:
Jim Gilbert Ministries
PO Box 141928
Gainesville, FL 32614

5/17/12

6/2/12

8/13/12

11/6/13

3/23/18 Cor

Additional copies of this book and other
book titles from DESTINY IMAGE are
available at your local bookstore.

Call toll-free: 1-800-722-6774

Send a request for a catalog to:

Destiny Image₍ₐ₎ Publishers, Inc.
P.O. Box 310
Shippensburg, PA 17257-0310

*"Speaking to the Purposes of God for This
Generation and for the Generations to Come."*

**For a complete list of our titles,
visit us at www.destinyimage.com**